Free Market Missionaries

Sharon Beder has written 9 books and around 140 articles, book chapters and conference papers, as well as educational monographs, consultancy reports and teaching resources. Her research has focused on how power relationships are maintained and challenged, particularly by corporations and professions. Her earlier books, some of which have been translated into other languages, are:

Suiting Themselves: How Corporations Drive the Global Agenda
Earthscan, London (2006)

Environmental Principles and Policies: An Interdisciplinary Introduction
UNSW Press, Sydney and Earthscan, London (2006)

Power Play: The Fight for Control of the World's Electricity
Scribe, Melbourne and the New Press, New York (2003)

Selling the Work Ethic: From Puritan Pulpit to Corporate PR
Zed Books, London and Scribe, Melbourne (2000)

Global Spin: The Corporate Assault on Environmentalism
Green Books, Devon, UK and Scribe, Melbourne (1997 and 2002)

The New Engineer
Macmillan, Melbourne (1998)

The Nature of Sustainable Development
Scribe, Melbourne (1996)

Toxic Fish and Sewer Surfing
Allen & Unwin, Sydney (1989)

Dr Beder is a qualified professional engineer and worked in this field until a career shift into researching and teaching environmental politics. She has held a number of appointments at Australian universities over the past two decades – most recently as professor in the School of Social Sciences, Media and Communication at the University of Wollongong in Australia.

Her website is http://homepage.mac.com/herinst/sbeder/home.html

Free Market Missionaries

The Corporate Manipulation of Community Values

Sharon Beder

EARTHSCAN
London • Sterling, VA

First published by Earthscan in the UK and USA in 2006

ISBN-13: 978-1-84407-334-4
ISBN-10: 1-84407-334-3

Typesetting by JS Typesetting Ltd, Porthcawl, Mid Glamorgan
Printed and bound in the UK by Bath Press
Cover design by Andrew Corbett

For a full list of publications please contact:

Earthscan
8–12 Camden High Street
London, NW1 0JH, UK
Tel: +44 (0)20 7387 8558
Fax: +44 (0)20 7387 8998
Email: earthinfo@earthscan.co.uk
Web: **www.earthscan.co.uk**

22883 Quicksilver Drive, Sterling, VA 20166-2012, USA

Earthscan is an imprint of James and James (Science Publishers) Ltd and publishes in association with the International Institute for Environment and Development

A catalogue record for this book is available from the British Library

Library of Congress Cataloging-in-Publication Data

Beder, Sharon.
Free market missionaries : the corporate manipulation of community values / Sharon Beder.
p. cm.
Includes bibliographical references and index.
ISBN-13: 978-1-84407-334-4
ISBN-10: 1-84407-334-3
1. Mass media and business. 2. Public relations. 3. Industrial publicity.
I. Corporations—Political activity. I. Title.
HD59.B375 2006
659—dc22

2005032451

The paper used for the text pages of this book is FSC-certified. FSC (the Forest Stewardship Council) is an international network to promote responsible management of the world's forests.

FSC
Mixed Sources
Product group from well-managed forests and other controlled sources
www.fsc.org Cert no. SGS-COC-2121
© 1996 Forest Stewardship Council

Contents

List of Boxes, Figures and Tables

Boxes

Figures

Tables

List of Acronyms and Abbreviations

AABO	Assembly of Australian Business Organisations
ABC	Australian Broadcasting Corporation
ABW	Australian Business Week
ACCI	Australian Chamber of Commerce and Industry
ADB	Asian Development Bank
AEF	American Economic Foundation
AEI	American Enterprise Institute
AFL	American Federation of Labor
AIG	American International Group
AIMS	Aims for Freedom and Enterprise (UK)
AIPP	Australian Institute of Public Policy
ALP	Australian Labor Party
APEE	Association of Private Enterprise Education
ASA	American Shareholders Association
ASI	Adam Smith Institute (UK)
AT&T	American Telephone and Telegraph Company
BA	Bachelor of Arts degree
BBC	British Broadcasting Corporation
BCA	Business Council of Australia
BHP	Broken Hill Proprietary Co.
BRT	Business Roundtable (US)
CBI	Confederation of British Industry
CED	Committee for Economic Development (US)
CEDA	Committee for Economic Development of Australia
CEO	chief executive officer
CFEE	Canadian Foundation for Economic Education
CIO	Congress of Industrial Organizations
CIS	Centre for Independent Studies (Australia)
CPS	Centre for Policy Studies (UK and Australia)
CRA	Conzinc Riotinto Australia
EA	Enterprise Australia
EC	European Commission
EQ	economics quotient

EU	European Union
FDI	foreign direct investment
FEE	Foundation for Economic Education (US)
FTE	Foundation for Teaching Economics (US)
GATT	General Agreement on Tariffs and Trade
GDP	gross domestic product
GM	General Motors
GNP	gross national product
GOP	Republican Party (US)
HOBSO	How Our Business System Operates (economic education programme)
IDB	Inter-American Development Bank
IEA	Institute of Economic Affairs (UK)
IMF	International Monetary Fund
IOD	Institute of Directors (UK)
IPA	Institute of Public Affairs (Australia)
JA	Junior Achievement Inc.
JCEE	Joint Council on Economic Education (US)
JOL	Job Ownership Limited
LSE	London Stock Exchange
MBA	Master of Business Administration degree
MDB	multilateral development bank
MP	member of parliament
NAIRU	non-accelerating inflation rate of unemployment
NAM	National Association of Manufacturers (US)
NCEE	National Council on Economic Education (US)
NCF	National Civic Federation (US)
NELA	National Electric Light Association (US)
NFTC	National Foreign Trade Council (US)
NFTE	National Foundation for Teaching Entrepreneurship (US)
NGO	non-governmental organization
NSW	New South Wales (Australia)
NZ	New Zealand
OECD	Organisation for Economic Co-operation and Development
ORC	Opinion Research Corporation (US)
PR	public relations
SIFE	Students in Free Enterprise (US)
SIFEE	Securities Industry Foundation for Economic Education
SIP	share incentive plan
TB	tuberculosis
TEL	test of economic literacy
TNC	transnational corporation
UCLA	University of California, Los Angeles

UK	United Kingdom
UN	United Nations
US	United States
USIC	US Industrial Council
WMC	Western Mining Corporation
WTO	World Trade Organization
YAA	Young Achievement Australia
YMCA	Young Men's Christian Association
YWCA	Young Women's Christian Association

Acknowledgements

I would like to thank Richard Gosden, who advised me, encouraged me and commented on draft chapters during the writing of this book. I would also like to thank Truda Gray for her research help on several of the chapters and assistance in writing Chapters 2 and 3. The research for this book was aided by an Australian Research Council (ARC) grant.

1

The Free Market Gospel

The conscious and intelligent manipulation of the organized habits and opinions of the masses is an important element in democratic society. Those who manipulate this unseen mechanism of society constitute an invisible government which is the true ruling power of our country.

EDWARD BERNAYS, FATHER OF MODERN PUBLIC RELATIONS[1]

Throughout the 20th century, business associations and coalitions coordinated mass propaganda campaigns that combined sophisticated public relations techniques developed in 20th century America with revitalized free market ideology originating in 18th century Europe. The purpose of this propaganda onslaught has been to persuade a majority of people that it is in their interests to eschew their own power as workers and citizens, and forgo their democratic right to restrain and regulate business activity. As a result, the political agenda is now largely confined to policies aimed at furthering business interests.

Nowhere has more effort been put into creating a capitalist, free market hegemony than in the US, where advocates of free markets have sought to identify every major institution with free enterprise. The Free Market 'remains the sacred cow of American politics and has become identified with America's claim to be a model for a universal civilization.'[2]

The weight of corporate propaganda has been augmented by the growth of business networks and coalitions aimed at shaping policy outcomes. Alex Carey, author of *Taking the Risk out of Democracy*, argued that the 20th century has seen three related developments; 'the growth of democracy, the growth of corporate power, and the growth of corporate propaganda as a means of protecting corporate power against democracy.'[3] However, viewed from a more recent perspective, it is clear that democratic power was progressively eclipsed by corporate power during the 20th century. This was the result of several factors: the growth of corporate influence; the public relations-orchestrated spread of free market ideology; and the proliferation of business networks and coalitions aimed at exerting political pressure (see Figure 1.1). As a consequence, corporations now completely dominate the political process.

corporate resources/influence + market ideology + public relations + political mobilization = corporate political power

Figure 1.1 *Corporate power equation*

PUBLIC RELATIONS

Rhetoric and deception have long been part of the arsenal available for people to persuade others of their own good qualities or the merits of something they would like to sell. However, the profession and industry of public relations originated in the US in the early 20th century when corporations sought to defend themselves in the face of public hostility and worker unrest. Until this time, American business had taken a relatively contemptuous attitude towards public opinion. Typical of the period was the infamous pronouncement attributed to railroad magnate Cornelius Vanderbilt that 'the public be damned'.[4] Similarly, in 1901 when banker JP Morgan told a reporter that he owed 'the public nothing', he demonstrated a commonly held business attitude.

However, the growth of democracy and the expansion of the voting franchise threatened business power. In the US, between 1880 and 1920, the voting franchise was extended from about 15 per cent of the adult population to around 50 per cent.[5] The defence of propertied interests had been easier when the vote was largely restricted to property owners. With the emergence of a political system in which power depended on the consent of non-propertied interests as well, the maintenance of this power became more problematic.

In the period when the voting franchise was being extended, the size and economic power of American business corporations increased both rapidly and very visibly. Financial and industrial capital became increasingly centralized and concentrated. Many people were concerned that the large corporations were cold, anonymous, impersonal, heartless and without soul or conscience. The corporation seemed to be 'driven by a cold economic logic that defined its every decision as a money equation'.[6]

By the early decades of the 20th century, a period sometimes referred to as the 'progressive era' or the 'muckraking era', public opposition to corporate economic power was increasing. So-called muckraking journalists effectively exposed the corruption, exploitation and inhuman working conditions by which the majority of the great corporations had prospered. Magazines such as *McClures*, *Everybodys*, *Cosmopolitan*, *Colliers* and *The American* carried exposés of big business activities. Authors such as Upton Sinclair, Ida Tarbells, Tom Lawson, Gustavus Myers and others revealed the realities of the power of these corporations.[7]

The respect once commanded by those who owned and headed these corporations was progressively eroded as the ruthless exploitation involved in building up their empires was disclosed. Public opposition was so great that as *Fortune Magazine* later observed of this period, 'business did not discover ... until its reputation was all but destroyed ... that in a democracy nothing is more important than public opinion'.[8]

As the company mergers continued and the influence of these large conglomerates on government became evident, there was increasing public concern about the centralization of so much power in so few hands, and the degree to which competition was being curtailed by these mergers. The huge corporations posed a threat to democratic principles, which were based on the dispersal of power. Under President Theodore Roosevelt (1901–1909) the US federal government responded to this public concern with a suite of new legislation aimed at regulating corporations and breaking up some of the large trusts such as American Tobacco, DuPont and Standard Oil.[9] This led to the adoption of defensive public relations strategies by American big business.

Many corporations undertook some reform measures in recognition that the more extreme abuses of the system would have to be ameliorated in order to secure basic cooperation from an already alienated workforce and a resentful public. However, the strategy of adopting programmes of social reform was limited because these corporations had no intention of actually restructuring power relations. Consequently, the technique of changing attitudes rather than changing business practices began to gain increasing currency amongst corporate leaders in the US.

Corporate public relations gave the corporation the appearance of a soul and a mission: to provide a service to the general public. Corporations such as Ford Motor Company, General Electric, Standard Oil and Goodyear Rubber emphasized their goals as service rather than profit, and their owners and chief executives portrayed themselves as public benefactors and statesmen.[10]

Many of the early public relations professionals who advised these leaders honed their skills while serving on the US Committee for Public Relations formed in 1917 to sell war bonds and promote support for the First World War. Propaganda was used by nations on both sides during this war – indeed, it was the first use of mass propaganda outside of religion (the term 'propaganda' comes from the Catholic Church's *Congregatio de Propaganda Fide* of the 17th century, meaning the 'congregation for propagating the faith'). During the First World War, propaganda was used for the first time 'as a systematic weapon of war'.[11]

Business leaders were not slow to learn from this demonstration of how public opinion could be shaped and harnessed, and they hired the very men who had achieved it to defend their public reputations and fight the unions.[12] These men included Ivy Lee and Edward Bernays, each of whom has been cited as the father of modern public relations.

Bernays was the first to write books on public relations and apply theory to their practice, seeking to utilize psychology, sociology and other social sciences to manipulate the desires and beliefs of members of the public in ways that went far beyond mere publicity and advertising. One of his most famous public relations strategies was the 1929 Torches of Freedom March he organized on behalf of the American Tobacco Company. It involved women marching through New York streets smoking cigarettes, thus associating women's rights and liberation with smoking without linking the march to his client.[13]

Bernays was a key proponent of the idea that 'changing the public's opinion – using public relations techniques – about troublesome social movements and labour unions, was far more effective than hiring goons to club people'.[14]

Despite a general improvement in public acceptance of large corporations, public relations expanded in the 1920s, as part of a 'conscious policy of managing public attitudes to retain' corporate power. By the end of the 1920s, public opinion with respect to large corporations had been turned around: 'most middle-class Americans had come to accept the giant corporation as a permanent feature of society', if not a benevolent institution serving the public welfare. They voted for pro-business presidents such as Warren Harding, Calvin Coolidge and Herbert Hoover. Bernays claimed that it was 'the deliberate use of propaganda' that had turned the 'mergers and trusts' from 'ogres' to 'friendly giants' in the minds of the public. The prosperity of the 1920s had also helped.[15]

POLITICAL MOBILIZATION

The formation of business networks and coalitions to achieve political goals through a combination of public relations and political lobbying also originated in the US. The National Association of Manufacturers (NAM), the leading US business organization in the earlier part of the 20th century, was one of the first general business coalitions to take advantage of the new public relations methods and use them to gain political power.

NAM had been formed in 1895 to promote foreign trade but in 1903 it shifted its focus to opposing labour unions and defending the right of employers to establish work conditions, fire employees at will, and set wages without interference from unions or government. It was opposed to any government intervention in the management of business. It lobbied against government legislation that aimed to help workers; disseminated anti-union propaganda; and sought to influence the outcomes of local elections to prevent pro-labour candidates being elected.[16]

In 1913 NAM was investigated by a committee of Congress for mass dissemination of propaganda and paying 'Congressmen to promote its legislative agenda'. The inquiry[17] found that NAM had:

- employed a House of Representatives' employee to spy for it;
- contributed large amounts of money to particular congressional candidates for their reelection campaigns;
- formed a front group called the Workingmen's Protective Association for the purposes of campaigning for Republican candidates;

- paid people to buttonhole Congressmen and waylay them on the way to the chamber so they would miss a vote;
- undertaken a 'disguised propaganda campaign through newspaper syndicates' and public education venues;
- distributed large amounts of propaganda to schools, colleges and civic organizations.

The inquiry report stopped just short of accusing the NAM of conspiracy:

> *The correspondence between officials and employees of the association laid before your committee and placed in evidence shows it to have been an organization having purposes and aspirations along industrial, commercial, legislative, and other lines so vast and far-reaching as to excite at once admiration and fear – admiration for the genius which conceived them, and fear for the ultimate effects which the successful accomplishments of all these ambitions might have on a government such as ours.*[18]

The private utility companies in the US also conspired to subvert democratic demands for public control through political manoeuvering, financial strategies and propaganda campaigns. During the 1920s they set aside their differences and formed coalitions and networks to coordinate a major campaign aimed at securing private ownership and minimal government regulation of essential public services. They sought 'to educate the American public about the dangers to the American Way of Life that would come if the utilities were ever allowed to slip from private enterprise to public control'. And in the words of one of the industry's own representatives, they did 'much to change and direct the economic thought and economic practice of the American people'.[19] In 1925 a utilities' spokesman boasted that American business had 'captured the government, and no other government in the world has been put to the service of business as ours'.[20]

Many of the gains made by business interests during the 1920s through their use of public relations were lost during the Great Depression when tens of millions of people lost their jobs and few could afford the goods and services that utilities and manufacturers could provide. This time, however, it was not just individual corporations and industries that were under attack from public opinion and threats of government regulation, but the entire capitalist system that was being called into question by an increasing number of people. Confidence in the ability of unregulated capitalism to provide for the social good reached an all-time low and was replaced by a 'profound distrust of business ... as trustee of the national economy'.[21]

Business responded with a coordinated nationwide public relations effort to promote the capitalist system and the values of free enterprise.[22] Trade and industry associations formed and coordinated these efforts. For the first time public relations, business coalitions and free market ideology were combined – in this case to defend corporate power from democratic power. Following the war, the same combination was used to fight union power as well as democratic power. These developments are described in the first three chapters of this book.

FREE MARKET SCRIPTURES

The power of an ideology is that it presents a view of the world as the 'truth' and, in particular, as the moral truth. In the past religion has provided the moral truth. Today the moral truth presented by economics is just as compelling as that offered by traditional religions. The ideology of the 'free market' derives from neoclassical economics, but it is a simplified and reduced version that actually distorts and exaggerates neoclassical economic theories.[23] Corporate executives who drive the Market and know how it really works, and how it varies from the ideology, nevertheless preach the free market gospel because it suits their political purposes.

Free market scriptures not only embody unrealistic, idealized assumptions about how humans actually behave, but also promote an ideal for how societies *should* be organized. They assume that in capitalist nations communities are little more than a collection of individuals who always act rationally to maximize their self-interest, which is usually a material/economic interest. They are buyers and sellers in the Market and they participate in a rational, impersonal way to get the most they can of what they want for the lowest price. They compete to do this rather than cooperate or collude. These one-dimensional individuals are not constrained or motivated by morality, nor a sense of duty/obligation, nor community expectations and norms. They do not seek other non-material goals nor do they act altruistically.[24]

This ideal of buyers and sellers freely competing in the Market to achieve their self-interest is considered to be the best of all possible worlds, 'a prescription for a socially and ethically desirable' world. Adam Smith was the first in a long line of economists who argued that the pursuit of economic self-interest by businessmen served the public good. He claimed that even though a businessman 'intends only his own gain … he is in this, as in many other cases, led by an invisible hand to promote an end which was no part of his intention.'[25] Thus the selfishness of the businessman in trying to get rich is beneficial to society, including workers and consumers:

> *It is not from the benevolence of the butcher, the brewer or the baker that we expect our dinner, but from their regard to their own self-interest. We address ourselves, not to their humanity but to their self-love, and never talk to them of our own necessities but of their advantages. Every individual is continually exerting himself to find out the most*

> *advantageous employment for whatever capital he can command. It is his own advantage, indeed, and not that of society, which he has in view. But the study of his own advantage naturally, or rather necessarily, leads him to prefer that employment which is most advantageous to the society.*[26]

The free market gospel claims that the Market is able to perfectly match production to consumer demand without the need for centralized planning, while keeping prices close to the cost of the most efficient production, and while encouraging innovation to extend the choice for buyers. It achieves this through competition.

Free market missionaries declare that the Market is democratic because it is driven by individual choices; it is efficient because of competition between sellers; and it is non-discriminatory because the price mechanism is impartial when it comes to colour, gender and race. *Choice, competition and efficiency* ensure everyone is better off because the economy produces all the goods that people want at the lowest possible price and available resources are supposedly fully and efficiently utilized.[27]

The ultimate test of general welfare within this view is of course wealth, where wealth refers to the bountiful 'production and sale of marketed goods and services'. Wealth is the goal because, as noted, each individual seeks only his or her own material self-interest. The need for cooperation and mutual support in healthy communities is ignored as is the role of government in a well-functioning economy.[28]

Issues of wealth distribution, the market power of large producers, collusion between producers, and the power of the wealthy to monopolize resources for themselves, disappear into the small print of free market scriptures. These assert that, despite evidence to the contrary over the last few decades, as a nation gets wealthier the wealth will 'trickle down' to the poor because it is invested and well spent, and therefore more jobs will be created and everyone will benefit.[29]

The idea that capitalism is about extracting wealth from production and systematically channelling it into the hands of a minority – and that wealth is used as a means to acquire social and political power – has no place in the free market scriptures. Economic texts treat excess profit as an aberration resulting from imperfections in a market not yet in equilibrium. They claim that the accumulation of profits is not at the expense of others in society but in fact enriches everyone because it is those profits, when invested, that create even more wealth.[30]

The greed of the individual, far from being the sin that it was in traditional religion, is necessary to the functioning of the Market. Market gospel says that any activity that makes a profit must serve society and so must be morally right.[31] This portrayal of the Market as a social ideal has suited business interests, which have promoted it and extended it to mean that all business activity is in the public interest and any restriction or regulation of business is undesirable because it distorts the Free Market.

In this view, government intervention in the management of the economy is unnecessary and unwise because the Market is a self-correcting mechanism. Competition is supposed to guarantee that those who raise prices to take unreasonable profits will be priced out of the Market by others who charge less. Those who pay workers low wages will lose them to those who are willing to pay higher wages. And these market transactions are carried out freely and voluntarily because people are free to pursue their own interests without interference or coercion. They can choose their jobs and they can choose the products they will buy.

The Market will find a natural equilibrium between prices and demand, between wages and employment levels, and that equilibrium is optimal, correct and just.[32] Similarly, if someone sells shoddy or dangerous goods, their reputation will be soured or they can be sued for the damage that ensues. Therefore there is no need for quality, price or wage controls, nor other government regulation of economic activity – hence the *Free* Market.

Whereas the term 'capitalism' denotes a particular form of social and political organization that can be critiqued and compared to other forms of organization, the Market is presented by business people and economists as a 'natural', innate, spontaneous form of human activity with its own immutable natural laws – that is, Market forces. When the real world does not conform to these laws, business people and economists refer to deficiencies and deformities in particular markets rather than discrepancies or incongruities in the Market view of the world.[33]

Business people have set out to conflate the individualism of the Market – that is, the individual's freedom to choose goods and a job – with the individualism that Anglo-Saxon cultures traditionally valued, which is a broader political concept altogether. Similarly, they correlate business freedom with economic freedom, and economic freedom with political freedom. They call consumer choice 'consumer democracy' and equate it with political democracy. They claim that 'shareholder democracy' ensures business enterprises are democratic and accountable (see Chapter 12).

Economists have long recognized, along with governments, that the market model has its limitations and failures. In the past, governments have intervened to provide goods that the Market failed to provide, particularly public goods. In other cases, families and communities have provided goods and services on a non-market basis. Governments have also intervened to protect the community against 'externalities' – that is, side-effects of market activities that are not factored into the buyer–seller transactions. These externalities include pollution and other environmental impacts, as well as health and other social effects of economic activities.

The problem for business owners is that governments represent a rival source of power in society. Although governments generally bend over backwards to facilitate business activities, they also have the potential, in democracies, to restrict and regulate them when pressured by the community. Yet governments are also still necessary to ensure law and order so that property rights can be protected and contracts enforced. Businesses have therefore mobilized and run public relations campaigns to reduce the power of elected governments.

Free enterprise has become the prevailing idea of our times, an idea without serious rival – although not without critics. It is an idea that equates business interests with the public interest and gives corporations increasing freedom to invest, produce and trade without government interference, despite the social, cultural and environmental consequences that are accumulating. The facilitation of market transactions increasingly takes priority over democratic process, and social and environmental decisions are increasingly left to the Market. Corporations are able to go about their business, increasingly free from democratic controls.

The 'Free Market' has become the dominant ideal and is given priority over democratic ideals whenever they are in conflict. Free enterprise propaganda has deprived its victims of the rationale to oppose it, credible alternatives to rival it, and the mechanisms to control it. This book does not argue that markets are undesirable. Rather, it seeks to explain how a free market ideal based on unrealistic dogmas and ideologies has vanquished all other ideals for human development.

NOTES

1 Edward L. Bernays, *Propaganda*, New York, Horace Liveright, 1928, p1.
2 John Gray, *False Dawn: The Delusions of Global Capitalism*, London, Granta Books, 2002, pp3, 104.
3 Alex Carey, *Taking the Risk out of Democracy*, ed. Andrew Lohrey, Sydney, UNSW Press, 1995, p18.
4 Thomas Cochran and William Miller, *The Age of Enterprise*, New York, Macmillan, 1942, p311.
5 Walter Lippman, *Essays in the Public Philosophy*, Boston, Little, Brown, 1955, pp39–40.
6 Louis Galambos, *The Public Image of Big Business in America, 1880–1940*, Baltimore, The Johns Hopkins University Press, 1975, p159; Roland Marchand, *Creating the Corporate Soul: The Rise of Public Relations and Corporate Imagery in American Big Business*, Berkeley, University of California Press, 1998, p8.
7 L. L. L. Golden, *Only by Public Consent*, New York, Hawthorn Books, 1968, p30; Alfred D. Chandler and Richard S. Tedlow, *The Coming of Managerial Capitalism: A Casebook History of American Economic Institutions*, Homewood, Illinois, Richard D. Irwin, 1985, p553; Carey, *Taking the Risk out of Democracy*, p80; Marchand, *Creating the Corporate Soul*, p7; Editorial, 'Business Is Still in Trouble', *Fortune*, May, 1949, p198.
8 Editorial, 'Business Is Still in Trouble', p198.
9 Marchand, *Creating the Corporate Soul*, p41; George Bittlingmayer, 'Antitrust and Business Activity: The First Quarter Century', *Business History Review*, Autumn, 1996, pp364, 369; John Stauber and Sheldon Rampton, *Toxic Sludge Is Good for You! Lies, Damn Lies and the Public Relations Industry*, Monroe, Maine, Common Courage Press, 1995, p19.

10 Marchand, *Creating the Corporate Soul*, pp90, 166, 200.
11 Don Bates, '"Mini-Me" History: Public Relations from the Dawn of Civilization', Institute for Public Relations 2002, pp6, 11; Andrew Lohrey, 'Introduction' in Carey, *Taking the Risk out of Democracy*, p1.
12 Carey, *Taking the Risk out of Democracy*, p22.
13 *Ibid.*, p81; Jeff Blyskal and Marie Blyskal, *PR: How the Public Relations Industry Writes the News*, New York, William Morrow and Co., 1985, p68; Bates, '"Mini-Me" History', p11.
14 Johan Carlisle, 'Public Relationships: Hill and Knowlton, Robert Gray, and the CIA', *CovertAction*, no 44, 1993, p22.
15 Carey, *Taking the Risk out of Democracy*, p79; Marchand, *Creating the Corporate Soul*, p162; Strother Holland Walker and Paul Sklar, *Business Finds Its Voice: Management's Effort to Sell the Business Idea to the Public*, New York and London, Harper & Brothers, 1938, p2; Bernays quoted in Stuart Ewen, *PR! A Social History of Spin*, New York, Basic Books, 1996, p215.
16 'Violations of Free Speech and Rights of Labor', Senate Committee on Education and Labor, 14 August 1939, pp208–9.
17 *Ibid.*, p209; American Federation of Labor, 'National Association of Manufacturers Exposed: Revelations of Senate Lobby Investigation', Washington, DC, American Federation of Labor, 1913, pp20, 23.
18 Quoted in American Federation of Labor, 'National Association of Manufacturers Exposed', p18.
19 Sharon Beder, *Power Play: The Fight to Control the World's Electricity*, Melbourne and New York, Scribe Publications and the New Press, 2003; Karl Schriftgiesser, *The Lobbyists: The Art and Business of Influencing Lawmakers*, Boston, Little, Brown & Co., 1951, p59; Carl D. Thompson, *Confessions of the Power Trust*, New York, E. P. Dutton & Co., 1932, p270.
20 Quoted in Alan R. Raucher, *Public Relations and Business 1900–1929*, Baltimore, The Johns Hopkins Press, 1968, p66.
21 Walker and Sklar, *Business Finds Its Voice*, p3.
22 Carey, *Taking the Risk out of Democracy*, p79.
23 Robert L. Heilbroner, *The Nature and Logic of Capitalism*, New York, W.W. Norton & Co., 1985, p107; Peter Self, *Rolling Back the Market: Economic Dogma and Political Choice*, London, Macmillan Press, 2000, p26.
24 James G. Carrier, 'Introduction', in James G. Carrier (ed) *Meanings of the Market: The Free-market in Western Culture*, New York, Oxford University Press, 1997, pp2–3; Lindy Edwards, *How to Argue with an Economist: Reopening Political Debate in Australia*, Cambridge, Cambridge University Press, 2002, pp54–5.
25 Self, *Rolling Back the Market*, p12; Adam Smith quoted in John Kenneth Galbraith, *The Anatomy of Power*, London, Hamish Hamilton, 1984.
26 Quoted in D. P. O'Brien, *The Classical Economists*, Oxford, Clarendon Press, 1975.
27 Edwards, *How to Argue with an Economist*, pp40–1, 77–8; Carrier, 'Introduction', pp2–3; Self, *Rolling Back the Market*, p7.
28 Self, *Rolling Back the Market*, pp26, 29.
29 *Ibid.*, pp14, 27.
30 Heilbroner, *The Nature and Logic of Capitalism*, pp33–5, 112; Locke cited in Heilbroner, *The Nature and Logic of Capitalism*, p113.

31 Sharon Beder, *Selling the Work Ethic: From Puritan Pulpit to Corporate PR*, London, Zed Books, 2000, pp19–22; Heilbroner, *The Nature and Logic of Capitalism*, p115.
32 Andrew Bard Schmookler, *The Illusion of Choice: How the Market Economy Shapes Our Destiny*, Albany, State University of New York Press, 1993; Edwards, *How to Argue with an Economist*, p78.
33 Carrier, 'Introduction', pp17–8; Edwards, *How to Argue with an Economist*, p65.

2

Promoting Business Values

Business, free enterprise, is the economic manifestation of the free society, the principal reason for America's pre-eminence.

EDITORIAL, *WALL STREET JOURNAL*, 1952[1]

... in so far as the countries of advanced capitalism are 'business civilisations', permeated by a business culture and a business ethos, business itself has played a crucial role in making them so. RALPH MILIBAND[2]

In the early 1930s, the heads of some of the largest US corporations –'the men who manage America's industry, trade and finance'[3] – started meeting regularly for dinner in New York. It was during the Great Depression, when public confidence in capitalism was at an all-time low and President Franklin Roosevelt was threatening to regulate corporations and curb their power. One of the diners was Robert B. Henderson, president of Pacific Portland Cement and vice-president of the National Association of Manufacturers (NAM). He described how the dinner meetings had been initiated at a conference where 'a few advanced thinking souls... realized that only top leadership would serve the purposes of business salvation'. He tells how, as a result of these meetings, 'gradually the gospel spread and the real leadership of American industry commenced to get into the front-line trench'. Members of the group called themselves the 'Brass Hats'.[4]

The entire project was original. Business men had sold goods and services; they had 'sold' individual companies, or industries, or even specific ideas (like the idea that the private ownership of utilities is best); but they had never undertaken to sell business-as-a-whole. Never before had they tried to sell that general philosophy which animates business, and which serves as a guide to social, political, and economic action.[5]

Companies that were supposed to be competitors colluded in a united effort to spread the free market message to the public using every available public relations avenue. To sell 'business-as-a-whole' they combined free market ideology, public relations techniques and business networks.

Franklin D. Roosevelt had been elected president of the US in 1932 with promises of a New Deal between government and the people, a deal that meant that government would intervene to help the people in times of crisis, such as the Depression. As part of the New Deal, Roosevelt's government instituted major legislative and institutional reforms, including regulations aimed at stabilizing and restoring confidence in the banks; a programme of public works projects that gave work to millions of the unemployed and modernized American infrastructure; and measures to reduce poverty.

These measures involved high levels of government spending, high taxes and increased government intervention in business affairs, all of which were abhorrent to leading business people. The president of the US Chamber of Commerce claimed that the government was in the hands of an 'organized mob'. Yet the government had so much popular support that business could not attack the New Deal directly without seeming to attack the public; 'and for business men to attack the public is for them to confess their inability to "serve" the public'.[6] The answer, business leaders realized, was to change public opinion and undermine the support for New Deal measures. To do this they sought to associate the New Deal with 'creeping socialism' and to promote the benefits of unregulated capitalism.[7]

In response to the decline in business confidence that accompanied the Depression and the New Deal programmes of the Roosevelt government, many US corporations had already made public relations a permanent part of their management structures. But business leaders realized that a more wholesale, coordinated effort was required if public opinion was to be turned around. They embarked on a full-scale battle that Alfred Sloan Jr of General Motors called 'a struggle between "political management" [government control] and "private enterprise" [corporate control]'. Sloan urged business leaders to 'fight to protect the very foundation of the American system'.[8]

NATIONAL ASSOCIATION OF MANUFACTURERS (NAM)

The Brass Hats chose NAM as their vehicle of battle, and in 1932 big business took over the association and restructured it, under the presidency of 'Brass Hat' Robert Lund of Lambert Pharmacal Co., to ensure that large corporations were well represented on the directorate. NAM claimed the right to call itself 'the voice of American industry' because it represented 35,000 manufacturers, employing around 5 million people.[9]

When Lund took over he established a public relations department and a director of public relations within NAM. Membership of NAM doubled over the following four years and the contributions of large corporations increased dramatically, so that 262 nationally known companies were contributing half of NAM's income. These included AT&T, Colgate-Palmolive-Peet, DuPont (the largest contributor), General Motors (the second largest contributor), Eastman

Kodak, General Foods, IBM, Johnson & Johnson, Monsanto, Procter & Gamble, Standard Oil, Texas Corporation and Westinghouse Electric.[10]

Following its reorganization, NAM's 'propaganda activities... became one of its most important functions, absorbing more time, effort, and money than all the other functions of the association put together.'[11] It set out to 'sell the "American way of life" to the American people' and coordinate business opposition to the New Deal.

NAM stated in its 1934 Annual Report that it was spreading 'fairly and at the same time vigorously and militantly' the 'true story of business'. In its less public documents it stated: 'Public policies in our democracy are eventually a reflection of public opinion. If we are to avoid disaster, it is essential that this public opinion be informed and able to discriminate between the sound and the unsound' and '[n]ow, more than ever before, strikes are being won or lost in the newspapers and over the radio'.[12]

Public relations expert Bruce Barton told NAM: 'The [business] story should be told, with all the imagination and art of which modern advertising is capable. It should be told just as continuously as the people are told that Ivory Soap floats...'.[13] The chair of NAM's National Industrial Information Committee called for business leaders in each state to get together to help with the campaign in order to 'meet the urgent need of preserving the private enterprise system... Summed up, the chief concern of business today is that it is not enjoying a favourable public.'[14]

NAM's campaign utilized all the techniques of persuasion that had previously been used to sell products 'to sell the business idea... the American System of Private Enterprise'.[15] These were supplemented by the techniques developed in the new field of public relations. Its National Industrial Information Committee put together a report entitled *Industry Must Speak* that set out what was involved in such a campaign (see Box 2.1) that 'Day after day, systematically and forcefully' hammered home its message to the American people.

BOX 2.1 ELEMENTS OF NAM'S CAMPAIGN

I. *Daily newspapers* – Realizing that public thought is shaped to a large degree by a country's newspapers, the National Association of Manufacturers' public information programme regularly covers the newspaper field to industry's advantage.
   a) *Bulletin to newspaper editors* – at regular intervals publishers and editorial writers of every daily newspaper in the country are furnished with an authoritative explanation of industry's viewpoint on current topics through the 'Voice of American Industry'.
   b) *Daily comic feature* – (Uncle Abner Says) – one of America's most popular comic features. Uncle Abner knows that if he can make his neighbours smile with his homely homespun comments on current problems, he can make them think.
   c) *You and Your Nation's Affairs* – popularizing economics for the masses. A group of outstanding authorities write this daily column for newspapers.

d) *News Stories* – industry's position on vital questions of the moment is explained to the public through spot news releases to local newspapers, press associations, radio stations and news syndicates.

II. *Weekly Newspapers* – To weekly newspapers go the following services carrying industry's story into the smaller cities and towns, reaching back to the grass roots:

a) *Weekly news clipsheet* (the nation's largest news feature syndicate) containing (1) Washington column (2) news and editorials on timely subjects (3) weekly article on Constitution.

b) *The country's largest cartoon service* drawn by Nate Collier, one of America's ace cartoonists – cartoons with a punch on current problems.

III. *Business Papers* – a) Bi-monthly clipsheet b) News releases c) Special articles

IV. *Advertising* – a) A series of full-page newspaper advertisements telling the facts about American industry and promoting community harmony. b) Outdoor advertising – proclaiming on the billboards of the nation that 'There Is No Way Like the American Way with Its "World's Highest Standard of Living", "World's Shortest Working Hours", "World's Highest Wages".'

V. *Radio* – Good will for industry is being engendered over the air in numerous ways.

a) *The NAM programme 'The American Family Robinson'* – the nation's largest dramatic radio programme, combining entertainment with simple facts about the American industrial system through a series of 15-minute electrical transcriptions, used for more than two years on stations from coast to coast.

b) *Foreign language transcriptions* – carrying the story of the accomplishments of American industry to the millions of Americans who listen to foreign language programmes.

c) *Speakers for special occasions* – giving the radio public an opportunity to listen to the views of leading industrialists on topics of current interest.

d) *Materials to news commentators*.

VI. *Public Speeches* – Speeches are one of the most effective ways of presenting the facts to the public. The NAM's information programme includes:

a) *Speakers' Bureau* – handling requests for speakers before conventions, clubs, on local radio programmes, etc.

b) *Special material for use by speakers* wherever needed.

c) *Professional speakers* to carry industry's message before groups of all types.

VII. *Motion Pictures*

a) *NAM 10-minute shorts*. Each picture has its own theme. One entitled 'America Yesterday, Today and Tomorrow', with narration by John S. Young, tells the story of progress under the American industrial system. Another, 'Men and Machines', with narration by Lowell Thomas, banishes the myth that machines are the principal source of unemployment. These films have been widely shown in (1) theatres (2) schools (3) industrial plants (4) clubs, etc.

b) *Newsreels* – carrying statements of the industrialists and others to the motion picture audiences of America through regular newsreel channels.

VIII. *Direct Mail* –

a) *'You and Industry'* library – a series of booklets to educators, professional men and women, schools and libraries and others throughout the country... The first attempt to popularize the facts about industry, making them attractive and entertaining.

b) *Shareholders' letter* – giving the owners of American industry – the shareholders – the facts about situations affecting the welfare of industry.

IX. *Foreign Language Contacts –*
 a) *Foreign Language News Service* – millions of workers in American industrial plants are readers of foreign language newspapers, and each week this programme reaches newspapers printed in four foreign languages.
 b) *Radio programmes in six languages*.

X. *Employee Contacts* – Believing that a fully informed employee is industry's greatest asset, the NAM supplies employers with a many-sided programme of employee information:
 a) *Leaflets* – a complete series telling employees the real facts about American industry.
 b) *Bulletin board posters* – for use on plant bulletin boards.
 c) *'Industrial Facts'* – carrying truth and knowledge to group leaders in industry – foremen, junior executives, superintendents – who help to shape the thinking of others.
 d) *Sound slide films* – one of the most effective mediums for employee information has been found to be sound slide films. Visually presenting the facts about the American industrial system, a series of NAM films has been seen by thousands of employees through the country. They are also used in schools and civic meetings. New films are ready for showing.
 e) *Plant publications* – a regular monthly editorial and news service reaching house organs which are read by employees from cover to cover.

Source: 'Violations of Free Speech and Rights of Labor'. Senate Committee on Education and Labor. 14 August 1939, pp160–161.

According to a 1939 Senate committee, this propaganda material reached millions of Americans (see Table 2.1).

Not satisfied with this comprehensive programme, the committee looked for ways to expand the campaign, and added a national radio show, more community programmes, and a strategy for getting material into schools and colleges 'where the thinking of our future generations should be shaped along sound lines'.[16] Motion pictures and sound slide films were thought to be particularly good for schools

Table 2.1 *Distribution of NAM propaganda*

Publication	*Circulation/Distribution*
Uncle Abner Says cartoon	2 million
'You and Your Nation's Affairs'	4.5 million
Foreign Language News Service	2.4 million
Employee leaflets	11 million
Motion pictures – *Let's Go America* and *Men and Machines*	6 million

Source: 'Violations of Free Speech and Rights of Labor'. Senate Committee on Education and Labor. 14 August 1939, pp162–166.

because they were 'the most impressive medium for leaving a lasting impression upon children. Here is an almost unlimited field of distribution in which we would be reaching children during their formative years.'[17]

In its effort 'to reach every group... through every channel' NAM was rather shy about owning up as the source of all this material. NAM's prepared editorials, columns, cartoons and news articles, which reached millions of people, were presented as originating with newspaper staff or independent individuals.[18] The same was true of its billboard posters, radio programmes and other materials.[19] For example, NAM advised in its manual for organizing civic progress meetings that the meeting should be 'organized entirely under local sponsorship, rather than under the auspices' of NAM and that 'we do not believe it is necessary to give local publicity to the fact that we supply the speaker. We believe it is more likely to attract a large audience if you announce him as Dr. So-and-So, of Blank University...'.[20]

The cost to NAM of the campaign was a fraction of what it would have been on a commercial basis because millions of dollars' worth of billboards, radio time and newspaper space were donated by business interests.[21]

The re-election of Roosevelt in 1936 came as a big shock to many businessmen who had invested in this massive propaganda campaign. The public relations techniques had come 'in certain quarters to command an exaggerated respect, as an infallible and almost automatic mechanism for directing public opinion, needing only to be properly financed'.[22] Yet Roosevelt's landslide victory had shown that public opinion was clearly on his side despite the business campaign.

The business community's response was to augment NAM's campaign with a more decentralized but coordinated local business campaign aimed more at local communities. Businesses, individually and under the auspices of NAM, used every medium of communication available to sell capitalism, as well as the more usual advertisements in newspapers and magazines that had the added bonus of winning friends in the press. US Steel noted in 1938 that 'The most important thing that faces a big corporation today is what the American people will think and what the American people will do about big business.'[23]

The refreshed campaign aimed, not just at production and dissemination of 'educational' materials, but also at strategies that utilized personal social pressures at the community level.[24] Figure 2.1 shows the way that NAM's National Industrial Council guided its local committees and publicity directors to ensure they would reach all sectors of the local community.

In addition, individual companies also adopted a more decentralized approach. For example, when General Motors decentralized its capital and administrative authority while keeping policy-making power centralized, it found it was not only economically advantageous but also politically useful. It meant that local communities competed to keep or attract local branches of GM and were opposed to any labour strikes or discord that might jeopardize this. Moreover, each local branch would carry out its own public relations activities, including establishing

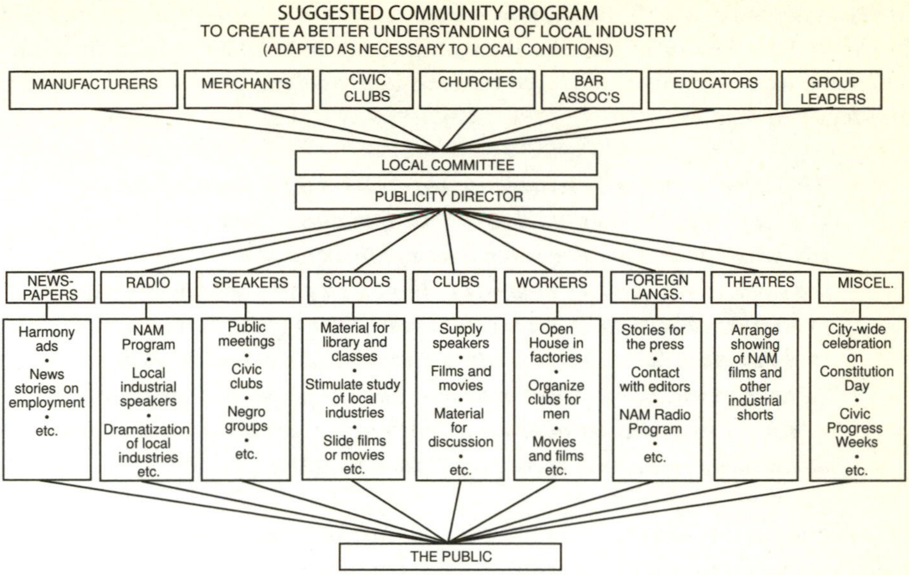

Figure 2.1 *National Industrial Council community program outreach*

Source: 'Violations of Free Speech and Rights of Labor'. Senate Committee on Education and Labor. 14 August 1939, p. 283.

friendly personal relations with local businessmen, bankers, newspaper editors, journalists and citizens. In this way 'plants begin to seem less like impersonal branches of big business; they take on the appearance of genuine, home-grown local industries, and drive their roots in among the people'.[25]

Similarly Ford's public relations director noted the importance of good public relations: 'Business sometimes move[s] ... because a town has become infested with the peculiar form of social, political, or unionistic philosophy which confused progress with the persecution of industry'. The steel industry also found decentralization offered 'the opportunity to control relations with local "publics"'.[26]

Some businesses found the NAM propaganda a bit too overpowering and obviously biased. One of NAM's own surveys in 1936 found that, although 'the majority of opinion heartily endorsed' it:

> *A smaller group took exception to the extreme tone and temper of most of the material sent to them ... thinking there might be the danger of antagonizing employees by leaflets and posters that were both partisan and biased ... too obviously propaganda on behalf of Industry and Management ...*[27]

Towards the end of the 1930s, the government's LaFollette Committee investigated NAM's public relations and labelled them propaganda rather than 'public education'. The LaFollette Committee surveyed business lobbying and promotional activities and reported that:

> *They asked not what the weaknesses and abuses of the economic structure had been, and how they could be corrected, but instead paid millions to tell the public that nothing was wrong and that grave dangers lurked in the proposed remedies. In addition to this broad political objective, the association considered its propaganda material an effective weapon in its fight against labor unions ... the committee deplores the failure of the National Association of Manufacturers and the powerful corporations which guide its policies to adapt themselves to changing times and to laws which the majority of the people deem wise and necessary.*[28]

In response to this further bad publicity, the NAM urged business to devote its entire public relations and advertising budgets to shaping public opinion in favour of the 'free' enterprise system.

The Free market message

Business propaganda coordinated by NAM presented an image of harmony between various interests – workers, bosses, consumers, stockholders – despite the obvious conflicts of interest: 'good times for industry mean good times for you' and 'you prosper when factories prosper'.[29] According to business, what was good for business was good for everyone.

The attempt to portray worker interest as being in harmony with business interest and to posit harmony as necessary for community prosperity – 'Prosperity dwells where harmony reigns'[30] – was not only a way of getting public support for business but a way of undermining support for unions on the part of both workers and the general public. NAM reprinted an article from *Printers' Ink* that stated: 'If manufacturers would invest one-tenth of the money in advertising preparation that they apparently quite willingly invest in labor spies, tear gas and other methods, which have proved worse than useless, they will stand a far better chance of winning public support than is possible under present circumstances.'[31]

The American economic system was portrayed as being just and delivering equal opportunity to everyone. It ensured that products improved and their prices came down, while good workers got higher wages and moved up in America's classless society. Capitalism was portrayed as 'an economic system of free men in which production and distribution is on personal initiative with the incentive of private profit'.[32] Also, the system was democratic because the price system meant that consumers determined what was produced and sold:

> *The customer has become the real Chairman of the Board of every progressive enterprise ... The public really determines the wages that can be paid. The fact is that all of us pay each other's wages. American business cannot be separated from America ... American business is our business ... 'business' is not a separate class ... it simply represents an extension of the public will, and the interests of management and of ordinary people are therefore identical ('What hurts business hurts you').*[33]

Business people portrayed themselves as striving to serve society. Everyone, it was argued, would be better off if industrial managers were given respect as the nation's leaders and allowed to carry on without government interference. The message to be emphasized was that political freedom, religious freedom, and 'economic' freedom were indivisible and any encroachment on economic freedom would reduce other freedoms.[34]

NAM opposed government expenditures and ridiculed bureaucratic efforts to cure economic problems. The NAM-sponsored cartoon character Uncle Abner espoused: 'Seems t'me like business could stand on its own feet a lot better if the politicians would get off'n its back.'[35] Uncle Abner was opposed to government regulations, taxes, public works, politicians and government loans.

The American economic system and American industry were declared the best in the world – 'There's no way like the American way.' It was claimed that this perfect system involved leaving business free to do as it wished without interference from government. In this way NAM sought to 'render public opinion intolerant of the aims of social progress through legislative effort'.[36] It told schoolchildren: 'It is essential, in a free system, that there should be no bureaucratic control of the citizens.'[37]

The appeal to nationalism was also evident in this and subsequent campaigns. By equating free enterprise with the national interest, citizens were supposed to feel that their own personal interests should not take priority over the greater national interest. Even if, individually, they were not materially well off as a result of free enterprise, the nation was, and this provided them with the opportunity to be better off in the future.

In reality, the large businesses that dominated NAM's agenda did not themselves believe NAM propaganda. A major purpose of business mergers was to overcome the uncertainty created by competition and so have more control over markets and therefore prices and sales. Despite the free market rhetoric about the benefits of competition, big business tried to avoid it and often found benefits in cooperating with each other against the interests of the consumer. A whole range of industry and trade associations, trusts and holding companies were formed for this purpose.[38]

While executives publicly extolled competition and the way it forced them to lower prices, the corporations they managed sought to control prices by swallowing up their competition. As a result the automobile, steel, rubber, tobacco, liquor, chemical and other industries all came to be dominated by a few very large companies (with names like International Nickel, International Salt, International Paper and United States Steel). A few marginalized smaller companies sometimes managed to hang on around the fringes. This industry concentration occurred in most industrialized countries.[39]

Despite antitrust legislation, by 1933 the 200 largest American corporations (not counting financing firms) and their subsidiaries controlled almost 60 per cent of the assets of all corporations. Not only were the large firms able to influence prices paid and received, but they often acted in unison rather than competition. Even where there was not explicit discussions about prices, a lead firm would often set the price that others would follow. Competition between firms was therefore based on attempts to differentiate products with the help of advertising and marketing, rather than on the basis of price.[40] Competition had shifted from competition between producers and sellers to competition 'between the business community on the one side and the consumers on the other'.[41] Contrary to the prevailing corporate propaganda, it was hardly a situation where business interests and public interest were synonymous.

Despite its discord with reality, free market ideology gained ground. In 1938 NAM president Robert Lund claimed credit for the shift of public opinion 'to the right'. He pointed out that:

> *... this program, five years ago, initiated a new era and a new formula in public contact by industry, that in volume of publicity the campaign has totalled more than all other similar programs combined, that it has continually – day by day and week by week – expounded to millions of people a certain set of principles, and that millions of our people believe today in these principles who did not five years ago.*[42]

Promotion of the free enterprise system did not cease with the advent of the Second World War. In November 1942, with the war as a backdrop to business's domestic battle, James Selvage, public relations director of NAM, gave a speech entitled 'Selling the Private Enterprise System'. In it Selvage asserted that 'ours is not a job today of selling merchandise ... we are selling America itself to Americans ... else freedom and its blood brother free enterprise will perish from the earth; make no mistake ... this is no sham battle that is going on behind the battle front'. Selvage pointed out that since corporations had little civilian merchandise to sell during wartime, 'selling the free enterprise system is the remaining reason for existence' of public relations and advertising. It is public relations and advertising, Selvage insisted, that 'must win or lose the battle for free enterprise'.[43]

A year later, the assistant director of public relations at General Motors, Fred Eldean, told an audience of newspaper publishers:

> *A manufacturer places a product on the market and gets a referendum from the people. The people in buying or not buying vote for or against the product. A free people expressing themselves in a free market, with an industry competing to serve them, brought the highest standard of living in the world ... Beyond selling his own company the local advertiser can sell the free American economy. He can sell it in terms that the local public can understand. He can sell it in terms of how it affects the people ... As Democracy requires a free press, a free people require a free market. The interpretation of the free market is the next job for institutional advertising.*[44]

These programmes to influence public opinion, although massive, were only the beginning. The chief significance of the period leading up to the Second World War was in the political coordination of business to defend the system as a whole from any change that threatened business control and power. The real free enterprise campaigns were yet to come.

COUNTERING GOVERNMENT REGULATION AND THE UNIONS

The Second World War, while restoring much confidence in the ability of business to deliver the goods, also demonstrated to many people that government controls, economic planning, and the public provision of welfare protection, could ensure a better society for all. During the war the vice-chairman of General Motors, Donaldson Brown, had written to NAM's president warning:

> *The public is profoundly conscious of the 'miracle of production' that industry is performing. Paradoxically enough, it is the very efficiency of our industrial system in turning out the goods required by the armed forces that endangers industry in the future through its threat to the system of free enterprise. Everyone knows that we are subject today to a high degree of governmental control, but too many may come to believe that the efficiency being displayed by industry derives from this war-time incident of centralized planning and administration, rather than the qualities inherent within industry itself.*[45]

In the immediate post-war period, key business organizations were concerned about government intervention and controls on the one hand, and union activity on the other – Big Government and Big Labour. Proposals for further government intervention included price controls, a rising minimum wage, expanded unemployment insurance and tax reforms. Unions were active and in some cases demanding not just improved pay and conditions, income security and full employment through government spending, but also a say in corporate decisions in areas such as pricing and investment. They were advocating social planning and expansion of the welfare state.[46]

The way in which business in the US used its power and resources to oppose unionism was unique in scale and comprehensiveness. In Britain unions were seen as necessary to containing radicalism and class struggle. The 1919 British Cabinet was told that 'trade union organisation was the only thing between us and anarchy'. Following the Second World War, when economic times were tough, British governments – both Labour and Conservative – expected trade unions 'to play a major part in maintaining industrial discipline, curbing militancy, and persuading their members to reduce their demands for higher wages'. In return, governments praised the role of trade unions, and union representatives were incorporated into government processes through representation on committees, royal commissions, inquiries and boards of nationalized industries.[47]

British trade union leaders tended to have narrow agendas, in terms of pay and conditions, rather than radical agendas aimed at the overthrow of the capitalist system. While the same was largely true of US trade union leaders, they and the measures they were promoting were nevertheless seen as a threat to the autonomy of business, and many US businessmen believed union demands were the beginning of the 'slippery slope towards socialism'.[48] The Opinion Research Corporation found in 1947 that 60 per cent of business executives said that 'business faces a real threat in the Socialistic trend'. An even higher percentage of executives in both large and small firms (80 per cent) agreed that more needed to be done to sell free enterprise to the American people.[49]

Business people 'shared a common commitment to halting the more radical features of the New Deal, such as public power, progressive taxation and pro-consumer regulation, and preserving the autonomy of corporate enterprise'.[50] Other problems for business, identified by the privately conducted polls, included the way that Americans were suspicious of the motives of corporate leadership; the lack of public 'understanding' of the role of corporations in providing America's high living standards; the belief of workers that technological progress was not in their interest; and the 'misinformation' put out by 'special-interest groups that needed to be counteracted'.[51]

Polls generally confirmed business fears that the public did not believe in the free enterprise system as wholeheartedly as business would wish. Although most people were in favour of private ownership and thought well of large corporations, a majority also thought that most businessmen did not have the good of the nation in mind when they made their decisions and therefore government oversight was necessary. Many believed that businesses made huge profits and, business leaders felt, few understood the relationship between profits and investment. Surveys showed that some 70 per cent of workers believed that the government should guarantee full employment. Many workers did not trust their employers and were not convinced of the value of free enterprise. A substantial number of workers, in fact, supported government ownership or control of the economy.[52]

Business sought to deal with these threats by selling free enterprise on the basis that 'if you control public opinion you have the government in your hand and labor behind the eight ball'.[53] Public relations consultants, eager for business, promoted the need for their services. Very large sums of money were spent on lobbying, institutional advertising, philanthropy, research sponsorship and other public relations activities. But the core of their efforts was 'economic education' – that is, the selling of free enterprise. All the major trade associations, foundations and corporations took part in this, including the US Chamber of Commerce, NAM and the Committee for Economic Development (CED).[54]

In her history of this period, Elizabeth Fones-Wolf explains how business groups countered the perceived trend towards socialism:

> *The business community ... set out to build an agreement around an alternative agenda. In doing so, it sought not only to recast the political economy of post-war America, but also to reshape the ideas, images, and attitudes through which Americans understood their world. Employers wanted support for the belief that economic decisions should be made in corporate boardrooms, not in legislative chambers. Prosperity was to be achieved through reliance on individual initiative and the natural harmony of workers and managers inherent in business's interpretation of the free enterprise system.*[55]

Fones-Wolf points out that in a two-pronged strategy, business organizations sought to discredit organized labour and unions by associating them with communism, which threatened individual freedom, and to promote business values by appeals to patriotism and American values.[56] Similarly, Alex Carey, in the article 'Managing Public Opinion: The Corporate Offensive', argued that corporations sought 'to identify the free enterprise system with every cherished value, and identify interventionist governments and strong unions (the only agencies capable of checking the complete domination of society by the corporations) with tyranny, oppression and even subversion'.[57]

Corporations, and the public relations people hired by them, identified business interests with national interest and 'the traditional American free enterprise system with social harmony, freedom, democracy, the family, the church, and patriotism', while they identified 'all government regulation of the affairs of business, and all liberals who supported such "interference", with communism and subversion'.[58]

Henry Link, head of the polling company the Psychological Corporation, argued that the promotion of free enterprise alone was not enough. What was needed to restore the legitimacy of business and prevent the interference of government was 'a transfer in emphasis from free enterprise to the freedom of all individuals under free enterprise; from capitalism to the much broader concept: Americanism'.[59]

What followed was 'the most intensive "sales" campaign in the history of the industry' according to Daniel Bell, then editor of *Fortune* magazine. What was being sold was free market dogma, and the full weight of business resources was poured into it: 'The apparatus itself is prodigious: 1600 business periodicals, 577 commercial and financial digests, 2500 advertising agencies, 500 public relations counsellors, 4000 corporate public relations departments and more than 6500 "house organs" with a combined circulation of more than 70 million.'[60]

Specific campaigns consumed huge resources. NAM spent over $3 million on one particular campaign after the war, opposing price controls. President Harry S. Truman described how:

> *The NAM spent a million and a half on newspaper advertising. They sent their own speakers to make a thousand talks before women's clubs, civic organizations and college students. A specially designed publication went to 37,000 school teachers, another one to 15,000 clergymen, another went to 35,000 farm leaders, and still another to 40,000 women's clubs. A special slipsheet with NAM propaganda went to 7500 weekly newspapers and to 2500 columnists and editorial writers . . .*[61]

NAM claimed that, as a result of this campaign, public support for price controls dropped from 85 per cent to 26 per cent.[62] President Truman strongly disapproved of NAM's campaign and in 1948 said of it: 'We know how the NAM organized its conspiracy against the American consumer.'[63]

NAM also raised several million dollars for its campaign against 'collectivism' in 1946 and 1947, along with additional funds to oppose particular pieces of legislation. However, the biggest efforts and the largest resources were spent selling the capitalist free enterprise system generally. Of course, all this advertising of the capitalist system was framed in terms of 'public education', a much more reputable and credible activity than advertising.[64]

New organizations were formed to promote business values, now labelled 'American' values. These included such organizations as the Foundation for Economic Education (1946), the American Heritage Foundation (1947) and the Industrial Information Institute (1947) which received funding from corporations such as DuPont, Republic Steel and Ford. However, at the forefront of the propaganda campaign was NAM, the Chamber of Commerce, the American Petroleum Institute and the American Iron & Steel Institute.[65] These bodies were themselves coordinated by the Advertising Council (see next chapter).

NOTES

1 A. Yarrow, 'The Big Postwar Story: "New Era" of "People's Capitalism" Dawns Where "Everybody's Rich in the U.S.," or So They Said', Mason University, http://mason.

gmu.edu/~ayarrow/economic%20journalismform. PDF accessed 2 January 2003, p2.
2 Ralph Miliband, *The State in Capitalist Society*, London, Quartet Books, 1969, p190.
3 Strother Holland Walker and Paul Sklar, *Business Finds Its Voice: Management's Effort to Sell the Business Idea to the Public*, New York and London, Harper & Brothers, 1938, p1.
4 Quoted in 'Violations of Free Speech and Rights of Labor', Senate Committee on Education and Labor, 14 August 1939, p44.
5 Walker and Sklar, *Business Finds Its Voice*, p1.
6 *Ibid.*, p5.
7 Alex Carey, *Taking the Risk out of Democracy*, ed Andrew Lohrey, Sydney, UNSW Press, 1995, p147.
8 Quoted in Roland Marchand, *Creating the Corporate Soul: The Rise of Public Relations and Corporate Imagery in American Big Business*, Berkeley, University of California Press, 1998, p203.
9 Walker and Sklar, *Business Finds Its Voice*, p53; NAM quoted in 'Violations of Free Speech', p3.
10 Walker and Sklar, *Business Finds Its Voice*, p53; 'Violations of Free Speech', pp49, 55–56, 212–3.
11 'Violations of Free Speech', p48.
12 Quoted in *Ibid.*, pp154, 158.
13 Quoted in Walker and Sklar, *Business Finds Its Voice*, p6.
14 Quoted in 'Violations of Free Speech', p159.
15 Walker and Sklar, *Business Finds Its Voice*, p1.
16 Quoted in 'Violations of Free Speech', p161.
17 Quoted in *Ibid.*, p165.
18 *Ibid.*, pp162–3.
19 *Ibid.*, pp166–7.
20 Appendix 3 in *Ibid.*, p285.
21 *Ibid.*, p170.
22 Walker and Sklar, *Business Finds Its Voice*, p59.
23 Richard S. Tedlow, *Keeping the Corporate Image: Public Relations and Business, 1900–1950*, Greenwich, Connecticut, JAI Press, 1979, p64; US Steel quoted in Marchand, *Creating the Corporate Soul*, p228.
24 Walker and Sklar, *Business Finds Its Voice*, p75.
25 *Ibid.*, pp66–9.
26 Quoted in *Ibid.*, pp69–70.
27 Quoted in 'Violations of Free Speech', p177.
28 *Ibid.*, pp178, 222.
29 NAM Billboards and 'educational' material quoted in *Ibid.*, p172.
30 MacDonald-Cook advertisements quoted in *Ibid.*, p185.
31 *Ibid.*, p178.
32 NAM pamphlets quoted in *Ibid.*, p173.
33 Walker and Sklar, *Business Finds Its Voice*, pp12–13.
34 Tedlow, *Keeping the Corporate Image*, pp64–5.

35 Quoted in 'Violations of Free Speech', p172.
36 *Ibid.*, p175.
37 NAM Billboards and 'educational' material quoted in *Ibid.*, pp172–3.
38 Louis Galambos, *The Public Image of Big Business in America, 1880–1940*, Baltimore, The Johns Hopkins University Press, 1975, pp9, 11.
39 John Kenneth Galbraith, *American Capitalism: The Concept of Countervailing Power*, Sentry edn, Boston, Houghton Mifflin, 1956, pp33, 35.
40 *Ibid.*, p42.
41 Veblen quoted in Dallas W. Smythe, *Dependency Road: Communications, Capitalism, Consciousness, and Canada*, New Jersey, Ablex Publishing, 1981, p58.
42 Quoted in 'Violations of Free Speech', p176.
43 James Selvage, 'Selling the Private Enterprise System', *Vital Speeches of the Day*, November, 1942.
44 Fred Eldean, 'The Next Job for Institutional Advertising', Paper presented at the Pennsylvania Newspaper Publisher's Association, Harrisburg, Pennsylvania, 4 October 1943.
45 Quoted in Tedlow, *Keeping the Corporate Image*, pp118–9.
46 Elizabeth A. Fones-Wolf, 'Beneath Consensus: Business, Labor, and the Post-War Order', Doctor of Philosophy, University of Massachusetts, 1990, pp3, 40, 422.
47 Ralph Miliband, *Capitalist Democracy in Britain*, Oxford, Oxford University Press, 1982, pp57–9.
48 *Ibid.*, p61; Fones-Wolf, 'Beneath Consensus', pp40–1.
49 ORC, 'The Company's Role in Selling Free Enterprise', Princeton, NJ, Opinion Research Corporation, January 1947, p8.
50 Robert Griffith, 'The Selling of America: The Advertising Council and American Politics, 1942–1960', *Business History Review*, Autumn, 1983, pp388–9.
51 Fred Norris, 'Basic Economics Courses for Industry', Los Angeles, adapted from Master's Thesis in Economics, 1954, p111.
52 Harvard Business Review article cited in Editorial, 'Business Is Still in Trouble', *Fortune*, May, 1949, p68; Surveys cited in Fones-Wolf, 'Beneath Consensus', pp47–8, 117.
53 Robert Lynd quoted in Fones-Wolf, 'Beneath Consensus', p39.
54 Griffith, 'The Selling of America', p389.
55 Fones-Wolf, 'Beneath Consensus', p422.
56 *Ibid.*, pp49–51.
57 Carey, *Taking the Risk out of Democracy*, p18.
58 *Ibid.*, p27.
59 Quoted in Stuart Ewen, *PR! A Social History of Spin*, New York, Basic Books, 1996, p360.
60 Quoted in Carey, *Taking the Risk out of Democracy*, p30.
61 Quoted in *Ibid.*, p34.
62 Quoted in *Ibid.*, p34.
63 Quoted in *Ibid.*, p34.
64 Fones-Wolf, 'Beneath Consensus', p54; John Kenneth Galbraith, *The Anatomy of Power*, London, Hamish Hamilton, 1984, p30.
65 Fones-Wolf, 'Beneath Consensus', pp52, 313.

3

Advertising Free Enterprise

It is as impossible to imagine a genuine democracy without the science of persuasion as it is to think of a totalitarian state without coercion.

FORTUNE MAGAZINE, 1949[1]

... there are lazy brains in many heads and the advertising and public relations people are the only mobile striking force for freedom, who can rapidly create zealots for the freedom way of life.

KEN WELLS, ADVERTISING COUNCIL DIRECTOR[2]

IN 1941, 600 MEMBERS OF THE AMERICAN ADVERTISING INDUSTRY GATHERED IN HOT SPRINGS, VIRGINIA. THROUGHOUT THE DEPRESSION, ADVERTISING, BOTH AS A SEPARATE INDUSTRY AND AS PART OF THE FREE ENTERPRISE SYSTEM, HAD BEEN SUBJECT TO INCREASING CRITICISM AND CHALLENGE. IN A ROUSING SPEECH ON THE FINAL DAY, JAMES WEBB YOUNG OF J. WALTER THOMPSON SUMMED UP THE PROBLEMS THAT THREATENED ADVERTISING AND BUSINESS GENERALLY:

And so we come to the area that troubles us most, where all is not quiet along the Potomac. I have suggested to you that the dangers that we see are not dangers to advertising per se, but dangers to the whole business structure of which we are a part ... Here is the crux of the problem ... What will it profit us to win the war of advertising and lose the war of business.[3]

Young, who as a young advertising copywriter in 1919 had made thousands of women conscious of their underarm sweat in the services of deodorant manufacturer Odorno, proposed that 'public service' advertising be undertaken as part of a public relations strategy to restore the image of advertising and of business more broadly.

We have within our hands the greatest aggregate means of mass education and persuasion the world has ever seen – namely, the channels of advertising communication. We have the masters of the techniques of using these channels. We have power. Why do we not use it?[4]

In response to Young's speech, the audience rose and clapped enthusiastically and pledged their support from the floor. However, less than a month later, America declared war on Japan. In response, Young helped to found the War Advertising Council, representing almost all the trade associations of the advertising and allied industries, to help with the war effort.[5]

Throughout the war years, the War Advertising Council carried out hundreds of publicity campaigns for the government and the war effort using donated time and space, to an estimated value of $1 billion. Sponsorship of the patriotic wartime advertising programmes improved the advertising industry's public image. In consequence, the council reorganized and continued its public service advertising after the war under the new name of the Advertising Council Inc., in the expectation that it could thereby maintain or advance a philanthropic image for both advertising and business. Its goal was to address 'societal problems through influencing and informing public opinion'.[6]

In the post-world war period, under the leadership of James Young, the Advertising Council, coordinating as it did the nation's entire structure of advertising agencies and associations, was brought to centre stage. NAM had been largely discredited by the pre-war disclosures of its propaganda activities at congressional hearings, and the business community was in need of a new untarnished image-maker and leader. Such a combination was found in the Advertising Council. The advertising industry, through the council, became the major coordinating centre of the entire nationwide corporate effort of moulding public opinion.

THE ROLE OF ADVERTISERS AND POLLSTERS

From the beginning, business had been encouraged in its free enterprise campaign by advertisers and public relations specialists who hoped for business opportunities from such a campaign. The American Federation of Advertising argued in the 1930s that the obligation 'to interpret what industry has done for the well-being of America' was more important than promoting company products. Public relations consultant Bruce Barton argued at the 1935 NAM convention that any manufacturer who declared his disdain for popular opinion was:

> *... a liability to all industry. No major industry has the moral right to allow itself to be unexplained, misunderstood or publicly distrusted; for by its unpopularity it poisons the pond in which we all must fish.*

He argued that business needed to be 'as diligent, as ingenious, and as resourceful' in its approach to 'the public as voters, as we have proved ourselves to be in our approach to them as buyers'.[7]

Paul Garrett, director of public relations at General Motors, told the American Association of Advertising Agencies:

> *The challenge that faces us is to shake off our lethargy and through public relations make the American plan of industry stick. For, unless the contributions of the system are explained to consumers in terms of their own interest, the system itself will not stand against the storm of fallacies that rides the air in this era of easy, world-wide and instantaneous communication.*[8]

For Garrett the 'fallacy of fallacies' was the belief that big companies were bad companies: 'as if size had anything to do with morality'. This arose because people ignored 'the fact that the consumer and nobody else determines that industry sometimes must be small and sometimes must be big to serve him well' and the fact that big businesses give rise to small businesses.[9]

During the 1930s, the advertising firm J. Walter Thompson demonstrated its skills at helping business educate the public about capitalism with an advertisement comparing State capitalism, where 'the *Politician* is the boss' with private capitalism where 'the *Consumer*, the *Citizen* is boss'. It argued that under the system of private capitalism 'The consumer is the voter, the juror, the judge and the executioner ... The consumer "votes" each time he buys one article and rejects another ...'. The fact that it was not the 'votes' in the marketplace but rather the 'votes' in the political sphere that were of concern to corporations was deliberately obscured. Similarly, advertising firm N. W. Ayer & Son produced 12 pamphlets explaining questions such as 'Why Business Is Big' to the public in an effort to get more advertising business from corporations.[10]

Radio networks, trade journals and magazines also offered to help business influence public attitudes. The National Broadcasting Company (NBC) advertised to business leaders in 1937:

> *Faced with new situations, new standards of economics, new attitudes of labor, business must campaign for public favor as never before. It must recognize public goodwill as the greatest possible force in Business, as it is in government. ... Use NBC to interpret your aims and ideals ...*[11]

New firms emerged that polled and surveyed public opinion on behalf of business leaders on a range of political issues of concern to them and gave them feedback about how well their propaganda was working. The Psychological Corporation began the 'Business Barometer', a series of surveys of attitudes to big business carried out twice a year and attracting clients such as General Motors, DuPont, Ford, General Electric, US Steel, Westinghouse, AT&T, Standard Oil and others. The Opinion Research Corporation, *Fortune* magazine, and others, also conducted surveys of public opinion about big business. This continuous feedback about the effectiveness of public relations campaigns enabled business to develop 'a new sophistication' in its propaganda techniques.[12]

For some people this polling offered a new scientific form of democracy whereby public opinion could be measured. Historian Stuart Ewen notes:

> *Pollsters would henceforth be the messengers through whom the public interest would be ostensibly articulated. Abstract, statistical renditions of democracy and of the public itself were appearing; ideals or memories of a participatory public were being annulled.*[13]

Of course, the results of polling could be easily influenced by the choice of questions and the way they were phrased, so that in reality, polls were frequently purchased by those who wanted to show that public opinion was on their side.

> *Reported in newspapers or cited on the radio, public opinion polls were becoming statistical applause tracks for encouraging those on the fence to join the crowd.*[14]

They were part of the public manipulation, a part that was all the more insidious because it purported to show the public was in charge.

Advertisers utilized pollsters in their work. Paul West, president of the Association of National Advertisers, explained why advertisers were the appropriate people for the job of selling free enterprise:

> *The advertising method, if properly utilized, can get our story across because, unlike any other method of communication, it starts by finding out through research what people want and what appeals they respond to, what they are confused about and where they are misinformed, it dramatizes and simplifies the message in terms of the other fellow's interests; it channels the messages to the desired audience in predetermined units of space or time at desired intervals; and it repeats and repeats until the message sinks in, until ideas are moved from one mind to another.*[15]

THE ADVERTISING COUNCIL CAMPAIGN

In 1947 the Advertising Council launched a nationwide public 'education' campaign to sell the free enterprise system to the American people. The programme was to operate at three levels:

1. at the factory or 'plant' level, in the form of economic education programmes for employees, with supporting public relations efforts in the community;
2. at the national level, with a nationwide advertising campaign in the mass media to put the business message across;
3. at the grassroots or local level.

Details of the plant-level programmes were to be largely determined by the individual corporations concerned, with the Joint Committee of the Advertising Council acting in a supervisory capacity. The national advertising campaign was to be coordinated by the Advertising Council.

The Advertising Council received 'unprecedented amounts of money' from business toward the $100 million economic education campaign to 'sell' the American economic system to the public, including $100,000 donations from General Foods and General Electric. General Motors, IBM, Johnson & Johnson, Procter & Gamble, Goodrich and Republic Steel all supported the campaign financially and various advertising agencies offered free services. The campaign started with over $3 million worth of donated time and space from the media and advertising agencies.[16]

According to Ken Wells, director of operations of the Advertising Council's Program on Economic Understanding, what was needed was:

> *A driving, hard-hitting ten-year campaign to sell and tell, and keep understood and sold, the positive and worthwhile principles of the American way ... Our job is putting the easily teachable definition of the economic system between the ears of 143,000,000 Americans.*[17]

According to the council, these 'principles of the American way' were:

- *The right to own private property*
- *The free market*
- *The profit and wage incentive*
- *Competition*
- *Government regulation but not government control*[18]

The free market was described as 'the most democratic institution ever devised by man – whereby all the people decide every day what goods and services are to be produced and in what quantities, making their decisions by establishing the prices they are willing to pay'. Competition was depicted as constantly forcing 'the seller to keep improving the goods and services he offers'. Government was supposed to be 'an authority which referees the game but does not play in it, enforces the rules but does not direct the play'.[19]

Ironically, the individualist message of competition and self-interest was sold through a campaign that sought to promote industrial harmony and the idea that we should all cooperate and work together to protect the system and achieve the prosperity it promised. The campaign explained why 'freedom and security go together', and argued that prosperity could be achieved by free enterprise, and increased production through mechanization and better efficiency and the cooperation of workers and management. The Advertising Council used token union support and the endorsement of the presidents of the AFL and the CIO to prove it was non-partisan. The campaign was also cheered on by Dwight D. Eisenhower both before and after he became president.[20]

The nationwide advertising campaign was launched in October 1947, and the *New York Times* reported that it:

> *... has stirred an enthusiasm that promises to make it a new weapon against Communist aggression ... Radio stations have pledged time for full-length dramatizations, the outdoor and car-card advertising industries have agreed to provide large space, as have leading Sunday newspaper supplements, business magazines and house organs. Value of the facilities is more than $1,000,000.*[21]

By October 1947, some 5000 business, community and educational organizations had been issued with a 'Plan for Action' kit. This kit was designed by the Advertising Council Joint Committee and a team of advertising agencies. The kit included a 'blueprint' that set out directions for the 'simple presentation of free enterprise fundamentals' aimed at teaching the value of the free enterprise economy and industry's role in it.[22]

As part of the 'plant-level programme' 9 million employees were put through 'evangelical' anti-union, anti-government courses of 'economic education' within a three-year period.[23] In June 1949, Ken Wells, operations director for the joint committee, estimated that the plant and community programmes 'combined with the advertising prepared for this phase of the campaign by the Advertising Council' had 'reached, to a greater or lesser extent, about 70 per cent of the American population'.[24] These factory-based programmes are described in more detail in the next chapter.

Business executives were also trained at intensive one-week seminar courses called Freedom Forums, which began in 1949. The first of these was described by an insider:

> *Over 100 important people from American industry journeyed to this small town to sit through long sessions of indoctrination in the fundamentals of our economic system and to discuss the most effective channels of communication needed to give an understanding of America to those who are confused or apathetic.*[25]

There they were taught about the free enterprise system and 'came away considerably more informed, and with a new and dynamic articulateness', according to Wells, who himself went on to become executive vice-president of the Freedom Foundation, which had just been formed.[26]

In the first two years of the Advertising Council campaign, 600 pages of ads had been published at no cost, newspapers had printed 13 million of lines of advertising free of charge, 8000 billboards had been erected, and radio messages were being broadcast into 'almost every home in America'. The advertisements offered a free pamphlet, *The Miracle of America* and 1.5 million copies of this were distributed by 1950. Many more had been reprinted in magazines and company publications.[27] By the end of 1949, the Advertising Council's campaign had blanketed the country with over 500 advertisements in national magazines, newspaper supplements and business publications, 8000 newspaper advertisements, 6000 outdoor posters and messages carried by almost all the network radio programmes, resulting in more than 2 billion 'listener impressions'.[28]

Auxiliary campaigns

The Advertising Council's work, though extensive, was not isolated. With the joint committee's coordination, NAM and the Chamber of Commerce, together with thousands of business and 'educational' organizations, undertook programmes on a scale that rivalled that of the Advertising Council. The free market message even appeared in comic books and on matchbox covers.[29]

NAM President Claude Putnam argued that 'to sell – to resell, if you will – to free Americans the philosophy that has kept us and our economy free' was a 'dire necessity'.[30] NAM enrolled hundreds more industrialists throughout the country in the campaign to reshape public opinion. The Opinion Research Corporation had identified ten 'ignorance areas that made a great deal of trouble for a good many companies' including the size of industry's profits; the share of profits going to workers; ownership of industry; the role of competition in reducing prices; and 'how capital earns its keep'.[31]

In its materials NAM addressed these concerns and also opposed unions, price controls, government spending and taxes. It produced films about how economic freedom and individual freedom were linked, about the benefits of wages paid by companies, and about the value of individual initiative and hard work. Millions of people viewed NAM motion pictures with titles such as *The Price of Freedom* – an alarmist film on 'creeping socialism'. Some 2.5 million people watched NAM films in 1948 alone.[32]

Churches were targeted through plant tours and conferences for clergy. NAM distributed millions of pamphlets (18 million were distributed between 1946 and 1950 to employees, students and community leaders) and supplemented its radio programmes with a television series, *Industry on Parade*, showcasing individual companies and demonstrating the benefits they offered to individuals, the community and the nation. It spent millions on 'paid advertisements, news releases, speeches, posters, leaflets, and magazines'. Thousands of papers and journals received material. These efforts were augmented by newspapers, which ran NAM material for free. Despite all this activity, NAM did not become a household name because it sought not to be identified with the materials.[33]

NAM sought to make use of business leaders and the respect they already wielded in the towns and cities to promote its goals with an Industry Leaders programme, which it launched in 1947. It recognized that if these business people were given the right messages and trained in how to deliver them to best effect, then they would be more effective in shaping public opinion than NAM spokesmen. They would be 'better champions of the American way'.[34]

NAM ran motivational conferences for 9000 selected business people in the first two years of the programme. At these conferences business people received a manual which explained the 'American Individual Enterprise System' and also source material for speeches and panel discussions directed at the local community. NAM told them how to sell free enterprise and how to appeal to the heart and to lead people 'through a thinking process'. These businessmen became the 'missionaries' for free enterprise, going to meetings such as the Young Men's Christian Association (YMCA), Young Women's Christian Association (YWCA), the Rotary, Exchange and parent–teacher associations, women's groups and church groups to spread the word. In the process they also increased their own influence in the community.[35]

NAM also targeted what it termed 'thought leaders' who were influential in shaping community opinion and encouraged local business people to do the same. These 'thought leaders' included educators, clergy, professionals, local officials and women's leaders. It produced publications aimed at particular groups, such as teachers or women's club leaders. Each publication was distributed to tens of thousands of people. Information packages, with speeches, sample news releases and advice on public speaking, were distributed to club directors. NAM held town meetings to which hundreds of clergy, educators, youth leaders and other 'thought leaders' came to be re-energized with the 'traditional concepts of American liberty'.[36]

In 1949 the US Chamber of Commerce launched programmes to provide training and resources to local chambers, and in 1954 it introduced Economic Discussion Groups with similar goals to NAM's Industry Leaders Conferences. Some 1500 groups of businessmen met weekly for 18 weeks to discuss materials supplied by the chamber.[37]

More moderate business organizations joined NAM and the Chamber of Commerce in their campaign. To counter growing concern that workers were being displaced by machines, their public relations material explained how machines create jobs and to promote opposition to government legislation on business activity, making a case for '[w]hy freedom [from government regulation] and security go together'. Advertising Council pamphlets were republished in company magazines and newsletters and in *Junior Scholastic* magazine, which went to thousands of school children.[38]

Many individual corporations also expanded their public relations efforts from radio to television and the production of films, which were distributed rent-free to schools, churches, clubs and theatres. Sometimes the films merely promoted an individual company and its products, but often they also promoted ideological messages. For example, General Motors funded films 'attacking communism, teaching the facts of the American private enterprise system and warning that government interference in the economy led to socialism'.[39]

Companies such as Ford, General Foods, General Electric and International Harvester also engaged in individual public relations campaigns to improve their own relationship with the community. By establishing goodwill in this way they intended to reinforce business economic leadership in the community. As part of this strategy they provided facilities to local communities and sponsored sports and other community activities.[40]

Individual companies encouraged employees at all levels to become involved in community organizations of all types and in some companies, such as General Electric, 'leadership of community organizations was seen as a prerequisite for professional advancement'. In this way, not only would the company have a voice in many community forums, but their personnel would become friendly with community 'thought leaders' and win some as supporters of business. Of particular importance was membership of policy-making boards such as school boards, where business interests could be protected and promoted.[41]

Individual companies also advertised the free market message. For example, Warner & Swasey (manufacturer of machine tools) advertised in *Newsweek*, *Business Week* and *United States News* in January 1947 that 'If you want a larger piece, bake a bigger pie':

> *The workmen already get by far the largest slice – 61% of all American corporations' production. The smallest slice (9%) goes to business to provide future jobs and a small part of it goes to the millions of people whose savings provide the factory and machines, without which there would be no jobs at all. Another slice goes for taxes; and for parts and materials. A very small slice for management, which keeps the business going. And that uses up the pie.*[42]

The Aluminium Company of America (Alcoa) gave employees and visitors a booklet that explained why the American economic system ensured freedom:

> *It is our freedom to work in a field of our own choice, for our own best interests, and those of society. It is our freedom to invest our earnings, to start and to build a business, to earn a profit, or to go broke. It is freedom from excessive government regulation, from the coercion of any group, public or private. It is our freedom to enter any market, any competition, limited only by the basic laws and rules of honesty and ethics. It is an aggressive system and one which gets results!*[43]

Alcoa also produced a series of colour advertisements for the *Saturday Evening Post* on 'the American economic formula, the heritage of a free people', and a documentary motion picture, *Unfinished Rainbows*, which was seen by over 23 million people. According to Alcoa's director of public relations, Charles C. Carr, this work was 'climate promotion', ensuring a favourable economic climate in which to do business.[44]

The election of Harry Truman to president in 1948, on a platform that included price controls and increased government spending, seemed to attest to the success of organized labour campaigns. It reinforced the fears of business people and caused them to increase their propaganda efforts. The chair of NAM's public relations committee and vice-president of DuPont, J. Warren Kinsman, stated that public relations tools were the only weapons 'powerful enough to arouse public opinion sufficiently to check the steady, insidious and current drift toward Socialism'.[45]

By the early 1950s, businesses and their allies were spending well over a $100 million each year on what was euphemistically called 'economic education' but was really public relations communications aimed at turning the public against government regulation and union demands.[46] In 1949 *Fortune* magazine claimed:

> *The daily tonnage output of propaganda and publicity ... has become an important force in American life. Nearly half of the contents of the best newspapers is derived from publicity releases; nearly all the contents of the lesser papers and the hundreds of specialized periodicals are directly or indirectly the work of PR departments.*[47]

In 1950 the Buchanan Committee, a House Select Committee on Lobbying, reported:

> *Organizations seeking to protect a privileged status for their members at the expense of the general welfare of all Americans use terms like 'socialism', 'statism', and 'welfare state' to forestall rational analysis of legislative proposals which they oppose ... Political freedom cannot live in an atmosphere of such hysterical oversimplification.*[48]

By 1951, corporate-sponsored films were being watched by 20 million people per week. Procter & Gamble, General Electric and Republic Steel also distributed free enterprise comic books. William Whyte estimated that American businesses were spending over $100 million each year on advertising, public and employee relations to sell the American free enterprise system in the early 1950s.[49]

> *Never before have businessmen appeared so gripped with a single idea; there is scarcely a convention that is not exhorted with it, and of all the*

> *general speeches made by businessmen, by far the greatest single category is that in which the audience is warned to spread the gospel before it is too late.*[50]

ECONOMIC 'ILLITERACY'

The Opinion Research Corporation (ORC), still a leading polling company today, was one of the pollsters that made a case for the need for the 'economic education' that the Advertising Council and others provided, and then later assessed the effectiveness of that 'education' on their behalf. In 1947 the ORC argued:

> *In the past few years it has been abundantly demonstrated that industry can operate under a system of competitive capitalism only if the public gives it support. Whether ten years from now the public will support capitalism or socialism depends importantly on what is being taught in America's schoolrooms today.*[51]

Various studies were made of high school students to prove that they were ignorant of economics and the fundamentals of the American economic system and needed economic education. However these studies were essentially surveys of how strongly business values were held in the community, rather than the objective studies of economic knowledge they purported to be. The sorts of questions that school students were asked, for example, were presented as questions of 'fact'. However, the answers required value judgements to be made – as can be seen by the sample of questions below. The 'correct' answers are shown with a tick:[52]

> *On the whole, workers make more money today than they did 30 years ago.*
> ( ) *But they are worse off because prices have gone up*
> ( ) *They are a little better off, but not much*
> ( ) *They are about 25% better off*
> (✓) *They are about 75% better off*
>
> *Money invested in new machinery and equipment has increased output. The workers have got some of the increase but the larger share has gone to the owners.*
> ( ) *I agree*
> (✓) *I disagree*
>
> *The wealth of this county is becoming more and more concentrated in the hands of the wealthiest 10% of the families*
> ( ) *True*
> (✓) *False*

In which of these industries is there practically no competition, or very little?
( ) *Steel industry*
( ) *Automobile industry*
( ) *Oil industry*
( ) *Rubber industry*
( ) *Chemical industry*
( ) *Radio-television industry*
(✓) *None*

The most secure jobs for employees are found in companies that....
( ) *Share profits with their employees*
(✓) *Make steady profits*
( ) *Pay high wages*
( ) *Have the most liberal benefits*

Consumers don't have much influence on prices. Companies set the price and the customer has to pay it.
( ) *I agree*
(✓) *I disagree*

The most practical way for workers to increase their standard of living is for....
(✓) *All workers to produce more*
( ) *All workers to get more of the money companies are already making*

If Social Security benefits are increased – say about double the present amount – the workers can be sure of a secure old age.
( ) *I agree*
(✓) *I disagree*

Not surprisingly, when given these same tests, executives scored much better than teachers or high school students.[53] In a series of such studies the ORC repeatedly found school students to be 'weak in economic understanding' in key areas. The low scores, claimed the ORC, indicated 'a high state of confusion and a serious lack of information' and 'untutored opinion'. The ORC stated that 'achieving a good score' not only required knowledge of basic historical facts but also 'a respect for the principles of individual freedom upon which our society is constructed'.[54]

In fact, such questions merely tested the degree to which high school students' opinions coincided with those of business people and conservative ideologues. Erroneous thinking amongst students was indicated by findings that the majority of senior students believed that virtual monopolies of one or two companies existed in some industries, that most companies make a profit in an average year, that owners received too much profit and that they got most of the gains from new machinery. Only a minority of seniors chose 'keeping the profit incentive alive' as being essential to survival of the American economic system.[55]

Worst of all, from a business point of view, over half the students agreed with the Marxist statement: 'The fairest economic system is one that "takes from each according to his ability" and gives to each "according to his needs".' This was even though most teachers disagreed with the statement. The failure of students 'to see through this Marxist doctrine' was taken to be evidence of 'how little high school Seniors comprehend the fundamentals of our system'.[56]

It was economic ignorance, ORC claimed, that led to an anti-business bias.[57] Thus, corrective education and propaganda was necessary and was aimed at schools, universities, company employees and also the public in general.

The ORC also argued that corrective education and propaganda was necessary to undermine the faith of the community in government and regulation:

> *The stress our high schools place on American history and government leads teenagers to believe that a government-directed economy, since it operates for the benefit of all, will best assure social and economic justice... Young people's support for enlarging the role of government in our lives is not likely to change without economic instruction.*[58]

While surveys found that workers recognized the importance of freedom, they also found that those same workers looked to government as protectors of freedom rather than as a threat to it, and this was of concern to business people who wanted minimal government regulation. For example, a 1952 ORC survey found that 80 per cent of manual workers said the main advantage of living in the USA was that people were free – free to speak, worship and vote as they chose and work where they chose. But what was of concern to businessmen was that these workers were complacent about these freedoms; they were 'asleep to the chipping away of freedoms' and did not understand the 'necessity for unceasing vigilance'. The researchers noted: 'Few workers view the government as anything but the benevolent protector of their rights. The idea that tyranny can come through government is not broadly recognized'.[59]

This meant, according to the ORC, that while workers were opposed to socialism they 'may well vote it in piece by piece' seeking the end advantage of each measure but without realising the 'loss of freedom entailed' in the means of attaining it. For example, they approved of social security, price controls and unions in terms of the benefits for themselves.[60] The lesson that the ORC suggested needed to be learned from this was that education needed to help workers redefine freedom in terms of means rather than ends.

The ORC argued that 'ignorance and lack of understanding of how the business system works go hand in hand with a willingness to vote for measures that undermine the system'. Clearly, it was best to correct such ignorance at school. Schoolchildren, it found, were more likely to view regulation of business and government control of prices favourably, but this could be corrected with simple 'education'.[61]

For example, after being taken on a three-day 'Dollars at Work' tour of various plants and offices, which was scripted and carefully planned, 'appreciable numbers changed their minds' on issues such as government control and the share of income that the worker gets. Similar changes in attitude were also noted after being shown a film entitled *Productivity* or a comic book on productivity. And the ORC concluded that 'far from charging industry with "propaganda", schoolchildren enjoy learning about industry through these new techniques'.[62]

Part of the aim of all this 'education' was to get people used to the idea that 'it is an appropriate part of business's role in democracy to judge what beliefs we must hold in order to be "economically educated"'. They juxtaposed personal, political and economic freedom, arguing that constraints on economic freedom were tantamount to reducing personal and political freedom and that those who sought to 'intervene excessively in the play of market forces', however well-intentioned they might be, posed a major threat to all those freedoms. Criticism of the economic system amounted to subversion of the political system.[63]

The economic education campaigns that resulted from this are described in the next chapter.

NOTES

1 Editorial, 'Business Is Still in Trouble', *Fortune*, May, 1949, p69.
2 Ken Wells, 'Remain Silent and Die', *PR Journal*, vol 4, no 10, 1948, pp9, 10.
3 James Webb Young, 'What Shall We Do About It?' Paper presented at the Special Joint Meeting of the AAAA & ANA, Hot Springs, VA, 14 November, 1941.
4 *Ibid.*
5 M. A. Mandell, 'A History of the Advertising Council', Doctor of Commercial Science, School of Business, Indiana University, p100.
6 J. Pimlott, 'Public Service Advertising', *POQ*, Summer, 1948, p211; Robert Griffith, 'The Selling of America: The Advertising Council and American Politics, 1942–1960', *Business History Review*, Autumn, 1983, p391; 'Advertising Council Archives', University of Illinois Archives, 19 August, 1998, www.comm.uiuc.edu/aca/Default.htm.
7 Quoted in Roland Marchand, *Creating the Corporate Soul: The Rise of Public Relations and Corporate Imagery in American Big Business*, Berkeley, University of California Press, 1998, pp203, 246 and Editorial, 'Business Is Still in Trouble', p200.
8 Paul W. Garrett, 'Public Relations – Industry's No. 1 Job', Paper presented at the 21st Annual Convention of the American Association of Advertising Agencies, White Sulphur Springs, West Virginia, 1938, p13.
9 *Ibid.*, p16.
10 Quoted in Marchand, *Creating the Corporate Soul*, pp213, 246.
11 NBC advertisement reproduced in *Ibid.*, p205.

12 Alex Carey, *Taking the Risk out of Democracy*, ed Andrew Lohrey, Sydney, UNSW Press, 1995, p147; Marchand, *Creating the Corporate Soul*, p247.
13 Stuart Ewen, *PR! A Social History of Spin*, New York, Basic Books, 1996, p186.
14 *Ibid.*, pp188–9.
15 Paul West, 'Needed Vitally: More Favorable Public Opinion of Corporations', *Printers Ink*, 14 September, 1945, p110.
16 Griffith, 'The Selling of America', p401.
17 Wells, 'Remain Silent and Die', pp9, 10.
18 *Ibid.*, p10.
19 Advertising Council quoted in C. C. Carr, 'Translating the American Economic System', *PR Journal*, vol 5, no 6, 1949, p4.
20 Griffith, 'The Selling of America', pp401, 404.
21 Brendan M. Jones, 'Nation-Wide Advertising Campaign Aimed at Combating Communism', *New York Times*, 17 October, 1948, p3F.
22 Brendan M. Jones, 'Community Drives in 150 New Plants', *New York Times*, 5 June, 1948, p3–1.
23 B. L. Cooke, 'Economic Education in Industry', PhD, University of Minneapolis, 1954, p105.
24 Jones, 'Community Drives in 150 New Plants', p3–1.
25 Carr, 'Translating the American Economic System', p2.
26 Jones, 'Community Drives in 150 New Plants', p3–7.
27 Griffith, 'The Selling of America', p402.
28 Mandell, 'A History of the Advertising Council', p248.
29 Jones, 'Nation-Wide Advertising Campaign', p3F; Griffith, 'The Selling of America', p403.
30 Quoted in William H. Whyte, *Is Anybody Listening? How and Why US Business Fumbles When It Talks with Human Beings*, New York, Simon & Schuster, 1952, p4.
31 ORC, 'The Company's Role in Selling Free Enterprise', Princeton, NJ, Opinion Research Corporation, January 1947, p24.
32 Elizabeth A. Fones-Wolf, 'Beneath Consensus: Business, Labor, and the Post-War Order', Doctor of Philosophy, University of Massachusetts, 1990, pp23–4, 56–7.
33 National Association of Manufacturers, 'Report to Members', NAM 1950, pp21–2; National Association of Manufacturers, 'Report to Members', NAM 1960; Carey, *Taking the Risk out of Democracy*, p28; Fones-Wolf, 'Beneath Consensus', pp55–6, 81–2; Karl Schriftgiesser, *The Lobbyists: The Art and Business of Influencing Lawmakers*, Boston, Little, Brown & Co., 1951, p95.
34 Fones-Wolf, 'Beneath Consensus', pp316–7.
35 *Ibid.*, pp316–9.
36 *Ibid.*, pp321–2.
37 *Ibid.*, p327.
38 *Ibid.*, pp80–1.
39 *Ibid.*, p83.
40 *Ibid.*, pp334–8.
41 *Ibid.*, pp339–40.
42 Reproduced in ORC, 'The Company's Role in Selling Free Enterprise'.
43 Quoted in Carr, 'Translating the American Economic System', p3.
44 *Ibid.*, pp3–4.

45 Fones-Wolf, 'Beneath Consensus', pp77–81.
46 Griffith, 'The Selling of America', p402.
47 Editorial, 'Business Is Still in Trouble', p69.
48 Quoted in Schriftgiesser, *The Lobbyists*, p152.
49 Fones-Wolf, 'Beneath Consensus', p82; Whyte, *Is Anybody Listening?* p7.
50 Whyte, *Is Anybody Listening?* p52.
51 ORC, 'Industry and the Social Science Teacher', Princeton, NJ, Opinion Research Corporation, April 1947, foreword.
52 Questions labelled factual in ORC, 'Why Too Many College Students Are Economic Illiterates', Princeton, NJ, Opinion Research Corporation, April 1960, p7.
53 *Ibid.*, p3.
54 ORC, 'The High School Market for Economic Education', Princeton, NJ, Public Opinion Research Corporation, June 1951, pp4, 24.
55 *Ibid.*, pp6–8.
56 *Ibid.*, pp11, 44.
57 ORC, 'Why Too Many College Students Are Economic Illiterates', p3.
58 *Ibid.*, p2.
59 ORC, 'Experiment in Employee Education. Courses in American Freedoms', Princeton, NJ, Opinion Research Corporation, May 1952, pp6–7, 25, 27.
60 *Ibid.*, pp7–8, 28.
61 ORC, 'School Children Learn About Industry', Princeton, NJ, Opinion Research Corporation, March 1950, pp6–7.
62 *Ibid.*, pp8–9, 11–12, 15.
63 Fred Norris, 'Basic Economics Courses for Industry', Los Angeles, adapted from Master's Thesis in Economics 1954, pp88, 119, 125.

4

Free Market 'Education'

Nothing is so important to the defence of the modern corporation as the argument that its power does not exist – that all power is surrendered to the impersonal play of the market. And nothing is more serviceable than the resulting conditioning of the young to that belief.

John Kenneth Galbraith[1]

In 1946 seven men met in the New York office of David Goodrich, chairman of B. F. Goodrich Company. They included a business association executive, Leonard Read, Donaldson Brown of General Motors, Henry Hazlitt of the *New York Times* and Claude Robinson of the Opinion Research Corporation, as well as Goodrich himself. This was the beginning of the Foundation for Economic Education (FEE), an organization that is dedicated to advancing individual economic freedom, private property, limited government and free trade through 'economic education'. It was possibly the earliest free market think tank and certainly provided a model for subsequent free market think tanks both in the US and internationally.[2]

Goodrich became FEE's chair, Hazlitt its vice-president, economist Ludwig von Mises was appointed its economic adviser, and Read became FEE's president and driving force. Read had been general manager of the Los Angeles Chamber of Commerce and then executive vice-president of the National Industrial Conference Board (a creation of the National Association of Manufacturers – NAM). Read found both organizations to be too moderate for his liking but his work with them supplied him with valuable corporate contacts.

The FEE was set up with the support of 20 of the largest corporations in the US, including General Motors, Chrysler, Southern California Edison, DuPont, and various oil and steel companies. Some 46 corporations had contributed a million dollars to FEE by the end of 1949. FEE also raised money by selling literature promoting free enterprise. Its articles were used by hundreds of newspapers and magazines, and *Reader's Digest* was particularly keen on reprinting its articles.

As the years went by, FEE's goals and leadership overlapped with that of the far-right John Birch Society, which was subsequently formed in 1958 by Robert Welch, a former long-term NAM director and chair of its Educational Advisory Committee. However, while many of the FEE's corporate donors would not want to be seen to be funding the John Birch Society, the FEE was a respectable recipient of their generosity.[3]

In a 1990 tribute to FEE, John Blundell, president of the influential UK free market think tank, the Institute of Economic Affairs (IEA), said: 'It is safe to say that had it not been for Leonard [Read] and FEE in the '40s, '50s, and '60s, those who followed and expanded the efforts on behalf of the free society in the '70s and '80s would have faced a much, much tougher battle.'[4]

FEE was one of several organizations formed around this time to promote free market economics. These groups, together with business associations and individual economists, sought to interpret the Depression in a way that left free market ideology unscathed and to oppose the New Deal on the grounds that it contradicted free market principles and undermined the incentive provided by the market. They continued to promote the competitive model of the market in books and articles.[5]

To economists the beauty of a free market based on competition was that it was efficient – the producer who could produce goods at the least cost won. But for business people the theory had its merit on a political level.[6] It disguised the power that they wielded, it re-labelled their drive for profit as public service, and it provided an argument against government regulation of business activities. Economics was presented as a science but was more often simply an argument for the promotion of free enterprise, with minimal government interference. Galbraith observes that:

> *...mainstream economics has for some centuries given grace and acceptability to convenient belief – to what the socially and economically favoured most wish or need to have believed. This economics, to repeat, is wholly reputable; it permeates and even dominates professional discussion and writing, the textbooks and classroom instruction.*[7]

To serve this function of making free enterprise beliefs acceptable, Galbraith notes that economic messages must have three aspects. Firstly, it needs to provide a rationale for minimizing government intervention. Secondly, it needs to justify 'untrammelled, uninhibited pursuit and possession of wealth' in terms of the common good. Thirdly, it needs to explain poverty and unemployment as resulting from the individual faults of those who find themselves in that situation.[8]

The massive campaign of 'economic' education that was undertaken by US businesses and their associations and front groups following the Second World War sought to achieve all three. Various organizations and individual companies established economic education programmes, including NAM, the US Chamber of Commerce, the Advertising Council and the Committee for Economic Development.[9]

The objective of 'educating' people about the economic system was to ensure that they would be more pro-business and accepting of market values. In his

1954 Master's thesis on the topic of economic education courses, Fred Norris explained:

> *A few businessmen have realized that popular acceptance of basic economics is essential for the preservation of their profit-and-loss habitat. These are the men who crusade with missionary zeal to popularize the system under which we operate.*[10]

This 'economic education' campaign largely succeeded in turning most Americans into free market believers, suspicious that government interventions eroded individual freedom and invited socialism into their midst.

PROLIFERATING FREE MARKET ASSOCIATIONS

Between 1942 and 1945, NAM facilitated the formation of various Committees on Cooperation with Education. By the late 1940s, the work of these committees in coordinating business and teacher exchanges was carried on at the national level by organizations such as the National Education Association, the American Council on Education, the American Vocational Association and others. The US Chamber of Commerce also established over 1300 Committees on Education between 1944 and 1949 that sought to bring together teachers and business people and others.[11]

Fred G. Clark founded the American Economic Foundation (AEF) in 1939. Before founding AEF, Clark was involved in broadcasting anti-socialist radio programmes for the Crusaders, which he headed. The AEF was financially supported by a number of industry and conservative interests, including the founders of *Reader's Digest* and NAM. Many utilities also contributed to it. From 1943 onwards, the AEF was heavily involved in providing economic training to millions of workers and thousands of teachers, as well as community groups. It produced films that were used by 7000 high schools in 41 states, as well as distributing editorials, promoting ideologically correct textbooks and organizing a speakers' bureau. It compiled the 'Ten Pillars of Economic Wisdom', which were promoted by other right-wing organizations, including the John Birch Society.[12] These Pillars included:

1. *Nothing is our material world [can be] free ...*
2. *Government is never a source of goods ...*
3. *The only valuable money that government has to spend is that money taxed or borrowed out of people's earnings ...*
4. *The only worthwhile job security is customer security ...*
5. *Customer security can be achieved by the worker only when he cooperates with management ...*

6 *Because wages are the principal cost of everything, widespread wage increases, without corresponding increases in production, simply increase the cost of everybody's living.*
7 *The greatest good for the greatest number means, in its material sense, the greatest goods for the greatest number which, in turn means the greatest productivity per worker.*
8 *All productivity is based on three factors: 1) natural resources .... 2) human energy ... 3) tools.*
9 *Tools are the only one of these three factors that man can increase without limit ... when there is a reward for the temporary self-denial that people must practice in order to channel part of their earnings away from purchases that produce immediate comfort and pleasure, and into new tools of production.*
10 *The productivity of the tools .... has always been highest in a competitive society in which the economic decisions are made by millions of progress-seeking individuals, rather than in a state-planned society ...*[13]

Corporations that funded FEE also funded the American Enterprise Association, the National Economic Council and the Committee for Constitutional Government. The Committee for Constitutional Government stated in its prospectus that its major purpose was to 'indoctrinate 10,000 college students' with 'facts' about 'their heritage of economic and constitutional freedom' and thus 'fortify our form of government against socialistic trends'. While FEE had been able to avoid registering under the Lobby Act by falsely claiming that its purpose was not to 'carry on propaganda or otherwise influence legislation', the Committee for Constitutional Government was unable to avoid it, and in 1949 it was recorded as having the second highest spending of all lobbies in the country.[14]

The committee also played a large part in popularizing the book, *The Road Ahead* by John T. Flynn, published in 1949. Flynn wrote pamphlets for the National Economic Council and was on the executive of the American Action. He was associated with the Committee for Constitutional Government and its offshoot, Fighters for Freedom.[15]

The Road Ahead, which was described in the *New York Times Book Review* as an extreme manifestation of 'an endemic hysteria presently affecting a considerable segment of our society', argued that socialism was the major threat facing America and 'our whole way of life'. This socialism was of the type emerging in England with the rise of the Labour Party and associated with the welfare state. Its advocates did not label themselves as socialists, but nevertheless they had the same goals. Flynn, noting that Truman looked like following these same goals, claimed: 'We cannot depend on any political party to save us. We must build a power outside the parties so strong that the parties will be compelled to yield to its demands.'[16]

The book first went on sale at $2.50 a copy and sold about 60,000 copies. It was then taken up by the Committee for Constitutional Government, which cut the price dramatically and sold 600,000 copies over the next five months. It sent out about 3.5 million postcard advertisements for the book and sold many in bulk lots to corporations and lobbying groups interested in promoting the book's message. It subsidized individuals and groups to finance its free distribution to key individuals such as clergymen and educators, businessmen, editors, judges, public officials and farm leaders.[17]

Reader's Digest printed a condensed version of the book in 1950 that was distributed to 9 million people, and it was also reprinted in condensed version in the *Congressional Record*, as well as various newspapers. The American Medical Association, which was fighting against a national health programme, also found it opportune to invest in the book and distribute free copies. Doctors' and dentists' surgeries had piles of free copies for waiting patients. Congressmen posted them out for free. In the end some 12 million or more were distributed.[18]

SCHOOL ECONOMICS EDUCATION

Businesses became very active in promoting free enterprise values in schools. Local businessmen were encouraged to find ways 'by which the concept of private enterprise and the details of its operation may be taught in the schools'. The use of school education to educate children to appreciate the free enterprise system was carefully thought out and a conscious strategy to win people over at an early and impressionable age.

When educators had become more critical of the free enterprise system during the Depression, some business people feared a growing socialist influence in schools.[19] Of particular concern to them were textbooks that they believed were critical of business and free enterprise. Several textbooks were condemned by organizations such as the American Legion and the Advertising Federation of America. Some texts were banned and even ceremoniously burned in a few communities.[20]

In 1940 NAM commissioned a review of social studies text books to find those that were anti-business or questioned the ideology of free enterprise. It also announced its intention to launch a major propaganda assault on schools throughout the US. Although most teachers were not communists, surveys showed that teachers tended to be more sympathetic than other groups to price controls, government ownership of utilities and railways, progressive taxation and the role of unions. So NAM and other business leaders sought to win these teachers over with financial support and personal meetings and tours.[21]

NAM set up an education department in 1949 especially for targeting schools and colleges. School students received posters, pamphlets with titles like *Who Profits from Profits?*, and leaflets that told 'in few words the cogent facts about profits, productivity, safety, individual freedom, taxes, security and other timely subjects'. NAM met with college presidents, deans, professors, school superintendents, student leaders and educational foundations and hosted college students and professors at their annual congress.[22]

Corporations took advantage of the need private colleges and universities had for funds to offer financial support and gain influence. The executives of a group of large corporations, including General Motors, Standard Oil, Ford Motor Company, International Harvester and United States Steel Corporation, formed the Council for Financial Aid to Education in 1952 to generate funds for this purpose and they succeeded in raising business donations from $24 million in 1948 to $280 million in 1965.[23]

In particular, corporations began to fund liberal arts and social sciences on top of their traditional support for science and technical courses in the hope of changing the political climate on campuses and winning educators to their cause, or at least winning their gratitude. This was aided by the activities of the Foundation for Economic Education and individual companies that set up exchange programmes, company tours, business speakers, conferences and seminars. These aimed to facilitate social contact between educators and business people and to give company executives the opportunity to promote free enterprise philosophy. Companies that became involved in these activities included DuPont, Alcoa, Firestone Tire and Rubber, Ford, Gulf Oil, Nabisco, Sears and Westinghouse and over one hundred others. NAM speakers were also active on campuses around the country reaching some 200,000 students each year in the mid-1950s.[24]

NAM continued to distribute its own materials into schools throughout the 1940s, including about 40 different pamphlets, and six motion pictures with titles such as *The Price of Freedom*, shown in 1946 to about a million students. A monthly magazine called *Trends* was also distributed to teachers promoting NAM policies with regard to labour, taxation, price control and inflation. NAM also adapted for high school students an educational course originally designed for employees entitled 'How Our Business System Operates' (HOBSO). The course identified economic freedom with political freedom and championed individual achievement over collective achievement through government measures (see below for its use with employees). Some 2000 teachers attended a one-week training course in the early 1950s to learn how to use the HOBSO materials correctly. One in eight high schools used another package: 'How we live in America' which was also adapted from employee education materials.[25]

A number of individual corporations also developed educational materials. For example, Coca-Cola prepared and distributed eight units of curriculum material on 'Our America' to some 30 million elementary school children, including posters and booklets and graphic material on various industry sectors such as transportation, electricity, steel, glass and oil. International Harvester and the American Petroleum Institute sponsored educational materials on the development of the US economy produced by the advertising agency, Byron G. Moon Company and distributed them free of charge.[26]

General Mills decided that even elementary school students were not too young to be taught free market economics, and it sponsored materials such as silk-screen panels telling the story of marketing bread; film strips; and the comic book *Freedom of Choice*. Although General Mills avoided advertising in the teaching materials, it recognized that there was advertising value with teachers in providing useful teaching aids. It was also interested that 'the formation of young minds in the direction of truth and clear economic thinking is an intangible but nonetheless valuable asset which amply repays the investment'. General Mills' Vice-President Samuel Gale was confident that 'given all the facts, teachers and students will arrive at sound conclusions' about 'the basic elements of our democracy'.[27]

Other companies pumping materials into schools – texts, filmstrips, teaching kits, movies – included US Steel, General Electric, General Motors, American Cyanamid, Standard Oil and many others. In fact, one in five corporations did so. In 1954 corporations were supplying about $50 million worth of free materials to schools, compared with an annual expenditure on regular textbooks in schools of $100 million. *Fortune* magazine observed that 'by 1950 the interest in selling free enterprise had grown so intense that many executives seemed to be spending more time considering comic books extolling profits than the more mundane problem of making profits'.[28]

Essay contests were held for school students offering large prizes for winning essays on topics such as 'Worker and Employer, Partners in Business' or 'What do Strikes Cost the Worker?' or 'Freedom is Everybody's Job'. Also, Junior Achievement Inc. ran workshops for high school students in which they played at being entrepreneurs and learned to 'appreciate the profit system'. Junior Achievement, a scheme that had been started in 1919 and was funded by corporations, had become very involved in selling the principles of free enterprise to teenagers.[29]

Other business initiatives included:

- Business–Industry–Education Day when schools would close and teachers visit factories, meet company executives and discuss business and economics issues relating to the firm and to the wider economic system;
- individual plant tours for teachers and students where 'a working model of capitalism in action' could be demonstrated;
- multi-plant tours;
- executive-teacher meetings;
- company courses in economics for teachers.[30]

Such activities were shown to improve the attitude of teachers and students towards business. During the 1950s, teachers were going on annual factory tours in more than 700 localities.[31]

Consumer education in schools, which had been heavily influenced by Consumers' Union reports, was also seen as a threat to business as 'students were learning to defend themselves against business'. This was viewed as an 'unhealthy attitude' towards business and therefore 'not good education'. Accordingly, a number of interested executives asked the National Better Business Bureau – an agency maintained by business for the protection of consumers – to step into the picture and determine what could be done in the way of improvement.[32]

The bureau arranged through the National Association of Secondary School Principals for a Consumer Education Study in 1943 to develop more pro-business curriculum materials for consumer education in schools. The Consumer Education Study prepared and published textbooks on consumer education based on advice and information provided by the bureau, and approved by the bureau as being completely fair to business. This was all funded by more than 50 businesses who willingly donated resources with 'little or no publicity'.[33] The Opinion Research Corporation (ORC) claimed:

> *A significant result of the programme has been to check the school use of many materials that are anti-business in nature. Another result has been an increased willingness on the part of teachers to use materials furnished by business ... Never before had teaching officialdom told teachers it was alright to use commercial materials provided they measure up to these criteria [educational and free of direct sales promotions] ...*
>
> *The Bureau believes an important public relations job for business is being done, and that teachers, consequently, are developing a much friendlier attitude toward American business.*[34]

A 1951 study found that 89 per cent of teachers surveyed used industry-sponsored materials in their classes. Another, a few years later, found that 77 per cent of all films shown in schools surveyed were donated sponsored films.[35] The ORC found that same year that three-quarters of social studies teachers reported receiving teaching aids from private corporations on the way business systems operate. Some described the material as 'one-sided, biased, smacks of propaganda, never admits any faults in the system'. However, most teachers tended to have high regard for the capitalist, free enterprise system, and social studies teachers were particularly open to receiving and using the corporate material.[36]

Some companies used consultants or teachers to design the materials so as to ensure their acceptability in the schools and give the impression that the materials, although sponsored, were neutral and independent. The National Education Association was not so particular, endorsing the use of all sponsored materials saying: 'No material is necessarily good or bad in itself. Probably nearly all free materials could serve a useful and constructive outlet in the classroom' provided it was used with care. The National Science Teachers Association admitted that by the late 1950s 'teachers and administrators have greater confidence in industry and in the motives behind industry's offerings to schools'. This was a major change from the immediate post-war years.[37]

The unions, however, did object to much of this material. In Ohio they unsuccessfully tried to stop a history text prepared by the Chamber of Commerce from being introduced. The text omitted reference to unions but devoted large sections to the rubber companies and to the Quaker Oats Company. Some unions tried to get their own materials into schools but without much success, since they 'had neither the resources nor the commitment to match business in the schools'.[38] They were too busy fighting more immediate battles in the workplace.

In 1954 FEE bought the magazine *The Freeman* and distributed it free, particularly to college students. Articles in *The Freeman* called for the abolition of income tax, the withdrawal of the US from the United Nations, and the withdrawal of the government from all public services – including post offices, education, roads, and electricity. An FEE textbook, *Understanding Our Free Economy*, was published in several editions. It argued that such things as minimum-wage laws, government control of interest rates and supervision of banks, and public ownership of land were all 'encroachments on free enterprise'.[39]

By the end of the 1950s, the business point of view had become the accepted truth in many schools and students were, in the words of economics professor Daniel Fusfeld, 'captives of the ideology of the right, ... indoctrinated' with the idea that an economy which was 'free, competitive and individualistic' had to be maintained.[40]

Despite this triumph, the need for economic 'education' continued to be promoted by business people in the 1960s. The president of the New York Stock Exchange told the National Association of Secondary School Principals in 1960 that the economic literacy of the American people was 'shockingly inadequate' and that it was up to the educational system to correct the situation. Economics professors at the college level complained that they had to 'unlearn' the students: 'We have a big job to do in just what you might call 'unlearning' the students who have all kinds of notions – they can't understand, for instance, how banks can create money.'[41]

Lucille Ford, in her 1967 PhD thesis, surveyed 90 organizations that were active in economic education and/or economic persuasion. Nearly all of these made their materials available to schools, and about a third specially designed materials for schools from elementary through to college level. She identified five types of organization providing this material:[42]

1 Business, industry and trade associations of industry who sought to show the role of industry and its products in the economic system. Examples included the American Bankers Association, the American Iron & Steel Institute, the US Chamber of Commerce, the New York Stock Exchange, NAM, the American Petroleum Institute and the Automobile Manufacturers which supplied materials to elementary and/or secondary schools.

2 Organizations advancing a particular economic philosophy such as The American Economic Foundation, Americans for the Competitive Enterprise System, Freedoms Foundation and the National Education Program.
3 Organizations seeking to sell educational materials for a profit such as the Industrial Relations Center.
4 Organizations set up for the purpose of changing people's understanding of economics such as the Joint Council on Economic Education and the Industrial Information Institute.
5 Think tanks and service organizations which concentrate on secondary schools and colleges such as the American Enterprise Institute, the Center for Information on America and the National Foundation for Consumer Credit.

These organizations produced teaching aids and also teaching units consisting of printed materials, films, record sets, text books, activity books, teacher's guides, wall charts, and tests. They also provided speakers, tours, awards programmes, and career conferences and programmes for secondary school students and symposia, seminars, workshops and panel discussions for college students.[43]

Some of these organizations were explicit in their ideology such as the National Economic Council which stated its commitment to 'prevent increases in government spending' and to 'unbuild the Federal bureaucracy' amongst other things.[44] Others maintained a veneer of objectivity.

Employee economic education

While many corporations attempted to influence school education, many more directed 'educational' efforts at their employees, who were captive audiences. Ninety-five per cent of large companies surveyed in 1947 approved of the idea of employee education, and in the following years, many large corporations, including Johnson & Johnson, IBM, Westinghouse, US Steel and DuPont developed educational programmes for workers or supervisors.[45]

As with the general public, it was assumed that undesirable worker attitudes towards business were related to their poor grasp of economic 'principles', in particular the following six economic principles:

1 Government control over production destroys free enterprise;
2 A man's real job security depends on how good his company is in meeting competition;
3 Highest pay should go to those who produce most;
4 The consumer, rather than the company, sets the price;
5 Labour-saving machinery makes jobs;
6 Stockholder and employee interests are allied.[46]

It was concluded from surveys that those who were ignorant of these economic principles were more likely to be dissatisfied at work and more likely to embrace 'collectivist' proposals. They were also more likely to favour price controls, limits on profits, limits on salaries, government ownership and stronger unions than those who were 'well-informed'. Company-based economic courses were therefore run to better inform workers and foremen so that they would have better attitudes towards business as well as more interest in company problems and working to solve them, increased productivity, and 'improved worker morale'.[47] The subjects most frequently covered in employee economic education courses were justifications for profits as supplying incentive, capital investment and job security; the ideology of competition and how it ensures 'the consumer is boss'; and the 'proper' and therefore limited role of government.[48]

By 1951, one out of every five large companies was giving formal courses in economics, and the majority of employee publications were 'carrying some material on freedom'. Their efforts were supplemented by those of educational and business organizations such as NAM, and the programmes of larger companies were often distributed to smaller companies. A 1952 ORC report noted that 'systematic company training in economics stands out as one of the fastest growing and most significant management developments in recent years'.[49]

A 1954 American Management Association (AMA) report found that employee education was found in almost all American industrial companies. It noted that 'employee education' and 'economic education' had 'become virtually synonymous to many people'. It also noted that some companies used the terms 'propaganda' and 'economic education' interchangeably and many were open about their wanting 'to influence our people to think "right"' and wanting 'to change their thinking'. Others were more circumspect, saying only that they wanted to present the pertinent 'facts' so that employees could draw their own conclusions.[50]

General Electric, when it introduced its own Economic Education Program, recognized the huge influence that employers could have through their own employees:

> *As employers in this country, businessmen are directly associated with more than 60 million people, more than a third of our population. If these 60 millions are made aware of the economic facts of life, we can be sure that they will, in turn, influence the thinking and knowledge of at least another third of the population.*[51]

Some companies confined their 'education' to economics, believing that with an understanding of economics, as taught by the company, 'they would quite naturally change their political and social thinking; thus management's basic goal would be attained'.[52] Others dealt more explicitly with social and political issues.

The HOBSO course developed by DuPont and adopted and distributed to other companies by NAM (mentioned earlier in this chapter) involved three 90-minute discussion sessions with groups of 20 employees on company time as follows:

Session One:	*Our American Business System (60 minutes)*
	Accomplishments of Our System (30 minutes)
Session Two:	*The Importance of Competition (60 minutes)*
	Individual Freedoms Under Our System (30 minutes)
Session Three:	*Proposed Changes in Our System (45 minutes)*
	Our Company – Its Story (45 minutes)[53]

The course taught ideology rather than economics or company operations, and emphasized the achievements of free enterprise while emphasizing the threat of socialism. It stressed the importance of profits, competition and economic freedom, and attacked government controls.[54] One critic stated:

> *HOBSO would be all right if its users were honest with themselves and with their employees about what it is. It is not an open or free discussion. It is directed, and the conference leader should say, 'I'm going to tell you these things', not say, 'We want your opinions' and then reject them or be selective in the opinions he accepts.*[55]

NAM trained personnel from companies using the HOBSO package as discussion leaders and provided the materials, including visual aids. The course contained 'no difficult-to-understand economic principles'. By the middle of the 1950s, more than 500 firms had participated in training sessions on HOBSO and its successor HOBSO II. This was despite it costing the average firm an estimated $1 million to run the programme in the workplace, including the cost of employee attendance during company time.[56]

DuPont also conducted attitude surveys, plant tours for the community, foreman visits to headquarters, talks by key executives, and produced newsletters in its efforts to foster 'improved understanding of business and economic fundamentals'. Its programme of propaganda was targeted at its employees, customers and shareholders whom it believed 'could reason rightly provided they had the information, facts and opinions necessary to start their thinking'.[57]

Stanolind Oil & Gas Company also adopted the 90-minute discussion format in its workplace programme entitled, 'Let's Talk It Over', which was mandatory for all employees, rank and file:

> *... we had become concerned over the growing drift toward socialism apparent in this country, and the apathy which too many Americans*

> *had assumed in connection with social, political and economic thinking. This course was devised as a tool to thwart that apathy and to stimulate greater interest on the part of Stanolind people in civic affairs.*[58]

Stanolind decided that since its target was socialism it would start with a discussion of the threat of communism, the tendency toward socialism in the US and how further government control would lead to socialism. By starting this way rather than launching immediately into a criticism of socialism the company felt that the course would be relieved 'of any aspect of company bias'.[59] The use of college professors as discussion leaders also reinforced the supposed impartiality of the course.

The course would then go on to discuss the 'American way of life', representative government and how 'individual thought and action influence law-making' and 'how most Americans are capitalists in one way or another' and 'why our standard of living is so high', as well as freedoms provided by the American system. Accompanying materials for employees to take home included the booklets *If you were Born in Russia*; *The Miracle of America*, produced by the Advertising Council; and *Good Citizen*, produced by The American Heritage Foundation.[60]

Sears Roebuck also produced its own economic education programme, which included a series of films and involved the training of 2600 meeting leaders. In 1952, these leaders conducted 71,000 meetings to put Sears' employees through the course, which consisted of three-hour sessions at weekly intervals, at a total cost of $6 million.[61]

The ORC surveyed the workers before and after doing the Sears Roebuck course. After the course, the percentage who agreed that 'the most practical way for workers to increase their standard of living' was for 'all workers to produce more' increased to 77 per cent. Eighty-seven per cent agreed that shorter hours had resulted from greater productive efficiency rather than union demands, compared with 69 per cent before the course. Their view of capitalists had also changed. The course managed to convince the workers that most Americans are actually capitalists. Seventy-four per cent (compared with 19 per cent before the course) agreed that most capitalists in the US are 'ordinary citizens who have savings and life insurance' and 94 per cent agreed that 'workers, management and stockholders are all really partners in the business. What hurts one group hurts the others also.'[62]

Ninety-six per cent agreed that 'One of the best things about our American business system is that, generally speaking, people get paid fairly in terms of their ability and how hard they work'. In addition, 99 per cent *disagreed* with the 'Marxist' statement that 'the fairest economic system is one that takes from each according to his ability and gives to each according to his needs', compared with 74 per cent before the course. And, according to the ORC, the tie between a citizen's personal freedom and the preservation of the free market system was strengthened.[63]

Other courses were equally successful in changing worker attitudes, according to the surveys. ORC did a before-and-after survey of workers undertaking a 'Freedom' course at the Connecticut Light & Power Company. More than 80 per cent agreed, after the course, that 'We are slowly losing important freedoms here in America' and that 'price control cannot be put in effect without affecting the average man's freedom'.[64]

Republic Steel Corporation aimed its economic education programme at the 6000 supervisors working for the company, rather than the 70,000 employees. It decided this was more cost-effective, as supervisors were 'likely to be more vocal than a rank-and-file worker in civic and community affairs'. Supervisors were tested before the course and questions that they most often got 'wrong' were 'singled out for corrective emphasis during the lessons'. The course consisted of 15 booklets and 15 hour-and-a-half guided group discussions. It was given legitimacy by the involvement of the University of Chicago so that 'Employees were less suspect of company slant in the material than they might have been had they heard the company's word alone.' The resulting increase in scores for 'economic knowledge' and for 'economic opinion' amongst supervisors led the Industrial Relations Center of the University of Chicago to adapt it for use by other companies 'at a price that even small ones can afford'.[65]

It was not only blue-collar workers who were subjected to indoctrination via workplace education. William Whyte describes in *The Organization Man* how young university graduates were trained to be able to fit into the organization. For example, the General Electric programme provided trainees, often engineering graduates, with intensive live-in training including DuPont's HOBSO programme.[66]

Apart from courses, companies used magazines, bulletin boards, pamphlets, meetings and advertisements to get their point across in the belief that by supplying information they could change workers' attitudes.[67]

Public relations experts went to a lot of effort to ensure employee communications were effective. For example, in 1960, the ORC published the report *Word Impact for Management's Communications*, which acknowledged the power of words and advised employers on which ones should be used. For example, the ORC tested the term 'Capitalism' on workers and found that 'Free Enterprise' was more likely to have a favourable connotation.[68] Words were tested for their familiarity, understandability and emotional impact.

Prominent industrial psychologist Morris Viteles was less sanguine than the ORC about the achievements of these programmes. He noted in his 1953 book *Motivation and Morale in Industry* that 'much remains to be done in establishing the relationships between economic indoctrination and attitude toward the economic system on the one hand, and net changes in ideology, morale, productivity, and the action of individuals as citizens of a commonwealth'. In his discussion of workplace propaganda Vitelli explained that 'an indirect or disguised approach to moulding attitudes and opinions is more effective than propaganda which is easily recognized as such'.[69]

In his chapter on 'Moulding and Modifying Attitudes', Vitelli considered whether it is better to give both sides of an issue or just one side in order to change workers' attitudes. Research suggested that better-educated people were more influenced by a presentation that appeared to be balanced than less-educated people so he recommended a one-sided programme for rank-and-file workers and a two-sided programme for supervisors and technical personnel.[70]

OUTCOMES

The PR aimed at selling the free enterprise system in the first half of the 20th century tended to be heavy handed and condescending. Corporations attempted to sell free market ideology in the same way as they sold their merchandise. Whyte, in his 1952 book *Is Anybody Listening?*, noted that although the businessman had never had 'so much paraphernalia with which to communicate his message', the free enterprise campaign was 'an insult to the intelligence' and a waste of money. He argued that the campaign was too abstract, defensive and negative and 'represents a shocking lack of faith in the American people, and in some cases downright contempt'.[71]

Nevertheless, all this campaigning seemed to pay off as the balance of public opinion shifted from organized labour to business. By 1950, most people, particularly the middle classes, had come to accept big business as an essential part of American life. A 1951 poll found that 76 per cent of those asked approved of big business compared with 10 per cent who disapproved.[72]

A million-dollar public relations campaign by organized labour in 1953 failed to counter the pro-free enterprise public relations effort. Anti-communist sentiment, fed by the revolution in China and developments in the Soviet Union, as well as McCarthy's anti-communist campaign in the US, tainted the unions in the public eye and caused division within the labour movement, weakening the power of the unions.[73]

By 1955, studies found that the community was much more supportive of industry. A majority of those surveyed agreed that the interests of employers and workers were the same, and the vast majority of Americans said they approved of large corporations. They were now more concerned about Big Labour and Big Government than about Big Business. One observer noted: 'the attitudes, opinions, arguments, values and slogans of the American business community are a familiar part of the landscape of most Americans. In recent years, the business point of view has found abundant expression in every kind of medium.'[74]

The earlier post-war business campaigns in the US were scaled down after President Dwight D. Eisenhower, a friend of business, was elected in 1952.[75] However, this was not the last of the campaigns to assert business values, and in the 1970s corporations again renewed their campaign to promote business values and policy goals (see next chapter).

NOTES

1 John Kenneth Galbraith, *The Anatomy of Power*, London, Hamish Hamilton, 1984, p120.

2 Mary Sennholz, 'Leonard Read, the Founder and Builder', *The Freeman*, May, 1996, www.libertyhaven.com/thinkers/leonarderead/readfounder.html; FEE, 'Foundation for Economic Education', Foundation for Economic Education, www.fee.org accessed 12 August 2004.

3 Karl Schriftgiesser, *The Lobbyists: The Art and Business of Influencing Lawmakers*, Boston, 1Little, Brown & Co., 951, pp169, 175; Lee Metcalf and Vic Reinemer, *Overcharge: How Electric Utilities Exploit and Mislead the Public*, New York, David McKay Company, 1967, pp181, 189; Chip Berlet and Matthew N. Lyons, *Right-Wing Populism in America: Too Close for Comfort*, New York, The Guilford Press, 2000, pp177–80.

4 John Blundell, 'Waging the War of Ideas: Why There Are No Shortcuts', Atlas Economic Research Foundation, January, 1990, www.atlasusa.org/toolkit/waging_war.php.

5 John Kenneth Galbraith, *American Capitalism: The Concept of Countervailing Power*, Sentry edn, Boston, Houghton Mifflin, 1956, pp22, 48.

6 *Ibid.*

7 John Kenneth Galbraith, *The Culture of Contentment*, London, Penguin, 1992, p95.

8 *Ibid.*, pp96–7.

9 Robert Griffith, 'The Selling of America: The Advertising Council and American Politics, 1942–1960', *Business History Review*, Autumn, 1983, p389.

10 Fred Norris, 'Basic Economics Courses for Industry', adapted from unpublished Master's Thesis in Economics, 1954, Los Angeles, pp59–60.

11 ORC, 'Industry and the Social Science Teacher', Princeton, NJ, Opinion Research Corporation, April 1947, pp38, 41; Elizabeth A. Fones-Wolf, *Selling Free Enterprise: The Business Assault on Labor and Liberalism, 1945–60*, Urbana and Chicago, University of Illinois Press, 1994, p201.

12 Metcalf and Reinemer, *Overcharge*, pp168, 170–8.

13 'Ten Pillars of Economic Wisdom: A Blueprint for Understanding', New York, American Economic Foundation, undated.

14 Quoted in Schriftgiesser, *The Lobbyists*, pp171–2, 199.

15 *Ibid.*, pp198–201.

16 Quoted in *Ibid.*, pp195–6.

17 *Ibid.*, pp202–4.

18 *Ibid.*, pp194–206.

19 S. Alexander Rippa, *Education in a Free Society: An American History*, New York, Longman, 1984, p300; Fones-Wolf, *Selling Free Enterprise*, p191.

20 Rippa, *Education in a Free Society*, pp297–8.

21 Fones-Wolf, *Selling Free Enterprise*, pp191–3; Rippa, *Education in a Free Society*, p299.

22 National Association of Manufacturers, 'Report to Members', NAM 1950, pp20–1, 24–6.

23 Fones-Wolf, *Selling Free Enterprise*, pp193–4.

24 *Ibid.*, pp194–7.
25 ORC, 'Industry and the Social Science Teacher', p39; Fones-Wolf, *Selling Free Enterprise*, p205.
26 ORC, 'Industry and the Social Science Teacher', p36.
27 Norris, 'Basic Economics Courses for Industry', pp125–132.
28 Fones-Wolf, *Selling Free Enterprise*, p204; *Fortune* quoted in Norris, 'Basic Economics Courses for Industry', p8.
29 Griffith, 'The Selling of America', p403; Fones-Wolf, *Selling Free Enterprise*, p203.
30 ORC, 'The High School Market for Economic Education', Princeton, NJ, Public Opinion Research Corporation, June 1951, pp18–19; Fones-Wolf, *Selling Free Enterprise*, p202.
31 ORC, 'Industry and the Social Science Teacher', pp48–9; Fones-Wolf, *Selling Free Enterprise*, p202.
32 ORC, 'Industry and the Social Science Teacher', pp42–3.
33 *Ibid.*, p43.
34 Opinion Research Corporation, 'Industry and the Social Science Teacher', Princeton, NJ, Opinion Research Corporation, April 1947, p44.
35 Lucille G. Ford, 'A Survey of Organizations Active in Economic Education', Doctor of Philosophy, Western Reserve University, Cleveland, Ohio, 1967, p67.
36 ORC, 'The High School Market for Economic Education', p15.
37 Fones-Wolf, *Selling Free Enterprise*, p204; Ford, 'A Survey of Organizations Active in Economic Education', p69.
38 Fones-Wolf, *Selling Free Enterprise*, pp209–10.
39 Metcalf and Reinemer, *Overcharge*, pp186–7.
40 Quoted in Fones-Wolf, *Selling Free Enterprise*, p211.
41 ORC, 'Why Too Many College Students Are Economic Illiterates', Princeton, NJ, Opinion Research Corporation, April 1960, pp1–4.
42 Ford, 'A Survey of Organizations Active in Economic Education', pp40–6.
43 *Ibid.*, pp42–3, 48, 53.
44 Quoted in *Ibid.*, p58.
45 ORC, 'The Company's Role in Selling Free Enterprise', Princeton, NJ, Opinion Research Corporation, January 1947; Elizabeth A. Fones-Wolf, 'Beneath Consensus: Business, Labor, and the Post-War Order', Doctor of Philosophy, University of Massachusetts, 1990, pp141–2.
46 Morris S. Viteles, *Motivation and Morale in Industry*, New York, W.W. Norton & Co., 1953, p423.
47 *Ibid.*, pp424–7.
48 Douglas Williams and Stanley Peterfreund, *The Education of Employees: A Status Report*, Management Education for Itself and Its Employees, New York, American Management Association, 1954, pp41–2.
49 ORC, 'Experiment in Employee Education. Courses in American Freedoms', Princeton, NJ, Opinion Research Corporation, May 1952, p31; Viteles, *Motivation and Morale in Industry*, p422.
50 Williams and Peterfreund, *The Education of Employees*, p31.
51 Quoted in Norris, 'Basic Economics Courses for Industry', p13.
52 *Ibid.*, p63.

53 *Ibid.*, p27.
54 Fones-Wolf, 'Beneath Consensus', pp143–4.
55 Quoted in Williams and Peterfreund, *The Education of Employees*, p38.
56 Norris, 'Basic Economics Courses for Industry', p27; Fones-Wolf, 'Beneath Consensus', pp142–3; Williams and Peterfreund, *The Education of Employees*, p40.
57 Norris, 'Basic Economics Courses for Industry', pp108–9, 111.
58 Quoted in *Ibid.*, p61.
59 *Ibid.*, pp66–7.
60 *Ibid.*, pp68, 70.
61 F. S. Cellier, 'The Story of Sears in America: An Economic Education Program', *American Management Association Personnel Series*, no 152, 1953.
62 ORC, 'Experiment in Employee Education', pp50–1.
63 *Ibid.*, pp49, 52; Norris, 'Basic Economics Courses for Industry', p81.
64 ORC, 'Experiment in Employee Education', pp55.
65 Norris, 'Basic Economics Courses for Industry', pp89-91, 105.
66 William H. Whyte, *The Organization Man*, 2nd edn, Harmondsworth, Middlesex, Penguin, 1960, p116.
67 Viteles, *Motivation and Morale in Industry*, pp414–5.
68 ORC, 'Word Impact for Management's Communications', Princeton, NJ, Opinion Research Corporation, January 1960, p3.
69 Viteles, *Motivation and Morale in Industry*, pp429, 431.
70 *Ibid.*, p435.
71 William H. Whyte, *Is Anybody Listening? How and Why US Business Fumbles When It Talks with Human Beings*, New York, Simon & Schuster, 1952, ppvii, 1, 8.
72 Richard S. Tedlow, *Keeping the Corporate Image: Public Relations and Business, 1900–1950*, Greenwich, Connecticut, JAI Press, 1979, pp16, 149.
73 Fones-Wolf, 'Beneath Consensus', pp85–6, 90.
74 *Ibid.*, p92; Sutton, quoted in Ralph Miliband, *The State in Capitalist Society*, London, Quartet Books, 1969, p192.
75 Fones-Wolf, 'Beneath Consensus', p332.

5

Economic 'Education' in the 1970s

For business, the turbulence of change was a nightmare of new regulations and increasingly vocal interest groups that needed pandering to. The rules of the game had changed, and new ways had to be found to at once get what one needed from government, shout down the opposition, and harness the power of interest groups for one's own benefit through persuasion.
JEFF AND MARIE BLYSKAL[1]

In 1971 Lewis F. Powell, Jr, a prominent corporate lawyer, sent a confidential memorandum to the chair of the education committee of the US Chamber of Commerce. Powell was a member of the board of directors of 11 corporations and had been president of the American Bar Association and chair of the Virginia State Board of Education.[2]

Powell's memo was a battle plan for the chamber to defend the free enterprise system from the 'broad attack' it was suffering 'from the college campus, the media, the intellectual and literary journals, the arts and sciences, and from politicians'. Powell noted that many of these institutions, particularly the campuses and the media, were financed or funded by business: 'One of the bewildering paradoxes of our time is the extent to which the enterprise system tolerates, if not participates in, its own destruction.'[3]

Powell argued for 'the wisdom, ingenuity and resources of American business to be marshalled against those who would destroy it' under the leadership of the Chamber of Commerce: 'It is time for American business – which has demonstrated the greatest capacity in all history to produce and to influence consumer decisions – to apply their great talents vigorously to the preservation of the system itself.' He outlined a number of strategies that an enlarged, restructured and better financed Chamber of Commerce could undertake with an increased staff that included 'highly qualified scholars in the social sciences who do believe in the system', competent lawyers, and 'speakers of the highest competency'. These strategies included:[4]

- action programmes tailored to high schools;
- monitoring national television networks in the same way as textbooks and complaining to the media and Federal Communications Commission when broadcasts are unfair;
- demanding equal time on current affairs and news programmes;
- publishing regularly in scholarly journals, and a range of magazines – popular and intellectual – and providing incentives for those scholars who believe in the system to publish also;
- devoting a significant proportion of the business advertising budget to selling the merits of the free enterprise system;
- becoming politically active, cultivating political power and using it 'aggressively and with determination – without embarrassment . . .';
- engaging in specially selected court cases to support business interests;
- mobilizing stockholders, perhaps through establishment of a national organization with enough corporate backing – 'muscle' – to be influential, and utilizing shareholder reports and magazines 'far more effectively as educational media' aimed at enlisting their political support;
- attacking critics of the system, such as Ralph Nader and Herbert Marcuse, and penalizing those who oppose free enterprise.

Powell's memorandum was circulated to members but the Chamber of Commerce decided it was unwilling to take the lead in such a campaign. Although the memo was confidential, it was leaked to the media and publicized when Powell was appointed by President Richard Nixon to the Supreme Court, as evidence of his inability to be objective. The publicity failed to prevent his appointment but served to inspire like-minded advocates of free enterprise, even extending as far as the Australian Chamber of Commerce.[5]

While the US Chamber of Commerce decided not to head the charge, the Advertising Council took on that role, as it had after the Second World War. It launched a major campaign in 1976 to promote free enterprise, or as the Council termed it: to 'create greater understanding of the American economic system'. The continuous campaign in favour of free enterprise has been described by Alexander Rippa, in his history of American education, as 'the most elaborate and costly public-relations project in American history'. The council itself referred to it as 'The Most Successful Introduction of a Public Service Campaign in Advertising Council History'.[6]

At the time, business was under attack, and public interest groups were challenging the authority of business and seeking government controls over business activities. Confidence in free enterprise was in decline. The first wave of modern environmentalists was blaming development and the growth of industrial activities for environmental degradation. Their warnings were capturing popular attention, resonating as they did with the experiences of communities facing obvious pollution in their neighbourhoods. Worst of all, from a business point of view, governments were responding with new environmental legislation.[7]

Public respect for business was at an all-time low and 'for the first time since the Great Depression, the legitimacy of big business was being called into question by large sectors of the public'.[8] A Harris poll found that between 1967 and 1977, at a time when the counter-culture movement brought with it a proliferation of public interest groups – including environmental and consumer groups – that challenged the authority of business and sought government controls over business activities, the percentage of people who had 'great confidence' in major companies fell from 55 per cent to 16 per cent.[9]

In various business meetings corporate executives lamented their decline in influence. For example, Carter Bales, director of McKinsey, New York, stated: 'Around the world, there have been challenges to the authority of each corporate actor – a breaking down, if you will, of their legitimacy.' And the president of the National Federation of Independent Business, Wilson Johnson, claimed 'we're losing the war against government usurpation of our economic freedom'.[10]

In response, the opinion shaping machinery set up in earlier times went into action and a great deal of money went into what was euphemistically called 'education', particularly education aimed at young people and children, to reassert the dominance of free market ideology.

THE ADVERTISING COUNCIL CAMPAIGN

In the 1970s the Advertising Council, with the support of the advertising industry, the media and American business, ran some 28 'public service' campaigns every year on topics such as 'America, it only works as well as you do', on productivity, and 'Help America Work', sponsored by the National Alliance of Businessmen. It was the largest single advertiser in the country. Its advertisements took up twice as much time and space as the top corporate advertiser, Procter & Gamble. It was able to do this on a tiny budget of $2 million a year because of the donated efforts of advertising agency executives and marketing people from top business corporations, as well as donated time and space for advertisements from media and publishing companies. For every dollar donated to the Advertising Council it received approximately $640 worth of free commercial time.[11]

The Advertising Council's extended campaign on economic education was far bigger and more ambitious than anything the council had previously attempted. It was supported by so many major corporations that the council boasted the list of supporters read like a 'who's who in American business'. It was also supported by the US Department of Commerce, not without some controversy at the time, since the money had been earmarked for jobs and minority business opportunities.[12]

According to *Fortune* magazine, the campaign was 'largely the brainchild of Barton A. Cummings, chairman of the executive committee at Compton Advertising'. Cummings would have preferred a campaign that directly advocated free enterprise but the Advertising Council's charter would not allow it to advertise anything controversial so a campaign aimed ostensibly at improving economic understanding was seen as a way of achieving the same goal.[13] Compton Advertising then designed the campaign.

The stated premise of the campaign was that people were economically illiterate and therefore needed economic education. According to the Joint Council on Economic Education (JCEE), 'The more one knows about economics, the more one is likely to be supportive of the American economic system.'[14] Of course, that knowledge had to be tailored to achieve such a result. The unstated premise was that if people were educated to view the free enterprise system as business people saw it, they would appreciate and defend it rather than criticize it.

Not everyone agreed that the campaign was impartial, and the Public Media Center threatened a counter campaign, which was subsequently undertaken by the People's Bicentennial Commission but with far fewer resources and therefore less effect. One result, however, was that two of the major television networks, ABC and CBS, initially declined to broadcast 'public service announcements' advertising Advertising Council booklets because they might have had to run free spots for opposing points of view. However, the NBC network and 300 individual television stations did run them, choosing to view them as objective and requiring no balancing point of view, despite a request from Jeremy Rifkin of the People's Commission for the opportunity to advertise an opposing booklet.[15]

In the lead up to the campaign, Compton Advertising undertook a survey of public attitudes to the economic system. The conclusion of this study was that most people didn't understand how the economic system worked and their part in it. They looked to government intervention for problems such as inflation and the growing size of corporations.[16]

Naturally those who were better off, with better jobs – professionals and business people – cited personal freedom and mobility as a key advantage of the US economic system more often than the poor, less-educated and blue-collar workers. More affluent people also tended to be less critical of the economic system and to see it as requiring fewer changes. Even so, according to the authors of the report, 'no evidence was found of any widespread overt feeling that fundamental structural changes are needed'.[17]

Compton Advertising undertook a more quantitative national study in 1976 that included 22 agree/disagree questions. Responses from the 3000 people surveyed were analysed as to their 'correctness' despite the heavy judgemental/attitudinal component to many of the questions.[18] Table 5.1 shows some sample questions. The 'correct' answers are shown with a tick.

Although the Compton survey found most people were in agreement with business values, indicating that the earlier employee and school campaigns had been successful, the Advertising Council believed that these positive attitudes needed to be more widespread and harnessed to ensure that people understood that protection of the economic system meant leaving it unregulated and unchanged.

The campaign juxtaposed personal, political and economic freedom, arguing that constraints on economic freedom were tantamount to reducing personal and

Table 5.1 *Survey of economic literacy*

	Agree	*Disagree*	*Don't Know*
Business alone decides what will be produced	38.6%	59.8% ✓	1.6%
The primary role of business is to provide goods and services the country needs	77.9% ✓	21.5%	0.6%
In general, when business profits are up, times are good and life is better for more people	81.1% ✓	18.3%	0.6%
Overall, the American economic system offers more freedom and opportunity to better oneself than other economic systems	91.6% ✓	7.3%	1.1%

Note: ✓ 'signifies correct response'

Source: Compton Advertising. 'Study on Advertising Awareness and Understanding of the American System: Benchmark, Phase I'. Compton Advertising. June 1976.

political freedom and that those who sought to 'intervene excessively in the play of market forces,' however well intentioned they might be, posed a major threat to those freedoms. Criticism of the economic system amounted to subversion of the political system.[19]

The Advertising Council told the media that 'every communications technique that is appropriate for such a campaign will be used in this effort, which we anticipate will carry over for a three to five year period'. The multi-million-dollar campaign included media advertisements, dedicated newsletters, films, teaching materials and training kits, booklets, point of sale displays, messages on envelopes, and flyers included with bank statements, utility bills and insurance premium notices. The media contributed $40 million of free time and space to the campaign in the first two years.[20]

The campaign sought to get maximum distribution of the booklet *America's Economic System ... and your part in it.* The booklet was in colour and illustrated with *Peanuts* cartoons. It described the economic system in simple, idealized terms (along the lines of the market story outlined in Chapter 1). It promoted the idea that everyone not only had a stake in the economic system, but also had a say in it. It argued that everyone helps to make decisions in the system – governments, producers and especially consumers: 'the key role that really makes everything work is played by you, in your role as consumer'. Ordinary people also play a role as producers – 'Workers are producers' – and as investors – 'if you have a savings account, own life insurance, or are in a pension fund, you are helping to generate funds for investment purposes'.[21]

The booklet emphasized the importance of hard work and increasing productivity 'if we are to maintain competitiveness in selling goods and services both at home and abroad'. It reinforced the need for consumers to spend their money buying goods to ensure the security of their jobs: 'Remember when we buy less than our economy is producing, eventually production goes down and unemployment increases.' Naturally, it also defended the role of advertising: 'Those who supply the best goods and services at the best prices generally will be the most successful. And it is through advertising that producers inform buyers about their goods and services . . .'.[22]

The booklet was careful to downplay the amount of profits made by corporations. It did this by using averages of all businesses and arguing that the profits made by corporations were small compared to the aggregate income of all individuals. It emphasized that the economic system was responsible for the high standard of living in the US and that personal freedom was intimately connected with economic freedom.[23]

The Advertising Council distributed millions of copies of these booklets to schools, workplaces and communities – some 13 million by 1979.[24] According to the council, advertisements for the booklets were sent to every media outlet and every magazine in the country. It was advertised free:

- on more than 400 television stations;
- on more than 1000 radio stations;
- in more than 3000 daily and weekly newspapers;
- in more than 400 business and consumer magazines;
- on thousands of counter cards in libraries, banks and stores;
- on more than 110,000 transit cards in subways and other transport venues (more than $25 million of measurable free time and space).[25]

The booklet was reproduced in full in more than 100 newspapers and magazines. More than 1800 companies, 1300 schools and 500 organizations ordered bulk copies for employees, students and members.[26]

After one year of the campaign, Compton Advertising did another survey asking the same 22 questions. It estimated by extrapolation from its surveys that 46 million people had been reached by the advertising about the economic system, and 10 million remembered the Advertising Council's campaign specifically. Those who were aware of the Advertising Council's campaign had 'a more positive attitude toward the economic system' and 'a more favourable attitude toward business' and in general the respondents had a 'better' knowledge of the economic system, 'more positive appraisal of the system', and 'less desire for government regulation of economic activities'.[27]

A second stage of the campaign launched in 1977 involved a huge advertising campaign centred around the idea of an Economics Quotient (EQ) – an obvious reference to IQ. Advertisements asked 'How high is your EQ?' or 'Do your kids have a higher EQ than you?' and included quiz questions and answers so people could test themselves. The idea was to make people feel ignorant so that they would write away for the booklet, while at the same time making an ideological point. The 'basic economic questions' in the advertisements included:

> **True or False?** *In 1975, the investment in equipment and facilities averaged almost $41,000 for each production worker in American industry.*
> *[Answer: true]*

> **True or False?** *If you have a savings account, own stock, bonds or life insurance, or are in a pension fund, you are an investor in the US economy.*
> *[Answer: true]*

The Advertising Council produced two more booklets that year, one on employment and one on inflation and these were also subject to mass distribution. Also, a picture book version of the original booklet was prepared for 'low-level readers' and children.[28]

COMPLEMENTARY CAMPAIGNS

The Advertising Council's 'economic education' campaign was supplemented by the efforts of many individual corporations, trade associations and chambers of commerce. Some companies offered their own employees economic 'education'. For example, the Clorox Company provided an economics course for its employees that counted towards a college degree. And Abbott Laboratories used internal publications to 'educate' its employees, as well as distributing the Advertising Council booklet to employees.[29]

Teacher education was also targeted by individual corporations because of the influence of teachers on millions of children. For example, American Cyanamid began an economic education programme for teachers in 1973, and by 1978, 600 teachers in four states had attended its 15-week course of seminars, earning in-service credit for doing so. Its manager of educational relations, William Elliott, noted that teachers started off as an 'adversary audience' but finished the course as 'pro-business'.[30]

The Continental Group, a manufacturer and distributor of metal, paper, and plastic packaging products, started its programme for teachers in 1974 and entitled it 'The Role of Business in a Free Society'. It was offered as a graduate course for teachers at colleges and universities in 30 states. It counted towards their masters or doctorates in education. The course featured lectures from leading businessmen from a variety of companies such as IBM, Standard Oil, W. R. Grace, Allied Chemical and Philip Morris, and seminars once a week for a session. Similar courses were offered to other 'opinion leaders' including journalists, clergy and MBA students. Continental also encouraged other firms to offer economic education courses and prepared a 200-page book on how to run such a programme. It established the Continental Institute to expand free enterprise economic education.[31]

Dow followed Continental's lead in establishing a teacher education course. In addition it produced a film extolling the superiority of capitalism; established a library of films and materials for teachers; organized business education exchange days; and set up a programme for college students to learn about free enterprise principles. Another company, Ryerson Inc., gave teachers summer employment so that they could learn how a business operates.[32]

Corporate-sponsored classroom materials were also produced for the purpose of selling the free enterprise system to schoolchildren. Four million packages of *Industry and the American Economy* (an 11-booklet package), were distributed to students and teachers all over the nation. Economic Ecology, an organization promoting free enterprise, produced a game called 'You Can Do It: Baseball' based on questions from the booklet *You Can Do It! The Story of What Makes America Tick*. Corporate money also financed a television show on economics featuring a leading free market economist, Milton Friedman (see Chapter 7) and another, *In Search of the Real America* featuring a Fellow from the conservative think tank the American Enterprise Institute.[33]

Sears Roebuck produced classroom materials for elementary and secondary school children, including textbooks, teachers' guides, audiovisual materials and classroom activities on economic and consumer education. Its booklet *Our Economic System – Essays and Teachers' Guides* included essays sponsored by the Business Roundtable. Eli Lilly and Company joined with the Indianapolis Chamber of Commerce to offer 'Opportunities to Learn About Business' to high school students. It involved nine full teaching days of lectures, reading, discussion; a simulated business game where students formed businesses and competed in the market; and contact with prominent business people. The game was also sponsored by General Motors and other businesses.[34]

Various oil companies also got involved. Phillips Petroleum Company supported the production of a series of five films entitled *American enterprise*, narrated by William Shatner (who played Captain Kirk on the popular television series *Star Trek*) with an accompanying teachers' guide. It cost $800,000 and reached over 8 million students. Amoco Oil Company also produced a 26-minute film and teachers' guide to explain how the free enterprise system works. The Exxon Company got together with Walt Disney Educational Media Company to produce a 22-minute film for high school students about two children who go into business.[35]

The US Industrial Council (USIC), a coalition of 4500 companies employing over 3 million people, ran its own campaign to defend free enterprise. It used 'radio broadcasts, national toll-free telephone lines, newspaper columns, economic research reports, pamphlets for professional groups and civic organizations, posters for display in factories and offices, and other forms of communication'. It distributed 3 million pieces of literature each year, including pamphlets such as *Who is a Capitalist?*, *What is Free Enterprise?* and *The Union Monopoly and the Abuse of Power*.[36]

The USIC Educational Foundation, the educational arm of USIC, also campaigned for free enterprise. It organized 'nationwide lecture tours by free enterprise spokesmen and leading free-market journalists'; offered prizes and awards 'to editorialists and political cartoonists for distinguished work'; and provided grants 'to academics and young scholars who are active in defence of free enterprise principle[s]'.[37]

The Booker T. Washington Foundation, recognizing that 'black Americans have almost an aversion to capitalism' and were inclined to see economics in terms of distribution and economic justice, set up Enterprise America to spread the gospel about free enterprise to black people.[38]

The Texas Bureau for Economic Understanding, which later became the American Enterprise Forum, produced an instructional programme that was used by 20 Texas universities. In one of the instructional booklets, produced with the Institute of Free Enterprise Education, it defended profits by arguing that: 'Without the hope for profit, America could not be a nation of free people because people wouldn't be willing to serve each other if the hope for gain were absent. The rulers would find it necessary to force people to work ...'.[39]

The National Education Program was another of the many organizations providing free enterprise educational materials for schools. It had been founded in 1936 and had established the Freedom Forum in 1949, becoming 'the cradle for a nation-wide educational movement supporting the American way of life and its three great pillars – Faith in God, Constitutional Government, and the Private Ownership of the Tools of Production'. By 1968 it was running annual Youth Forums in 12 states where high school students learned about 'the incomparable advantages of the American system, why and how it produces far more than any form of Socialism or Communism, and how it must be protected from the Communist conspiracy which seeks to destroy it'.[40]

In the 1970s, while continuing its annual Freedom Forums and their Youth equivalents, the National Education Program also produced 'full-color animated cartoons'; flannel board presentations; a monthly newsletter; a weekly column for newspapers and trade publications; audio-taped and printed speeches; a Do-It-Yourself Materials Kit for organizing a one-day forum; and a number of films on topics such as *A Look at Capitalism* and *The Spirit of Enterprise*. One film – *The Truth about Communism* – was hosted and narrated by Ronald Reagan.[41] It distributed 'Activity Suggestions for Citizenship Leaders' with advice on how to form a group and recruit people to it and become politically active:

> *High School Juniors and Seniors are mature enough to join the crusade to eliminate citizenship ignorance and apathy. Some of the National Program films, or others on citizenship subjects, should be scheduled for school assembly periods, or in history, civics, and economics classes. ... Study groups of Juniors and Seniors could be formed, to meet in homes ...*[42]

> *Assign some of your group to attend school board meetings, town council sessions, county board or quorum court meetings, and report on problems confronted and the proposed solutions... Seek to get citizenship education programs carried to every family – in school affairs, at clubs, fairs, community-wide events ... Write letters-to-the-editor (but do not overdo it). Write carefully composed, well-documented, restrained letters on matters of concern that are being debated...*[43]

The US Chamber of Commerce, despite its reluctance to lead a campaign as envisioned by Powell, was happy enough to take part. It produced films, teaching materials and booklets on the economic system and a package entitled 'Economics for Young Americans' that included film strips, audio cassettes, lesson plans and text on productivity, profits and the environment.[44] Local chambers of commerce also participated in the campaign.

For example, the Los Angeles Area Chamber of Commerce put together a catalogue of expert speakers on issues including government/business relations, commercial and industrial development, and the environment. The Bergen County Chamber of Commerce set up the Bergen Chamber Economic Education Foundation, which sponsored college symposia, developed high school curricular and teacher education programmes. Various Invest in America councils set up scholarship programmes, speech competitions, school and college conferences and workshops for teachers on economic understanding.[45]

In Texas, a law was passed in 1973 making it mandatory to teach public high school students about 'the essentials and benefits of the free enterprise system ... for at least one semester or quarter ...'[46] In response, the Institute for Free Enterprise and the Texas Bureau for Economic Understanding put out a booklet explaining that the motivation for this law was a realization that the American Free Enterprise System 'has a basic moral foundation' which the booklet tried to associate with the Bible.[47]

UNIVERSITIES

Powell had called for various actions to be taken with respect to universities, including evaluating social science textbooks for their ideological stance, insisting on the right to be heard on the college speaking circuit and urging that pro-business people be included in university administrations and on boards of trustees.[48]

Many took up Powell's call for selective corporate funding of universities. David Packard made the same plea to a Committee for Corporate Support of American Universities in 1973, and a couple of years later, James J. Kilpatrick, a columnist with *Nation's Business*, reiterated that it was a bizarre custom that 'corporations, whose future depends upon the preservation of a free enterprise system' would 'give large sums of money to institutions whose faculties regard free enterprise with contempt'.[49]

William Simon, a former Treasury Secretary, also attacked universities for criticizing capitalism and, as Powell had, argued that corporations should not fund universities that were critical in this way but rather put their money into those universities that were business friendly. Many academics saw this as a form of blackmail but others submitted. By 1977 the Joint Council on Economic Education (JCEE), an umbrella group for the state Councils on Economic Education, was funnelling money from business to some 155 university centres and 360 school district programmes that helped teachers give instruction on the free enterprise economy.[50]

The conservative foundations who were pouring money into think tanks and other advocacy groups also funded conservative university programmes, chairs of free enterprise and private enterprise, college and university newspapers and student publications with the right slant, and scholarships for the right sort of people. In this way, 'by strategically leveraging their resources', they 'engineered the rise of a right-wing intelligentsia that has come to wield enormous influence in national policy debates'.[51]

By 1979, corporations were underwriting more than 40 academic centres and chairs of free enterprise. For example, Goodyear Tire & Rubber financed the chair of free enterprise at Kent State University, where market economics was taught to undergraduates, and Pepsico, Phillips Petroleum and Dow Chemical funded Texas A&M University's Center for Education and Research in Free Enterprise, which trained high school teachers in economics.[52]

Simon became president of the Olin Foundation in 1977, as well as being on the boards of the Heritage Foundation and other neoconservative think tanks. With Simon at the helm, the Olin Foundation funded a number of programmes, including economics programmes, fellowships and chairs at leading US universities such as Yale and Harvard. It funded 33 new student publications.[53] Simon and Irving Kristol also established the Institute for Educational Affairs (IEA):

> *Its purpose is to seek out promising PhD candidates and undergraduate leaders, help them to establish themselves through grants and fellowships and then help them get jobs with activist organizations, research projects, student publications, federal agencies, or leading periodicals. IEA received start-up grants of $100,000 from the Olin, Scaife, JM and Smith Richardson foundations, as well as substantial contributions from Coca-Cola, Dow Chemical, Ford Motor Co., General Electric, K-Mart, Mobil and Nestle corporations.*[54]

The University of Texas established an Institute for Constructive Capitalism in 1979 that aimed 'to construct a modern ethical and philosophical basis for capitalism'. Mobil, Shell Oil, Tenneco and other corporations donated millions of dollars to it. Similarly, the University of Southern California established a Center for the Study of Private Enterprise in 1976 with the aim of enlisting business leaders in 'political activism'. The center published pamphlets explaining how employers could 'educate' employees to influence government policy. It also distributed bumper stickers saying 'The American Economic System: It works when we do.'[55]

It was claimed that teachers who did Georgia State University's teachers' courses not only increased their knowledge of economics, but subsequently spent three times as much time teaching economics to their school students after the course as they had before. The University of Miami put on workshops for journalists 'and others who interpret economics for the public' as well as lawyers and judges. Dr Marilyn Kourilsky, the Willard Eccles Chair of Economics at Weber State College (Utah), developed a programme of environmental education for kindergarten children entitled 'Kinder-Economy'. This involved half an hour a day teaching economic concepts with the children playing at running businesses.[56]

OUTCOMES

In the late 1970s, US business was spending a billion dollars each year on propaganda of various sorts 'aimed at persuading the American public that their interests were the same as business's interests'. The result of all this expenditure showed in the polls in 1980 when the percentage of people who thought that there was too much regulation soared to 60 per cent (up from 22 per cent in 1975).[57]

The anti-materialism of the hippie generation gave way in the late 1970s to a more consumerist orientation amongst the young, who happily sported advertisements on their T-shirts, often paying for the privilege. Corporate executives were welcomed onto campuses around the country to teach 'sought-after courses on the free enterprise system'. By 1978, US business had 'clearly regained the political initiative' and defeated many of the regulatory measures hard won by public interest activists. They achieved the abolition of the consumer protection agency, reduction of automobile-emissions standards, the deregulation of energy prices and the lowering of corporate taxes.[58]

By 1986, 27 states required some form of economics education in primary and/or secondary schools on the assumption that 'popular misconceptions lead to bad policies'. The JCEE provided materials for school economic courses and acted as a professional body for those teaching in them. The JCEE recommended that all school teachers be required to do a course on economic principles as part of their training; that all teachers involved in teaching subjects with economic content receive instruction in how to teach economics; and that all prospective teachers be tested to ensure they have the right understanding of economics.[59]

Part of the aim of all this 'education' was to get people used to the idea that 'it is an appropriate part of business's role in democracy to judge what beliefs we must hold in order to be "economically educated"'.[60] Glenn K. Hirsch argued that the Advertising Council served the corporate ruling class by:

> *Providing an inexpensive and effective means of mobilizing the populace and insuring the ideological hegemony of the 'power elite' over the people through the legitimation of the corporate order; by defining the parameters of public debate; and by acting to prevent the presentation of opposing ideologies.*[61]

The Advertising Council also performed the function of think tank and forum for top corporations, generating 'ideas to be used in the effort to articulate the ideology of capitalism'.[62] In his network analysis of the Advertising Council, Hirsch found that its governing bodies and committees included hundreds of top executives from the Fortune 500 banks and corporations. Nearly one-third of the Advertising Council members were also members of one or more of the three major elite policy groups at the time: The Committee for Economic Development, The Council on Foreign Relations, and the Business Council. Other 'interlocks' included the International Chamber of Commerce, the US Chamber of Commerce, and NAM. The Advertising Council's Public Policy committee, which decided what campaigns to pursue, while supposedly representing people from all sectors of American society including labour, education and religion, nevertheless drew half of its membership from the corporate world. These people also tended to be members of the three think tanks listed above.[63]

The campaign also sought to challenge and prevent the spread of opposing ideas and values. The Advertising Council's massive media campaigns left little room for those with opposing ideologies to present their messages. It utilized all the free community time that the media had to offer and drowned out all other voices. In this way capitalist hegemony was preserved: the overall political objective being neatly summed up by Hirsh: 'Public knowledge of inequality and injustice isn't so damaging as long as these perceptions are not drawn together into a coherent, opposing ideology.'[64]

NOTES

1 Jeff Blyskal and Marie Blyskal, *PR: How the Public Relations Industry Writes the News*, New York, William Morrow and Co., 1985, p153.

2 Jerry M. Landay, 'The Powell Manifesto', Mediatransparency.org, 20 August 2002, www.mediatransparency.org/stories/powell.htm; Linda Greenhouse, 'Lewis F. Powell Jr., Who Became the Quiet Centrist of the Supreme Court, Is Dead at 90', *New York Times*, 26 August 1998.

3 Lewis F. Powell, 'Confidential Memorandum: Attack on American Free Enterprise System', 23 August 1971.

4 *Ibid.*

5 ACC, '70th Annual Report 1973–74', Canberra, Australian Chamber of Commerce, 1974, p8.

6 Advertising Council, 'Program to Last Three to Five Years', *Economic Communicator*, May, 1976, p1; S. Alexander Rippa, *Education in a Free Society: An American History*, New York, Longman, 1984, p306; Advertising Council, 'A Status Report on the Advertising Council's Public Service Campaign on the American Economic System', New York, Advertising Council, undated.

7 Sharon Beder, *The Nature of Sustainable Development*, 2nd edn, Melbourne, Scribe Publications, 1996, pxii.

8 Michael Parenti, *Inventing Reality: The Politics of the Mass Media*, New York, St Martin's Press, 1986, p67.

9 Cited in David B. Burks, 'Disenchantment with Business: A Mandate for Christian Ethics', *The Entrepreneur*, August, 1977, p1.

10 Quoted in ACC, '74th Annual Report 1977–78', Canberra, Australian Chamber of Commerce, 1978, p11 and 'Why Business Finds It Tough to Polish Its Own Image', *US News & World Report*, 19 September 1977, p64.

11 Glenn K. Hirsch, 'Only You Can Prevent Ideological Hegemony: The Advertising Council and Its Place in the American Power Structure', *The Insurgent Sociologist*, vol V, no III, 1975, pp64–5.

12 Advertising Council, 'Program to Last Three to Five Years', p1; Advertising Council, 'Corporate Effort: Economic Education', *Economic Communicator*, May, 1976, p1; Advertising Council, 'On the Issues', *Economic Communicator*, September/October, 1976, p3.

13 'The Last Great Free Enterprise Campaign', *Fortune*, June, 1977, p188.

14 Quoted in 'Teaching the Teachers', *Chemical Week*, 18 October 1978, p27.

15 'The Last Great Free Enterprise Campaign', p188; Herbert Stein, 'Expert Reviews "AES" Booklet', *Economic Communicator*, September/October, 1976, pp1–2; Advertising Council, 'On the Issues', p3.

16 Barton A. Cummings, 'The Advertising Council's Campaign on Economic Education', April, 1979.

17 Compton Advertising, 'National Survey on the American Economic System', New York, Advertising Council, 1974, p14.

18 Compton Advertising, 'Study on Advertising Awareness and Understanding of the American System: Benchmark, Phase I', Compton Advertising, June 1976.

19 Alex Carey, *Taking the Risk out of Democracy*, ed Andrew Lohrey, Sydney, UNSW Press, 1995, pp119, 125.

20 Advertising Council, 'Program to Last Three to Five Years', p6; Advertising Council, 'Corporate Effort', pp1, 5; Cummings, 'The Advertising Council's Campaign on Economic Education'.

21 Advertising Council, *The American Economic System And Your Part in It*, New York, Advertising Council and the US Department of Commerce, 1976, pp3–5.

22 *Ibid.*, pp10–11.

23 *Ibid.*, pp15–18.

24 Carey, *Taking the Risk out of Democracy*, pp87–88, 105, 112, 114; Cummings, 'The Advertising Council's Campaign on Economic Education'.

25 Advertising Council, 'A Status Report'; Advertising Council, 'Highlights of Results and Progress', New York, Advertising Council, 1 November 1977.

26 Advertising Council, 'Highlights of Results and Progress'.

27 Compton Advertising, 'Study on Advertising Awareness and Understanding of the American System: Post Study, Phase II', Compton Advertising, June 1977.
28 Cummings, 'The Advertising Council's Campaign on Economic Education'.
29 Advertising Council, 'Corporations Set up Employee Eco-Ed Programs', *Economic Communicator*, September/October, 1976, p4.
30 'Teaching the Teachers', p27.
31 Advertising Council, 'Corporate Effort', pp4–5; 'Teaching the Teachers', p27.
32 *Ibid.*
33 Rippa, *Education in a Free Society*, p308; Advertising Council, 'Spring Fever: Baseball & Economics', *Economic Communicator*, May, 1976, p2; Ann Crittenden, 'The Economic Wind's Blowing toward the Right – for Now', *The New York Times*, 16 July 1978, p3.1.
34 Advertising Council, 'Corporate Effort', p5; Advertising Council, 'Some Academic Efforts Aim at Secondary School Teachers', *Economic Communicator*, July, 1976, p7.
35 Advertising Council, 'Corporate Materials to Build Economic Understanding', *Economic Communicator*, July, 1976, p3; Crittenden, 'The Economic Wind's Blowing toward the Right', p3.1.
36 Chauncey W. Lever, 'Fighting for Free Enterprise in America: The USIC Approach', in Michael Ivens (ed) *International Papers on the Revival of Freedom and Enterprise*, London, AIMS, 1978, p71.
37 *Ibid.*, p72.
38 William Raspberry, 'Do Blacks Have an Aversion to Capitalism?' *Houston Chronical*, 6 November 1987, p26.
39 Leon B. Blair, 'American Enterprise Forum', in *The Handbook of Texas Online*, Austin, Texas, Texas State Historical Association, 2002; Tom Rose, *Free Enterprise Economics: A Resource Unit for Instruction in America's Free Enterprise System*, Dallas, Texas, The Institute for Free Enterprise Education and the Texas Bureau for Economic Understanding, 1974, p17.
40 National Education Program, 'The Origin and Purpose of the National Education Program', Searcy, Arkansas, National Education Program, undated, p2.
41 *Ibid.*
42 National Education Program, 'Activity Suggestions for Citizenship Leaders', Searcy, Arkansas, National Education Program, undated.
43 *Ibid.*
44 Advertising Council, 'Chambers of Commerce Get Involved', *Economic Communicator*, September/October, 1976, p7.
45 *Ibid.*, p7; Advertising Council, 'Non-Profit, Community Groups Work to Create "Economics" Interest', *Economic Communicator*, July, 1976, p4; Advertising Council, *The American Economic System*, p6.
46 Instruction in Free Enterprise System 1973, 21.1031 of Texas Education Code, State of Texas, 63rd Legislature, 27 August.
47 Tom Rose, *Free Enterprise Economics*, Dallas, Texas, The Institute for Free Enterprise Education and the Texas Bureau for Economic Understanding, 1974.
48 Powell, 'Confidential Memorandum'.
49 James J. Kilpatrick, 'Why Students Are Hostile to Free Enterprise', *Nation's Business*, July, 1975.

50 Merrill Sheils, 'Capitalism 101', *Newsweek*, 30 April 1979, p62; 'Why Business Finds It Tough to Polish Its Own Image', p64.
51 'Buying a Movement: Right-Wing Foundations and American Politics', Washington, DC, People for the American Way, 2002, pp3, 13; David Callahan quoted in 'Buying a Movement: Right-Wing Foundations and American Politics', pp3, 13.
52 Crittenden, 'The Economic Wind's Blowing toward the Right', p3.1; Sheils, 'Capitalism 101', p62.
53 Jerry M. Landay, 'Simon Said', Mediatransparency.org, 23 June 2004, www.mediatransparency.org/stories/neocons.html; Sidney Blumenthal, *The Rise of the Counter-Establishment: From Conservative Ideology to Political Power*, New York, Time Books, 1986, p67.
54 'Buying a Movement: Right-Wing Foundations and American Politics', p14.
55 Sheils, 'Capitalism 101', p62.
56 Advertising Council, 'Corporate Effort', p5; 'Why Business Finds It Tough to Polish Its Own Image', p64; Advertising Council, *The American Economic System*, p6.
57 Carey, *Taking the Risk out of Democracy*, p89; Parenti, *Inventing Reality: The Politics of the Mass Media*, p74.
58 Anthony Sampson, *Company Man: The Rise and Fall of Corporate Life*, paperback edn, London, HarperCollinsBusiness, 1996, p130; Crittenden, 'The Economic Wind's Blowing toward the Right', p3.1; David Vogel, *Fluctuating Fortunes: The Political Power of Business in America*, New York, Basic Books, 1989, p193.
59 James Tobin, 'Economic Literacy Isn't a Marginal Investment', *Wall Street Journal*, 9 July 1986.
60 Carey, *Taking the Risk out of Democracy*, p88.
61 Hirsch, 'Only You Can Prevent Ideological Hegemony', p65.
62 Quoted in *Ibid.*, p75.
63 *Ibid.*, p69.
64 *Ibid.*, p79.

6

Exporting Free Market Education

We believe that young people should leave school with an adequate understanding of how wealth is created in our society and an appropriate evaluation of the essential role of industry and commerce.

CONFEDERATION OF BRITISH INDUSTRY, 1984[1]

The voice of private enterprise has for so long been too muted and fragmented. It must become more audible. Too few proponents of the system are informed and articulate.

E. S. OWEN, ENTERPRISE AUSTRALIA, 1983[2]

Economic education spread from the US to other English-speaking countries during the 1970s and 1980s with the active help of key US public relations people. In Britain in the 1970s the Department of Education and Science (DES) stated that young people needed to be taught 'how industry creates national wealth' and that they 'need to reach maturity with a basic understanding of the economy and the activities, especially manufacturing industries, which are necessary for the creation of Britain's national wealth'.[3]

The British Aims for Freedom and Enterprise group (AIMS) held an international conference in London in 1978 on 'The Revival of Freedom and Enterprise', and organized a Free Enterprise Day.[4] At the Conference, F. Clifton White, a director of the US Public Affairs Council and adviser on all presidential campaigns between 1948 and 1976, argued that those who supported increased government intervention – 'the enemies of freedom' – had 'proved more adept' at influencing the political process and should be put on the defensive. He pointed out that the decline in voter participation in elections in Western societies provided an opportunity for those committed to promoting free enterprise: 'Fewer people are participating in elections, which increases our ability to influence the outcomes of elections, and thus to change rules which we find to be detrimental to freedom.'[5]

Conference-goers were also exhorted to use the media to promote the free enterprise message. One speaker suggested that not only could advertising time be used to support free enterprise – 'announcements can be purchased to expose young people to the good points of our system' – but also free public service announcements could be used for the same purpose:[6]

> *[A]ll of us must ask the philanthropies that we do support, be they youth organisations, athletic clubs, medical research groups, hospitals, universities, etc., to incorporate in their radio public service announcements a recognition of the contributions of freedom and enterprise to their success. Separately, radio stations should receive from business people and professionals the encouragement and assistance to schedule announcements which tell the story of freedom and enterprise.*[7]

Similarly, Kenneth Giddens, a former director of Voice of America, argued at the same London conference for the use of international radio to promote free enterprise. Apparently unaware of the irony of what he was saying, Giddens accused international radio broadcasts from 'authoritarian nations' of censoring and distorting their news 'to try to manipulate and control the thinking of people of other lands through their international broadcasts' and therefore being primarily propagandist. In contrast, he said, international broadcasters such as the BBC, Canadian Broadcasting, Radio Australia and Voice of America had large audiences because of their adherence to truth and because they do not slant the news. He then went on to say such news media 'offer an extremely useful potential instrument to carry the stories of the blessings of free enterprise and capitalism, to both the free and authoritarian worlds ... for the story these free enterprise international broadcasters can tell is both thrilling and inspiring evidence of the superiority of our system'.[8]

School and university education was also addressed at the conference. Frank Broadway, director of Facts about Business, a UK firm that supplied educational material for schools and employees, claimed that 'apathy and hostility towards free enterprise begin in the schools'. He argued that this was not because teachers were Marxists but rather because they didn't know enough to provide children with a good understanding of free enterprise and its benefits. The solution was to provide teachers with this material and his experience was that most teachers were willing to use 'quality material supplied by business'.[9]

Facts about Business had its own schools programme launched in 1975, 'Business and Profit', which included a free booklet and purchasable wall charts and study folders. By 1978, the programme was being used in a quarter of all secondary schools in Britain; the organization then launched another, called 'Discover British Industry', which was taken up by over 400 schools in the first four months.[10]

Broadway argued that while companies provided literature and speakers to schools and arranged school visits to factories, 'a more intensive, widespread and sustained effort' was needed to equip school leavers with 'a substantial understanding of free enterprise'. This would involve employer organizations, chambers of commerce, trade associations, and big companies at the national level as well as companies at the local level, all explaining the achievements of free enterprise. Such materials would have to be attractive to teachers and students, have some educational content, and 'be intellectually respectable factual explanations of profit-earning' rather than 'obvious political apologia for capitalism ... The prize is not only the survival of free enterprise, but in many cases survival of the individual company.'[11]

Michael Forsyth, former chair of the Federation of Conservative Students, argued that Freedom Groups be established on university campuses to counter the left; to mobilize students to join in student 'representative' bodies; to 'communicate the positive arguments for a free society'; and 'to monitor examination papers, booklists and the content of courses, in consultation with groups of teachers and lecturers, for bias and one-sidedness'.[12]

In 1984, the Confederation of British Industry (CBI) criticized schools for failing to give students a more positive attitude towards business and industry. It accused schools of promoting 'negative attitudes to authority, entrepreneurial activity and the fundamental concept of a market-driven, profit-oriented economic system'.[13]

In its early years, the Institute of Economic Affairs (IEA – see Chapter 8) had some influence in the universities and produced undergraduate and secondary school texts. The Association of British Chambers of Commerce also argued in the 1980s that teachers should be encouraged to seek business experience and be rewarded by increases in salary and promotion for having it.[14]

A Foundation for Economic Education was also set up in Canada (CFEE) in 1974 because, business activists claimed, 'the level of economic education and economic literacy across Canada was woefully low'.[15] Similarly, the Institut der Deutschen Wirtschaft (Institute of the Germany Economy) called for businesses to offer economic education to teachers as well as business experience.[16]

ECONOMIC EDUCATION IN AUSTRALIA

In Australia, after the election of a 'progressive' Labor government in 1972, the Australian Chamber of Commerce (ACC) reacted with a nationwide 'economic education campaign' to promote free enterprise.[17] Its 1972 annual report stated:

> *The National Chamber sees, as its major objective, the need to promote and safeguard the interest of free enterprise, in its broadest, most constructive sense ... the exercise of normal business prudence will not in itself ensure the survival of the free enterprise system ... The free enterprise story has to be told in a way that will obtain public recognition and understanding of the role of profits and individual initiative in the progress of this country.*[18]

ACC President in 1974, K.D.Williams, claimed that the 'apparent increase of animosity towards business in Australia' was 'part of an international phenomenon' and business was being 'made the scapegoat for much of what people feel is wrong in Australia and in the Western world today'.[19] He claimed:

> *... there has been too great an emphasis on the differences instead of the similarities of interest of employees and management. This has hindered us in reaching the kind of national consensus needed to raise standards of productivity and to combat the insidious problem of inflation ... we should remember that a company consists of employers, employees and shareholders, and their fortunes are bound up with the future of enterprise.*[20]

ACC's Economic Education programme was the 'centre piece of our activities in public opinion forming about the role of business in the community, especially amongst the young' and, like the US campaigns, was a response to a supposed 'widespread lack of understanding of economic facts of life by the general public'. ACC ran a series of essay competitions for students; surveyed and evaluated existing economics and commerce courses in Australian schools; and recommended changes to the Departments of Education in each state to ensure that students would learn the 'correct' view of how private enterprise works.[21]

ACC produced 15 videos and films 'for instructional use in schools' in cooperation with the Productivity Promotion Council of Australia, the Institute of Public Affairs (a conservative think tank – see Chapter 9), the Sydney Stock Exchange and 'two of Australia's major companies'. Its first series of videos, entitled *Business in the Community*, was on the contribution of companies and specific industries to the well-being of Australian society with an emphasis on the role of adequate profit in maintaining employment and economic growth. The ACC wanted to 'counter the view that the only concern of business is profits'.[22]

The departments of education in each state agreed to use ACC materials and to include them in Department Resource Centres. The ACC also claimed 'good relations with Teachers' Associations throughout Australia' and support from them for ACC programmes. The ACC encouraged and facilitated city-based chambers of commerce to undertake their own educational programmes. It produced a 'Guide to Employee Economic Information Programmes' for employers to undertake economic education with their employees and distributed it to some 450 companies.[23]

The ACC targeted the media with paid radio and television time, as well as free time on public (ABC) and commercial radio and television networks. Visual aids in the press were aimed at explaining to the public the 'real' level of profits and the criteria they should be judged by, as well as the disincentive effect of taxation; the impact of inflation; and the importance of productivity. Business spokespersons were given media training and others were provided with speakers' kits and materials and background papers expostulating the business viewpoint for use in debate.[24]

In 1975 the ACC formed the Assembly of Australian Business Organisations (AABO) 'for the purpose of discussing the grave problems facing private enterprise caused by socialistic Government policies and for determining a concerted action programme on a national level'. The ACC was concerned about the government's 'policy of intrusion into the private sector' and asked that the government 'abolish the Prices Justification Tribunal and withdraw proposals for the national compensation scheme' and various other measures.[25]

The formation of the AABO went unannounced because the ACC wanted to keep it quiet to start with. The AABO went on to sponsor a National Private Enterprise Convention in 1976 with the support of the Australian Chamber of Manufacturers, the Australian Mining Industry Council, the Australian Farmers' Federation, and the Australian Wool Growers' and Graziers' Council.[26] It was organized by the ACC and supported by the newly elected conservative Liberal government. Several senior government ministers participated, and the Prime Minister, Malcolm Fraser, told the convention that a concerted effort to sell the benefits of the free enterprise system was needed:

> *It is good to see that an increasing number of people are taking action to see that there is a growing appreciation of the common interests of everyone in a profitable and efficient private sector.How can I explain to people that private enterprise is the best system for the average Australian if managements cannot be bothered explaining it to their own employees?*
>
> *It needs to be explained even more clearly that new plant, new equipment, new jobs, are created out of profits.*[27]

John Howard, then Minister for Business and Consumer Affairs, told the convention that he too was concerned that the public was suspicious of business and that it thought more government control was needed. He said that the government welcomed self-regulation by business and that he believed 'the principal responsibility of business to the community is to survive and prosper'. The Treasurer, Phillip Lynch, told the convention that the voice of business in Australia was too fragmented and that there needed to be a single business group like the Confederation of British Industry, to enable government to consult effectively with private enterprise.[28]

Sir Robert Norman, head of the Bank of New South Wales (now Westpac), also told the convention of the need to sell the free enterprise system:

> *We must convince our employees in particular that the only form of society where Trade Unions can flourish is in a free enterprise democracy . . . We must continue to justify our corporate existence in terms that the public can understand and appreciate.*[29]

The convention resolved that an action committee be appointed 'to devise and coordinate a programme' to communicate to various publics about the importance of profits and free enterprise. The formation of a National Business Council for Community Affairs was mooted. The convention also supported the government in its efforts to 'restrain growth in public expenditure; to cut back direct government involvement in traditional areas of private enterprise activity; and to provide new opportunities for private business to compete for government projects'.[30]

Another organization that responded to the perceived crisis of free enterprise in Australia was the Institute of Directors, which had 'always aimed to be an influential body in business and political circles'. Sir Robert Crichton-Brown, its president, presented the institute 'as a proponent of private enterprise' and an 'adviser to government on behalf of the private-enterprise corporate system'. He argued that its role needed to be enlarged: 'We must be constantly vigilant in countering moves to wreck the present private enterprise system.'[31]

Crichton-Brown hoped that the institute could play a role in encouraging and facilitating 'a better understanding between the work force and management – a recognition of the common goal – a respect for profit and incentive; and an understanding that only by increasing the size of the cake can we increase the size of the slices'.[32] He claimed that the institute: 'must publicise and sell the benefits of the system... [through] such bodies as Enterprise Australia ... We cannot relax until we have convinced society at large that our influence is indeed for its good.'[33]

Other organizations that actively sponsored economic education in Australia included the Australian Bankers Association, the Australian Mining Industry Council, the Australian Industries Development Association (later merged with the Business Roundtable to form the Business Council of Australia), the American Chamber of Commerce in Australia, and conservative think tanks such as the Centre for Economic Development in Australia (CEDA) and the Institute of Public Affairs (IPA). The activities of these organizations included conferences and presentations to teachers, business people and school students.[34]

The IPA also distributed publications to some 1200 high schools about union power and the growth of government, as well as distributing publications to workers via employers. The IPA had been established by 'prominent businessmen' in response to the election of a Labor government in 1943 and it aimed to 'resist the trend to socialism' that these businessmen felt the election represented. It sent its secretary to the US to study economic education programmes as early as 1955 and he had been particularly impressed with their employee education programmes (see Chapter 4).[35]

During the 1980s, the Queensland branch of the IPA organized Business–Teacher Workshops that involved 7000 teachers and business people in after-school discussion groups. In 1988 the IPA set up an Education Policy Unit to influence school curricula and critique the education system. It was funded by more than 70 companies and headed by Dame Leonie Kramer. A couple of years later, Kramer was appointed by the state government to the NSW Board of Studies, which sets school curricula. She later became Chancellor of Sydney University.[36]

Centre 2000, a marginal right-wing think tank, sponsored student competitions and donated text books advocating free markets to schools and universities. It ran 'Sponsor an Intellect', a project aimed at raising money to buy the free market books to donate.[37] A Foundation for Economic Education was established in Brisbane in 1976, modelled after FEE in the US and using its materials to promote the free market and principles of *laissez-faire* economics. It provided teaching materials, films and speakers to schools and also to service clubs and political parties.[38]

The Centre for Independent Studies (CIS), another free market think tank, established an Economics Education Resource Centre for economics teachers in 1989. It aimed to 'promote an understanding of the role of markets in creating wealth through an efficient allocation of resources in the Australian economy'. To this end it produced a bimonthly newsletter, *The Economics Education Review*, subscribed to by 800 schools and libraries; organized an annual national conference for economics teachers; and held professional development days that were attended by some 600 teachers.[39]

ENTERPRISE AUSTRALIA

Enterprise Australia (EA) was set up in 1976 as an offshoot of the Australian Free Enterprise Association, which had been established in response to perceived threats to free enterprise – including the election of Gough Whitlam's Labor government – with funding from CIG, Esso, Kodak, Ford Motors and IBM.[40] Keavney, CEO of EA, saw two main threats to free enterprise in Australia. One was the encroachment of government into 'areas best left to the productive private sector' and the other 'the widespread public misconceptions' about business such as the size of profits and who benefits from them.[41]

> *Enterprise Australia's message is basically this – that the main beneficiary of free enterprise is the community itself. In addition, it believes that a much greater community of interest exists between management and employees than is normally understood. Recognition of these points will reduce conflict and confrontation and promote co-operation and consensus.*[42]

EA presented itself as being unaligned with any political party and representing the public interest, not just that of employers. It sought to make alliances with 'moderate' unions in order to bolster the credibility of this claim. However, its literature was clear about the role it played in helping business 'to tell its own story' and it admitted that its 'sole responsibility is to raise the level of community understanding about how free enterprise works'. EA sought to show that free enterprise contributed to 'Australia's way of life' and standard of living and to 'emphasise the dangers to our society of unnecessary regulations'. This was the message it spread to educational institutions, the media, small business and employees.[43]

The ACC and EA, like their US counterparts, used surveys of school leavers to find the 'deficiencies' in their attitudes to the free enterprise system and then circulated corrective material through schools. The similarities with the US economic education campaign were not accidental. 'In its first few years E.A. brought a succession of American "economic educators" to Australia to provide guidance. Keavney repeatedly toured the US, giving progress reports to the N.A.M. and the US Chamber of Commerce, among others.'[44] In 1979, EA brought Barton Cummins, a key architect of the Advertising Council's free enterprise campaign, to Australia to describe that campaign so it could serve as a model in Australia. Cummins told a business audience:

> *In Australia – as in America – there are people who want to destroy the free enterprise system. They believe in government control of the lives of all of us, particularly the business community. They do not believe in competition. They do not believe in the profit motive. They do not believe in freedom for businessmen like you and me ... More regulation by government is their answer ... It is important to remember that economic freedom and personal freedom go hand in hand ...*
>
> *In short, you've got to educate the Australian people about your economic system. When they really understand it, they'll appreciate it more ...*[45]

EA's schools and colleges programmes were 'developed within school systems in official association with Departments of Education' in each state. These included:[46]

- a core text book *The World of Business in Australia* (an adaptation of a Canadian text[47]) with teacher's guide, student's workbook and audio-visual material;
- topic books for primary schools;
- a 22-module audio-visual course on economic concepts for secondary schools ('produced in cooperation with NSW Department of Education');
- work-experience programmes for teachers and for students; conferences for secondary school students; workshops for teachers;
- a magazine for teachers;
- a clearinghouse of industry-provided 'educational' materials for schools;
- a programme in which business executives spent one or two weeks in schools.

EA also produced 15 videos and films with titles such as *Profits, Advertising and The Market Economy*. Their material was made available to school resource centres with the approval of the departments of education in each state. It convened a committee of 13 professional organizations working in schools to ensure that school leavers would have a proper understanding of the commercial world. EA's annual Enterprise Week, modelled on that of the British Aims for Freedom and Enterprise, was opened by the Prime Minister, Malcolm Fraser, in 1977, and was accompanied by a great deal of media attention and editorials on free enterprise.[48] EA also arranged for Friedrich von Hayek (see Chapter 7) to give seminars in universities and other tertiary educational institutions, and identified key Australian academics who could deliver a similar message.[49]

Various teachers' unions attacked EA materials as propaganda, and teachers' journals ran articles under headlines such as 'Fanatical Believers in Private Enterprise' and accompanied by satirical cartoons. David Bell wrote in *Education* that 'the interests of the Big Businessmen behind Enterprise Australia have nothing in common with the students we teach. Rather, they see them as a future, exploitable, labour force, and politically passive citizenry!' One politician, Joan Coxsedge, called for 'investigations into the way in which Enterprise Australia, an American-modelled, mind-managing outfit, has infiltrated school systems in other States ... as part of its expensive attempt to bolster the so-called free enterprise system'.[50]

Nevertheless, the educational authorities seemed to welcome this material into schools, and EA was careful to get the endorsement of selected teachers, public servants, academics and politicians of both major parties. An attempt by the teachers' union to get the NSW Department of Education to stop cooperating with EA in 1982 was unsuccessful. Even after the Labor government was elected again in 1983, Enterprise Australia continued to have government support, and Prime Minister Bob Hawke's public endorsement.[51]

EA had an economic education programme for women from business and women's groups. And it sponsored a board game, 'Poleconomy', with sales of over 100,000. Its speakers' programme was divided into two categories: for 'the unconverted' and for 'the converted'. The converted were told how to explain private enterprise to others, and Keavney sought to encourage missionaries for free enterprise in the manner that Christianity was spread in the first century by 'believers' becoming committed 'explainers'.[52]

For the media, EA wrote reports and feature articles; gave awards for enterprise; held a series of briefings with 'media decision-makers'; made two television documentary series (broadcast by some 40 television stations); offered a syndicated column for free local newspapers; had simple 'facts' broadcast on radio and television about business and economics; and made regular media comment on topical issues.[53] EA produced a series of television programmes called *Making it Together* and broadcast commercials promoting the benefits of free enterprise on over 100 radio stations.

The ease with which EA could access the Australian media is aptly demonstrated in a boast by Keavney in 1978 that:

> *Enterprise Australia is in the process of producing 12 half-hour documentaries ... [that] will be shown by a national network channel, free, as a public service in good viewing time ... In association with the Australian Federation of Commercial Broadcasters, Enterprise Australia is having a series of eight radio spots broadcast, at no charge, throughout Australia, giving brief but telling messages about the benefits of free enterprise.*[54]

EA also produced a series of television spots on the benefits of free enterprise. One of EA's television ads stated:

> *A world survey has found that only one country in ten has all the freedoms Australia enjoys.*
> *Australia has free speech, freedom of assembly, free elections, freedom of movement – and free enterprise.*
> *The danger lies in taking these freedoms for granted.*
> *We must value each one – and work together to keep them.*[55]

The message to employees was the 'essential commonality of interests of managers and employees' and this was transmitted through annual employee reports (for which EA gave awards); audiovisual economics courses; distribution of information on existing company programmes; visits by tame US union leaders; and training courses for managers.[56]

EA also provided speakers for Rotary clubs and such like. It produced a supplement for 2.5 million Australian *Reader's Digest* subscribers and a document on consensus and cooperation between employers and employees aimed at inclusion in church publications and sermons. According to EA, some churches consequently organized 'industrial harmony' services with business and union leaders reading the lessons.[57]

EA brought a number of speakers to Australia to gain the attention of television current affairs programmes and to attract union and Labor Party members to their cause, so as to bolster EA's credibility as representing the broader community interest. Speakers were also brought to Australia to run seminars for senior business executives in order to promote free enterprise to employees.[58]

By 1979, the proportion of people who thought the government should cut taxes rather than spend more on social services had increased to 59 per cent, compared to 26 per cent in 1967, and the proportion of people who thought more should be spent on social services had declined from 68 per cent to 36 per cent. Similarly, the percentage of people who thought unions had too much power had increased from 47 to 78.[59] Such a reversal of opinion was unusual and could be largely attributed to the onslaught of business propaganda in the late 1970s.

UNIVERSITIES

In Australia, EA recognized that 'tomorrow's public opinions are being largely forged in today's tertiary institutions' and it sought to develop 'beachheads' in universities, technical colleges and other tertiary institutions through conferences; addresses to academics; forming 'Students Industrial Groups' in which students could interact with business people; and executives-in-residence.[60] Monash University hosted one such executive-in-residence in 1983, and by 1984, 12 universities had similar arrangements in place whereby business executives explained the free enterprise system to academics and students at formal meetings. Monash also employed a person full time from 1983 'with special duties which include encouraging schools to use Enterprise Australia materials'.[61]

The conversion of many university economics courses to the conservative neoclassical economics pushed by organizations such as EA had a profound effect in Australia. Michael Pusey, in his 1991 book *Economic Rationalism in Canberra*, found that 54 per cent of the top public servants in the federal government had degrees in economics, commerce, business administration or accounting, or called themselves economists. This was particularly true of the central government departments of Prime Minister and Cabinet (PM&C), Treasury, and Finance, where 72 per cent of Senior Executive Service people had an economics/commerce/ business administration education. This was in contrast to the British Civil Service, where they were more likely to have a liberal arts education, and in Europe, where they were likely to have a law education.[62]

Because of the conservative nature of economics courses at most Australian universities, these senior public servants expressed more conservative economic thinking than those with different types of education. They were more likely to favour a deregulated labour market; to argue that Australian GDP was biased towards wages rather than towards capital; to claim that relations between capital and labour tended to be complementary and equal; and to argue that trade unions had more power than business interests. They also favoured small government, less provision of social services, less government intervention in the economy and more individual initiative and incentives to encourage it.[63]

Pusey noted in his study that these economically trained public officials in the central agencies set the agenda:

> *... they had captured the promotions system from about 1982 onwards and used it to favour their own kind. From undisturbed positions of power in the central agencies they had – with successive waves of rationalisation and restructuring – demoralised, colonised, and in many cases driven out the real problem-solvers in the public service ... In this way they obtained an overwhelming domination.*[64]

NOTES

1 Quoted in Harold J. Noah and Max A. Eckstein, 'Business and Industry Involvement with Education in Britain, France and Germany', in Jon Lauglo and Kevin Lillis (eds) *Vocationalizing Education: An International Perspective*, Oxford, Pergamon Press, 1988, p47.
2 Enterprise Australia, 'The Capitalist Crisis: Meeting the Challenge', Enterprise Australia 1983.
3 Quoted in Colin Wringe, 'Education, Schooling and the World of Work', in David Corson (ed) *Education for Work: Background to Policy and Curriculum*, New Zealand, 1988, Dunmore Press, p33.
4 Michael Ivens (ed) *International Papers on the Revival of Freedom and Enterprise*, London, AIMS, 1978, pv.
5 F. Clifton White, 'How to Go on the Political Offensive', in Michael Ivens (ed) *International Papers on the Revival of Freedom and Enterprise*, London, AIMS, 1978, pp1–2.
6 Norman Knight, 'Using Commercial Radio on Behalf of Freedom and Enterprise', in Michael Ivens (ed) *International Papers on the Revival of Freedom and Enterprise*, London, AIMS, 1978, p39.
7 *Ibid.*, p39.
8 Kenneth R. Giddens, 'International Radio and Free Enterprise', in Michael Ivens (ed) *International Papers on the Revival of Freedom and Enterprise*, London, AIMS, 1978, pp36–7.
9 Frank Broadway, 'Defending Free Enterprise: An Approach to the Schools', in Michael Ivens (ed) *International Papers on the Revival of Freedom and Enterprise*, London, AIMS, 1978, p63.
10 *Ibid.*, p63.
11 *Ibid.*, p64.
12 Michael Forsyth, 'Defending Freedom in Higher Education', in Michael Ivens (ed) *International Papers on the Revival of Freedom and Enterprise*, London, AIMS, 1978, p65.
13 Noah and Eckstein, 'Business and Industry Involvement with Education in Britain, France and Germany', p47.
14 *Ibid.*, p50.
15 Garry Rabbior, 'Knowledge: The Key to Economic Success', *Canadian Banker*, January/February, 1998, p20.
16 Noah and Eckstein, 'Business and Industry Involvement with Education in Britain, France and Germany', p50.
17 Alex Carey, *Taking the Risk out of Democracy*, ed Andrew Lohrey, Sydney, UNSW Press, 1995, pp87–88, 105, 112, 114.
18 Australian Chamber of Commerce, 'Sixty-Eighth Annual Report 1971–72', Canberra, Australian Chamber of Commerce, 1972.
19 K. D. Williams, 'The Image of Business in Australia Today', Canberra, Australian Chamber of Commerce, 1974.
20 *Ibid.*

21 Australian Chamber of Commerce, '72nd Annual Report 1975–76', Canberra, Australian Chamber of Commerce, 1976, p7; Australian Chamber of Commerce, 'Economic Education Campaign Phase 3', Australian Chamber of Commerce 1978; Australian Chamber of Commerce, 'Economic Education Campaign Phase 2: Three Year Action Programme 1976–1978', Australian Chamber of Commerce 1976, pIII.
22 Australian Chamber of Commerce, '72nd Annual Report 1975–76', p16; Australian Chamber of Commerce, 'Economic Education Campaign', pI.
23 Australian Chamber of Commerce, 'Economic Education Campaign', ppI–II; Australian Chamber of Commerce, '74th Annual Report 1977–78', Canberra, Australian Chamber of Commerce, 1978, p19.
24 Australian Chamber of Commerce, 'Economic Education Campaign', pIV–VIII.
25 Australian Chamber of Commerce, '72nd Annual Report 1975–76', pp4, 14.
26 *Ibid.*, p4.
27 Quoted in *Ibid.*, p8.
28 Quoted in *Ibid.*, p8.
29 Quoted in *Ibid.*, p9.
30 *Ibid.*
31 Robert Crichton-Brown, 'Looking to the Future – the Institute's Role in the Corporate Sphere', *The Australian Director*, October/December, 1977, pp11, 15.
32 *Ibid.*, p11.
33 Quoted in Alex Carey, 'Conspiracy or Groundswell?' in Ken Coghill (ed) *The New Right's Australian Fantasy*, Fitzroy, Victoria, McPhee Gribble and Penguin Books, 1987, p17.
34 Alex Carey, 'The Ideological Management Industry', in E. L. Wheelwright and K. D. Buckley (eds) *Communications and the Media*, Sydney, Allen & Unwin, 1987; Carey, *Taking the Risk out of Democracy*, pp113, 116–7.
35 Bette Moore and Gary Carpenter, 'Main Players', in Ken Coghill (ed) *The New Right's Australian Fantasy*, Fitzroy, Victoria, McPhee Gribble and Penguin Books, 1987, p148; Carey, 'The Ideological Management Industry'.
36 Damien Cahill, 'The Right Values in Education: Neo-Liberal Think-tanks and the Assault Upon Public Schooling', *Overland*, June, 2005.
37 Tim Duncan and Anthony McAdam, 'New Right: Where Is Stands and What It Means', *The Bulletin*, 10 December 1985, p45; Moore and Carpenter, 'Main Players', p151.
38 Marian Sawer, 'Political Manifestations of Australian Libertarianism', in Marian Sawer (ed) *Australia and the New Right*, North Sydney, George Allen & Unwin, 1982, p7.
39 Cahill, 'The Right Values in Education'.
40 Carey, 'The Ideological Management Industry'.
41 Jack Keavney, 'Enterprise Australia: A Case Study in Mobilisation', in Michael Ivens (ed) *International Papers on the Revival of Freedom and Enterprise*, London, AIMS, 1978, p66.
42 *Ibid.*, p66.
43 *Ibid.*, p66; Enterprise Australia, 'Action 1982', Enterprise Australia 1982.

44 Carey, *Taking the Risk out of Democracy*, pp112–3; Carey, 'Conspiracy or Groundswell?'
45 Barton A. Cummings, 'The Advertising Council's Campaign on Economic Education', April, 1979.
46 Enterprise Australia, 'Action 1982'.
47 Carey, 'The Ideological Management Industry'.
48 Carey, *Taking the Risk out of Democracy*, pp112–3; Keavney, 'Enterprise Australia', pp66, 68.
49 Keavney, 'Enterprise Australia, p69.
50 Quoted in Enterprise Australia, 'The Facts of the Enterprise Australia Schools and Colleges Programme', Enterprise Australia, September 1982.
51 *Ibid.*; Carey, 'The Ideological Management Industry'.
52 Enterprise Australia, 'Annual Report', Enterprise Australia 1982.
53 Enterprise Australia, 'Action 1982'; Enterprise Australia, 'Annual Report'.
54 Keavney, 'Enterprise Australia', p67.
55 Quoted in Enterprise Australia, 'Annual Report'.
56 Enterprise Australia, 'Action 1982'.
57 Keavney, 'Enterprise Australia', p67.
58 *Ibid.*, pp67–8.
59 Don Aitkin, 'A Sea-Change on Tax Cuts', *National Times*, 10–16 February 1980b; Don Aitkin, 'Why Labor Should Cut Union Ties', *National Times*, 17–23 February, 1980, p32.
60 Enterprise Australia, 'Action 1982'.
61 Carey, 'The Ideological Management Industry'; Enterprise Australia, 'Annual Report'.
62 Michael Pusey, *Economic Rationalism in Canberra*, Cambridge, Cambridge University Press, 1991, pp59, 78.
63 *Ibid.*, pp60–4.
64 Michael Pusey, 'What's Wrong with Economic Rationalism', in Donald Horne (ed) *The Trouble with Economic Rationalism*, Newham, Victoria, Scribe, 1992, p64.

7

Pro-Business Policies as Ideology

> *... when I was a young man, only the very old men still believed in the free-market system. When I was in my middle ages I myself and nobody else believed in it. And now I have the pleasure of having lived long enough to see that the young people again believe in it. And that is a very important change.* FRIEDRICH VON HAYEK, 1978[1]

> *Ideologies perform essential political functions of informing the public, mobilising supporters and energising leaders and other activists ... An effective ideology will mobilise political supporters to share the general beliefs and goals of a party, interest group or politician.* PETER SELF[2]

In 1947, a group of 37 like-minded people from the US, Britain and Europe – economists, historians and journalists – met in a fashionable resort at Mont Pèlerin in Switzerland. They had been invited there by Friedrich von Hayek, an Austrian-born economic theoretician who worked at the London School of Economics.

Hayek's 1944 book *The Road to Serfdom*, was said to be 'the first intellectually respectable defense of free-market doctrine to have appeared in decades'. The book, which argued that government planning leads to dictatorship and that free markets should reign, was republished in condensed form by *Reader's Digest*. The Book-of-the-Month Club distributed over a million copies. In it Hayek looked back to the glories of free market England in the 19th century, ignoring the mass poverty and atrocious working conditions of the 'dark satanic mills'. Nor did he recognize the role of colonies, tariffs, export bounties and government legislation in maintaining this *laissez-faire* idyll.[3]

Joining Hayek at Mont Pèlerin was Ludwig von Mises, an Austrian libertarian economist and mentor to Hayek, whose writings at this time were being promoted and disseminated by the Foundation for Economic Education (FEE – see Chapter 4); Leonard Reed who had founded the FEE in the previous year; and Henry Hazlitt, FEE vice-president. FEE was said to have been the inspiration for Hayek to start his own group to 'train an army of fighters for freedom'. Another guest was American economist Milton Friedman. Like Hayek, Friedman promoted ideas that had been generally thought by contemporary economists to be discredited relics of the past. Together they worked to foster a 'belief in the superiority of markets over other ways of organizing economic activity'.[4]

The meeting was funded in part by the William Volker Fund, which paid the travel expenses of the ten Americans attending the meeting. William Volker had been a Kansas City businessman who became a millionaire by the time he was 43, selling household furnishings. He set up the William Volker Fund in 1932 and placed his nephew and employee, Harold Luhnow, in charge in 1944. Under Luhnow, who was friendly with various free market advocate businessmen – including Jasper Crane of DuPont and B.E. Hutchinson of Chrysler, both trustees for FEE – the fund gave money to a number of conservative free market causes including FEE, for which Luhnow also became a trustee.[5]

Luhnow used the fund to help free market economists who had been unable to get positions at US universities, including von Mises, whose salary it paid while he was a visiting professor at New York University for many years, and Hayek, whom it helped to get a position at the University of Chicago. The fund also paid for a series of lectures by Milton and Rose Friedman, and helped all these free market activists to meet and plan their strategies in places such as Mont Pèlerin.[6]

It was at a time when European nations were nationalizing public services and some industries and Hayek and his friends believed that this trend towards increased government planning and involvement in the economy needed to be stopped. At a subsequent meeting that year they formed the Mont Pèlerin Society to strive for the wider adoption of free-market policies. The society, which continued to meet regularly, and was presided over by Hayek until 1961, enabled extreme market ideologues who might otherwise have felt isolated or alienated to come together and plot change. It was a long-term project, and Hayek warned the others that they should expect a long-term, but winnable, struggle: 'What to the contemporary observer appears as a battle of conflicting interests decided by the votes of the masses,' he said, 'has usually been decided long before in a battle of ideas confined to narrow circles.'[7]

The Mont Pèlerin Society was the seed that started a network of some 78 institutions. The society forged links with like-minded think tanks, corporations, governments and university economics departments, becoming the intellectual and ideological inspiration for economic fundamentalists around the world. Although the society itself has a very low profile it has exercised a strong influence through its more than 500 members – who hold key positions in government, government bureaucracies and in an array of think tanks – as well as its informal networks.[8]

The efforts of the Mont Pèlerin Society would have come to nothing, however, had business interests not embraced their ideas and poured money into their networks and think tanks from the 1970s. These networks and think tanks combined neoclassical economic theories and economic liberalism in a way that suited corporate interests. Neoclassical economic theories, which were a development of the classical economic theories of Adam Smith and his followers in the 19th century, were revived as a way of giving increased legitimacy to unrestrained market forces and increasing the potential for profit-making. These theories put great faith in the ability of markets and prices to allocate resources efficiently and ensure optimum productivity.[9]

Liberalism was a political philosophy that promoted the freedom of individuals to follow their own desires with a minimum of interference or constraint from society. Free market economists co-opted the term to apply to their own opposition to government intervention or regulation, calling this view 'economic liberalism'. It provided the argument that 'if the competitiveness and rivalry of unrestrained egoism existed in a capitalist market setting, then this competition would benefit the individuals involved and all society as well'. Their emphasis was on freedom of the individual to make money rather than freedom from oppression, exploitation and poverty.[10]

This fundamentalist combination of neoclassical theories and economic liberalism came to be referred to as neoliberalism in Europe, neoconservatism in the US, and economic rationalism or economic fundamentalism in Australia. Advocates promoted the replacement of government functions and services with those provided by private profit-seeking firms operating in the market (privatization); deregulation of labour and financial markets; deregulation of business activities; free trade; and smaller government through reduced taxes, spending and regulation. These policies were advocated in the name of free markets, competitiveness, efficiency, economic growth and the public interest.

Until the 1980s, most OECD governments subscribed to Keynesian economic theory which promoted government spending as a way of keeping market demand high enough to ensure high levels of employment, and therefore high levels of income and spending. In this way, they sought to avoid the downward spiral into depression that had occurred in the 1930s. Budget deficits and surpluses were used to regulate economic activity and manage the economy. Governments therefore had a strong social and economic role which they sometimes used to achieve greater equity through progressive taxation and the free provision of welfare and social services, such as health and education.[11]

Keynesian economics did not sit well with business interests since it gave a significant role to governments in running the economy. Similarly, conservatives were uncomfortable with it because they disliked governments intervening in the economy and the ensuing growth of government power. Although government spending was supposed to be cut back during boom times, the large central bureaucracies that were responsible for welfare, education and health acquired their own impetus.

Keynesian economics suffered a pronounced decline in popularity during the 1970s when economic growth in affluent countries slowed as oil prices escalated following the oil crisis. Stagflation, the combination of low economic growth and inflation, contradicted Keynesian theories, which seemed to offer no solution to the problem. Opponents argued that the welfare state was the problem because social security, and the high taxation it required, degraded the incentives to work hard and take business risks. Business people feared that the rising government deficits would cause interest rates to go up, making private investment more expensive and adding to inflation. At the same time free market advocates disparaged the benefits of government intervention and planning through spurious reference to the failures of the planned economies of the Soviet Union and other communist nations.[12]

Today the argument against government intervention and for small government and reduced government spending is particularly strong in all English-speaking countries and tends to be an article of faith rather than an empirically based rationale.[13] Economic 'education' campaigns had helped to shift opinion at the community grassroots level but a subsequent major shift at the government policy-making level required the more theoretical economic arguments that economists like Hayek and Friedman supplied.

After Hayek moved to the University of Chicago to join Friedman in 1950, the economics department there became a focal point of free market economics, attracting adherents to its faculty and graduating free market advocates. As a result, the term 'Chicago School' came to be synonymous with free market economics. There were also free market economists associated with other universities, particularly the University of Rochester, UCLA, the University of Virginia, the University of Washington at Seattle, as well as the London School of Economics.[14] However, they were particularly concentrated at the University of Chicago, where the few economists of different persuasion, like Paul Douglas, felt out of place:

> *I was disconcerted to find that the economic and political conservatives had acquired an almost complete domination over my department, and taught that market decisions were always right and profit values the supreme ones. The doctrine of non-interference with the market meant, in practice, clear the track for big business. Inequalities of bargaining power, knowledge, and income were brushed aside, and the realities of monopoly, quasi-monopoly, and imperfect competition were treated as either immaterial or nonexistent.*[15]

The Chicago School's policy prescriptions included maximum freedom of choice for entrepreneurs and producers; minimization of taxation, welfare and government intervention; the removal of tariffs; the privatization of government services; deregulation of labour markets and the denationalization of money. Friedman was credited with being the leader of the Chicago School economists and was taken up and promoted by Hayek-inspired networks: 'more than anyone else, he was responsible for reviving' and popularizing free market ideas.[16]

For many years these free market economic ideas were considered marginal and obsolete in other universities. But they gradually moved from the margins of economic thought towards the centre of orthodoxy because these ideas became useful to business interests seeking to minimize government interference in their activities; achieve a better low-tax business climate; and expand markets into realms of government business. Both Hayek and Friedman received Nobel prizes in the 1970s. Friedman went on to be an adviser to several government leaders, including US Presidents Richard Nixon and Ronald Reagan, UK Prime Minister Margaret Thatcher and, most controversially, Chilean dictator Augusto Pinochet, who had overthrown the democratically elected Allende government (see Chapter 10).[17]

MONETARISM AND THE NATURAL RATE OF UNEMPLOYMENT

Friedman was most closely identified with monetarism, a theory that had been discredited following the Great Depression.[18] Its renewed appeal in the 1970s came because it claimed to explain the stagflation that many countries were experiencing. Following Keynes, governments put up with a certain amount of inflation so as to promote economic growth and keep employment levels up. In times of low economic growth, they increased government spending and therefore the budget deficit, and this was often paid for by printing more money and thereby increasing the money supply. With more money in circulation, more money was spent and more jobs created.

However, in the 1970s, inflation increased while economic growth stagnated and employment levels fell. Monetarists such as Friedman blamed inflation on increases in the money supply. They argued that governments should keep the money supply steady so as to avoid inflation, and that if this was done, depressions would also be avoided. They explained the new phenomena of stagflation in terms of people's expectations of inflation. This expectation, monetarists argued, caused producers to charge higher prices and employees to demand higher wages when money supply was increased, thus using up the extra money that was supposed to create new jobs and extra production.

They also argued that there was a trade-off between unemployment and inflation and that some unemployment was necessary to keep inflation down because a certain level of unemployment kept wages down. This was because workers were not in a position to demand higher wages if the demand for their labour was reduced by the presence of others willing to do their jobs. The level of unemployment necessary to prevent inflation was named the 'natural level of unemployment' because it was supposedly determined by the market.[19]

Monetarism was not taken seriously at first. Friedman's methods were considered to be not very rigorous and 'faintly disreputable'.[20] Paul Diesing describes the sort of tactics that Friedman would use to ensure that the data fitted his hypotheses:

> 1 *If raw or adjusted data are consistent with [the hypothesis], he reports them as confirmation ...*
> 2 *If the fit with expectations is moderate, he exaggerates the fit ...*
> 3 *If particular data points or groups differ from the predicted regression, he invents ad hoc explanations for the divergence ...*

4 *If a whole set of data disagree with predictions, adjust them until they do agree ...*
5 *If no plausible adjustment suggests itself, reject the data as unreliable ...*
6 *If data adjustment or rejection are not feasible, express puzzlement. 'I have not been able to construct any plausible explanation for the discrepancy ...'* [21]

However, in the 1970s, when governments were at a loss to know how to deal with stagflation, Friedman's theories were taken seriously. Monetarism was at its most popular in the late 1970s in economic and policy circles as businesses homed in on inflation as a major economic problem. Inflation was of most concern to the wealthy who had a lot of money invested and businesses that had to pay higher wages and borrow money at increased interest rates. Workers were more concerned that unemployment levels were kept low and government services adequate. Monetarism and the natural rate of unemployment were therefore policies that aimed to serve the top end of town.

Monetarism appealed to free market ideologues because it reduced the role of government in the economy. Similarly, it aided the argument against government spending and social programmes, which free market advocates railed against. Friedman was against all government interventions in the market including tariffs, rent controls, minimum wages, regulation, social security, public housing, national parks, and government provision of infrastructure and services such as post offices and roads. Monetarism was also attractive to free market advocates because it explained the Great Depression in terms of government failure rather than market failure – that is, the failure of the Federal Reserve to manage money supply properly, rather than declining demand, overproduction and income inequality in the market.[22]

The pursuit of monetarism also had a marked political agenda. Nigel Ashford, writing in the think tank magazine *Policy*, argued that the interest in monetarism was clearly seen by some as a way of reducing union power:

> *In the 1970s British governments of both parties believed that the only solution to the problem of inflation was an incomes policy, which required the support, or at least the acquiescence, of the trade unions in a corporatist style of decision-making. The governments were then forced into a dependency relationship with the unions. The pursuit of an anti-inflation strategy that depended on the money supply, which was within the control of the government, reduced that dependency relationship and thus the power of the unions ...*[23]

The idea of a natural rate of unemployment also suited governments that wanted to be absolved from responsibility for unemployment. It provided the rhetoric to obscure the plain fact that people were being thrown out of work so that those still in work would not be in a position to demand higher wages.[24] It was later labelled with a more politically neutral term, the non-accelerating inflation rate of unemployment (NAIRU). But far from being determined by the market, NAIRU was decided by economists. John Kenneth Galbraith noted:

> *The estimated NAIRU tracks the actual unemployment. When unemployment goes up, conservative economists raise their NAIRU. When it falls, they predict inflation, and if inflation doesn't happen they cut their estimated NAIRU. There is a long and not-very-reputable literature of such estimates . . .*[25]

Most significantly, when implemented, monetarism failed to deliver, even for the top end of town. The Nixon administration had a brief experiment with monetarism in 1969 when the Dean of the University of Chicago business school, George Shultz, was budget director. The result was that inflation grew by 6 per cent and unemployment increased from 3.5 to 5 per cent. The experiment was abandoned, and in 1971 Nixon froze wages, prices and rents and declared 'I am now a Keynesian'.[26]

Margaret Thatcher applied monetarism during the 1980s in the UK and the resulting economic disaster meant that the system was largely discredited. Instead of low inflation and stable economic growth, the economy went into recession. Manufacturing output declined by 10 per cent between 1979 and 1984, and at the same time, investment in manufacturing plunged by 30 per cent. Unemployment more than doubled to almost 12 per cent and did not recover when the recession ended. The social outfall caused riots, and Thatcher's level of support fell dramatically, even within her own party. Her political career was only saved by the Falklands War. The Bank of England abandoned monetarism in 1986.[27]

Ronald Reagan, like Thatcher, was an admirer of Friedman, and publicly declared Friedman to be a close economic adviser. When he was elected US president in 1980 his administration embraced monetarism and reduced the money supply. This caused deflation and unemployment. The *Wall Street Journal*, a supporter of monetarism, editorialized:

> *The economic downturn set postwar records in unemployment and hit some states like a depression, but it is also bound to produce benefits . . . as the 'Austrian school' of economics teaches, recessions play an important part in economic growth. They weed out inefficient, outmoded enterprises and free resources for new ones. The Reagan administration is the first in memory to adopt this school of thought and to deal with a slump by doing nothing.*[28]

However, business was not so sanguine, and pressed Reagan to do something. Monetarist policies were soon reversed with Reagan's big budget deficits. The Federal Reserve officially abandoned monetarism in 1982. 'Interest rates fell, the stock market boomed, and the monetarists were bitterly disappointed.' They claimed that monetarism hadn't been given enough time to work its magic.[29] However, the same could not be said of the British experiment with monetarism, nor that of Chile (see Chapter 10).

For corporations, monetarism was a failed experiment aimed at controlling inflation, a clear business priority. However, its proponents were useful in discrediting Keynsianism and the idea that governments should try to spend their way out of recessions by creating money.

SUPPLY-SIDE VOODOO

Supply-side economics was supposed to be another way of solving stagflation. Proponents advocated incentives for the wealthy to invest in productive activities through lower taxes and reduced government spending on the poor and social services. Like monetarism, it represented the revival of an old, obsolete and discredited theory[30] and, like monetarism and the natural rate of unemployment, it came to dominate public policy.

Higher marginal tax rates and greater government regulation were said, by supply-siders, to impede economic growth by reducing incentives for work, saving and investment and therefore reducing productivity. The higher incomes that would ensue from tax cuts were supposed to be spent by entrepreneurs on investment that would increase production, and therefore jobs would be created. As a result, more taxes would be collected by the government in the long run, despite being paid at a lower rate. This was because profits would be higher and more workers would be paying taxes.

Supply-siders assume government is wasteful, inefficient and unproductive, and the more a government spends, the more the economy slows. Governments, they argue, divert resources away from 'productive private-sector ventures'. Welfare in particular, provides disincentives for people to work. Taxes and regulations raise the cost of entrepreneurship while reducing the high returns that can be made from economic ventures. This reduces the willingness of entrepreneurs to take risks, so causing the economy to stagnate. Inflation also acts like a tax in that it diminishes earnings, savings and investments: 'inflation is a clandestine tax that damages economic growth and opportunity'. Supply-side economists accept the monetarists' explanation of inflation as 'too much money chasing too few goods'.[31]

Supply-side arguments did not have much credence amongst most economists, not even conservative economists like Friedman, but were politically popular amongst higher-income earners and businesses for obvious reasons. It was promoted by journalists at the *Wall Street Journal*, which became the major supply-side debating forum. Other advocates included Irving Kristol, editor of the neoconservative journal *The Public Interest*; some congressional staffers; consulting firms; and conservative think tanks (see next chapter).[32] Economist Paul Krugman claimed with respect to supply-side economics:

> *... a handful of wealthy cranks can support an impressive-looking array of think tanks, research institutes, foundations, and so on devoted to promoting an economic doctrine they like ... The supply-siders will always have a safe haven in the world of Free Enterprise Institutes and Centers for the Study of Capitalism, outlets in the pages of Forbes and the Wall Street Journal, and new recruits who never tire of saying the same things again and again.*[33]

Similarly, Sidney Blumenthal, in his book *The Rise of the Counter-Establishment*, argued that supply-side economics 'travelled from lunatic panacea to official catechism in a few short years'.[34] It also had popular appeal because of its 'have your cake and eat it too' message:

> *Supply-side economics provided the theoretical underpinnings for old-fashioned optimism. The doctrine restated the free-market myth with verve and originality. In an era when the 'limits to growth' were proclaimed, the gnostic supply-siders made claims to knowing the secret of endless wealth: the magic of the marketplace... a theory for the multitude of go-getters, promising that the cornucopia was bottomless.*[35]

This optimism helped Ronald Reagan to get elected, despite George Bush labelling supply-side theories as 'voodoo economics' when he was a rival candidate for presidential nomination in the 1980 primaries. Reagan's campaign advertisements promised tax cuts that would make everyone better off:

> *Ronald Reagan believes that when you tax something, you get less of it. We're taxing work, savings, and investment like never before. As a result, we have less work, less savings, and less invested.*[36]

Like monetarism, supply-side economics failed to deliver on its promises in practice. Reagan's tax cuts did not lead to higher incomes, greater economic growth, increased employment nor increased savings. Therefore less tax was collected and, because government spending was not reduced accordingly, budget deficits increased with a tripling of the national debt.[37]

Reagan's budget director, David Stockman, later told the *Atlantic Monthly* that the 1981 tax cut 'was always a Trojan horse to bring down the top [tax] rate' for the wealthy. Supply-side theory was just a reformulated version of 'trickle down' theory that if the rich are richer they will invest more and the economy will grow, and the extra wealth created will eventually 'trickle down' to the poor: 'if one feeds the horse enough oats, some will pass through to the road for the sparrows'.[38] However, the reality was that corporations did not spend their tax savings on job-creating investments. On the contrary, they downsized in a major way throughout the 1980s and 1990s, despite having to pay very minimal taxes.

CONTESTABILITY THEORY

Classical economic theory was based on the idea that prices and outputs are kept within reasonable levels by competition. If prices and profits are too high, more firms will enter the market and drive them down. If they are too low, some firms will go out of business enabling the remainder to raise prices and profits. However, government measures to ensure competition, such as anti-trust legislation, were very much opposed by large corporations which preferred not to have to compete.

Contestability theory, or contestable markets theory, claimed that competition did not have to be real or actual for the market to keep prices down; all that was needed was the potential for competition to ensure that prices and profits did not go too high. So, according to this theory, even a monopoly could be kept in check by the potential of competition.[39]

Contestability theory, originally formulated by William Baumol and others, was taken up by the Chicago School and then by the Reagan administration. Contestability theory was used to favour deregulation policies for monopolies by a 'a group of economists, in particular associated with the Bell Lab. of the American Telephone and Telegraph Company, and with the US Civil Aeronautics Board'.[40] Contestability was also cited in the UK when British Telecom and British Gas were privatized as monopolies.

Normally, a monopoly is thought to need regulation, to ensure prices are kept within reason and ensure good service. Contestability theory, however, claims that the best government policy is to remove regulations that might hinder the potential of low-risk entry and exit of firms into the market. Regulations, it is argued, tend to keep prices and services high, and sometimes foster cross-subsidization to ensure equity. They limit the operations of companies and do not provide incentives for them to operate efficiently.[41]

Contestability theory assumes that it is easy for firms to enter a market without expending large amounts of money on technology and production capacity. It assumes that the new firm can withstand price-cutting strategies by established firms hoping to prevent its establishment. And it assumes that companies leaving the market will not incur costs.[42] All these assumptions are demonstrably unrealistic for most industries but this did not stop the adoption of this theory by policy-makers.

Such theories were used in the 19th century to oppose anti-trust legislation aimed at preventing monopolies, and again in the 1980s by economists of the Chicago School for the same purpose. They argued that there was no need for government interventions to prevent mergers, concentration and vertical restraints on trade because the potential for competition remains. Such trends towards monopoly merely reflect the drive for economic efficiency.[43]

Douglas Greer notes that contestability theory has been adopted by policy-makers despite having very little empirical support: 'Notwithstanding its inconsistencies, implausibilities, non-robustness, empirical immateriality, and impracticality of application, contestability has had a significant impact...'. Greer argues that ideology and ignorance are the main explanations: 'contestability quickly won influence in the US not on its merits. Rather, it rode on the coattails of compatible Chicago views embraced by Reagan's political and judicial appointees.'[44]

Even Baumol and his colleagues were angry with the way their theory was used by the Chicago School, denying that it 'offers a carte blanche to mindless deregulation and the dismantling of antitrust safeguards ... Contestability theory does not, and was not intended to, lend support to those who believe (or almost seem to believe) that the unrestrained market automatically solves all economic problems and that virtually all regulation and antitrust activity constitutes a pointless and costly source of economic efficiency.'[45]

PUBLIC CHOICE THEORY

Another theory that has been very influential and has become central to free market economics is public choice theory. While ideas such as contestability theory give reasons for favouring the market to provide government services, public choice theory provides a means to discredit government decision-making and intervention as being self-interested rather than in the public interest. It stresses political failure rather than market failure, which had been central to Keynesianism. 'In particular it has helped to erode the optimistic post-1945 belief in government planning and the welfare state, and to substitute the conclusion that the less governments do, the better.'[46]

The intellect behind public choice theory was James Buchanan, who co-founded the Public Choice Society in 1963 with Gordon Tullock. Buchanan and Tullock at the Virginia School and others at the Chicago School 'explained political behaviour in terms of the self-interest of political actors, such as politicians seeking election, bureaucrats seeking size maximisation (or empire building) or interest groups seeking to use the power of government to further their own interests'.[47]

Public choice theory applies classical economic assumptions about human behaviour to the study of government. It likens politics to the market in that bureaucrats and politicians are seeking to serve their own self-interest and voters are like consumers who use their votes to buy packages of policies from political parties that are in their self-interest. Public choice, as embodied in government decisions, is merely an aggregate of individual self-interest and personal agendas. And the electorate is assumed to be ignorant and greedy.[48]

Public choice theorists highlight the faults of government decision-making while presenting an idealized view of the market with which to contrast it. Some, such as Buchanan, even suggest that decisions made by the majority are best avoided in some situations.[49]

The problem, public choice theorists say, is that voting is a weak way of expressing consumer preferences compared with consumer behaviour in the market.[50] What is more, organized minority interests – that is, special-interest groups – are able to distort the process by offering inducements to politicians or, in the case of public-sector unions, non-governmental organizations (NGOs) and other pressure groups, exerting pressure disproportionate to their numbers. Politicians who want to secure political support find it is in their interests to provide political favours to particular constituencies. Such favours may benefit a narrow group of people, but the costs are spread thinly over the wider public and so the politicians do not lose votes in the process. In this way, politicians are somewhat unresponsive to the requirements of individuals even when the majority of the population is represented by such individuals.

In recognizing the distorting influence of interest groups, the business supporters of public choice theory do not include themselves as special interests as they maintain that general business interests and the public interest are synonymous. For example, Roger Kerr, executive director of the NZ Business Roundtable, agreed that other groups' 'political lobbying was now the prime threat to democratic government because the process led to the advancement of private interests at the expense of the general public interest'. In contrast, lobbying by the NZ Business Roundtable 'explicitly committed itself to the promotion of overall national interests rather than sectional interests'. He claimed that others who lobbied government tried to achieve redistribution of economic benefits rather than the goal of making the pie larger, that is the creation of wealth.[51]

According to public choice theory it is not only politicians and interest groups who are at fault. Bureaucrats also distort the democratic process because they are primarily motivated by considerations such as pay, status, and ambition. This means they may distort or withhold information from politicians and they have an interest in large budgets and big departments, which leads to a growth of government and, according to these economists, that is not in the public interest. Without market pressures, government managers have no incentive to reduce waste or become economically efficient. In this way, governments tend to oversupply public goods, or supply them in a wasteful way.

However, critics do not accept the assumption that motivations in the political sphere are the same as those in the market place. Surveys seem to back this up:

> *In almost every case there is a relationship between the way the individual views the state of the economy or the competence of the government and how she votes; but little relationship between her vote and her personal financial status . . . Of course the voter will hope that what is best for the*

> *national prosperity will also in due course benefit him or herself but this is a different kind of judgement from 'pocketbook voting'.*[52]

Ideology, which also plays a key role in politics, cannot easily be explained in terms of self-interest. Bureaucrats do not always seek to increase budgets and build empires. In fact, there is much evidence in more recent times of bureau heads presiding over and championing dramatic cutbacks in government services and personnel.

The policy prescriptions that follow from public choice theory include:

- reducing the size and power of government through government spending cuts and deregulation;
- making what remains of government subject to market discipline as far as possible through full cost accounting, ensuring private competition, introducing user pay fees and changing the structure of rewards for managers.

Privatization of government services, of course, achieves both goals at once.[53]

Peter Self, in his book *Government by the Market?* notes that while public choice theory may seem to be somewhat simplistic or exaggerated, 'it has enough plausibility in common experience to pass muster without close examination'. The credibility of the theory is enhanced by a contrived 'scientific' methodology and spurious equations. 'Thus the highly critical picture of the political process can be influential without necessarily being fully believed or altogether consistent with the original theories.'[54]

The resurgence of market faith was not merely a manifestation of the naïvety of economists. Their theories were embraced by big business because they provided a legitimation for their pursuit of self-interest – business activity – and avenues for business expansion. The policy prescriptions that suited business best – including reductions in taxes, minimal regulations, and freedom to trade and invest anywhere in the world – were justified by this body of economic theory that represented such policies as being in the public interest.

There was some appeal in free market ideology for governments, too, in that it absolved them of responsibility for economic performance: 'In a nutshell, the new classical policy package gave politicians the chance to abdicate, with a clear conscience, many of the responsibilities which the State had assumed in the preceding decades ... Politicians in many countries seized eagerly upon the alibi thus offered for their failure to meet the economic expectations of their electorates.'[55]

NOTES

1 William Cran and Daniel Yergin, 'The Commanding Heights: The Battle for the World Economy', Public Broadcasting Service, 2002, www.pbs.org/wgbh/commandingheights/.

2 Peter Self, *Government by the Market? The Politics of Public Choice*, Hampshire and London, Macmillan, 1993, p55.

3 Sidney Blumenthal, *The Rise of the Counter-Establishment: From Conservative Ideology to Political Power*, New York, Time Books, 1986, pp16–7.

4 Henry Hazlitt, 'Leonard E. Read, RIP', *National Review*, 10 June 1983, p668; Hayek quoted in Damien Cahill, 'In the Vanguard', *Workers Online*, August, 2004, http://workers.labor.net.au/features/200408/b_tradeunion_neocons.html; Blumenthal, *The Rise of the Counter-Establishment*, p88; Daniel Yergin and Joseph Stanislaw, *The Commanding Heights*, 1997, p141.

5 Henry Hazlitt, 'The Early History of FEE', *The Freeman*, March, 1984, www.libertyhaven.com/theoreticalorphilosophicalissues/history/earlyhistory.html; John Blundell, 'Waging the War of Ideas: Why There Are No Shortcuts', Atlas Economic Research Foundation, January, 1990, www.atlasusa.org/toolkit/waging_war.php.

6 Blundell, 'Waging the War of Ideas'; Disinfopedia, 'Harold Luhnow', Center for Media & Democracy, 19 August 2004, www.disinfopedia.or/wiki.phtml?title=Harold_Luhnow.

7 Yergin and Stanislaw, *The Commanding Heights*, p144.

8 Richard Cockett, *Thinking the Unthinkable: Think-Tanks and the Economic Counter-Revolution 1931–1983*, Harper Collins, 1994, p304; Greg Lindsay, 'Threats to Freedom Then and Now', *Policy*, Autumn, 1997, www.cis.org.au/Policy/mps.html, p20.

9 Christopher Sheil, *Water's Fall: Running the Risks with Economic Rationalism*, Annandale, NSW, Pluto Press, 2000, p23.

10 *Ibid.*, p26; E.K. Hunt quoted in Helen Noyes, 'Economic Rationalism', Bachelor of Economics (Social Science) Honours, University of Sydney, 1995, p10; Frank Stilwell, 'Economic Rationalism: Sound Foundations for Policy?' in Stuart Rees, Gordon Rodley and Frank Stilwell (eds) *Beyond the Market: Alternatives to Economic Rationalism*, Leichhardt, NSW, Pluto Press, 1993, p34.

11 Greg Whitwell, 'The Power of Economic Ideas? Keynsian Economic Policies in Post-War Australia', in Stephen Bell and Brian Head (eds) *State, Economy and Public Policy*, Melbourne, Oxford University Press, 1994, p120.

12 Brian Easton and Rolf Gerritsen, 'Economic Reform: Parallels and Divergences', in Francis G. Castles, Rolf Gerritsen and Jack Vowles (eds) *The Great Experiment: Labour Parties and Public Policy Transformation in Australia and New Zealand*, Sydney, Allen & Unwin, 1996, p28; John Carroll, 'Economic Rationalism and Its Consequences', in John Carroll and Robert Manne (eds) *Shutdown: The Failure of Economic Rationalism and How to Rescue Australia*, Melbourne, The Text Publishing Company, 1992, p8; Peter M. Jackson and Catherine M. Price, 'Privatisation and Regulation: A Review of the Issues', in Peter M. Jackson and Catherine M. Price (eds) *Privatisation and Regulation: A Review of the Issues*, London and New York, Longman, 1994, p3.

13 John Kenneth Galbraith, *The Culture of Contentment*, London, Penguin, 1992, p82.
14 Brian Easton, 'From Reaganomics to Rogernomics', in Alan Bollard (ed) *The Influence of United States Economics on New Zealand*, Wellington, NZ-US Educational Foundation and the New Zealand Institute of Economic Research, 1988, p74; Blumenthal, *The Rise of the Counter-Establishment*, p93.
15 Quoted in Blumenthal, *The Rise of the Counter-Establishment*, p96.
16 Sheil, *Water's Fall*, p27; Peter Vintila, 'Markets, Morals and Manifestos', in Peter Vintila, John Phillimore and Peter Newman (eds) *Markets, Morals & Manifestos: Fightback! & the Politics of Economic Rationalism in the 1990s*, Murdoch, WA, Institute for Science and Technology Policy, Murdoch University, 1992, p9; Blumenthal, *The Rise of the Counter-Establishment*, pp88–9.
17 Marian Sawer, 'Political Manifestations of Australian Libertarianism', in Marian Sawer (ed) *Australia and the New Right*, North Sydney, George Allen & Unwin, 1982, p2; Sheil, *Water's Fall*, p27; Cran and Yergin, 'The Commanding Heights'.
18 Blumenthal, *The Rise of the Counter-Establishment*, p88.
19 Steve Kangas, 'Milton Friedman and the Natural Rate of Unemployment', Liberalism Resurgent, www.huppi.com/kangaroo/L-chinairu.htm accessed 15 August 2004.
20 Paul Krugman, *Peddling Prosperity: Economic Sense and Nonsense in the Age of Diminished Expectations*, New York, W.W.Norton, 1994, p40.
21 Quoted in Steve Kangas, 'Milton Friedman and Monetarism', Liberalism Resurgent, www.huppi.com/kangaroo/L-chimonetarism.htm accessed 11 June 2001.
22 Blumenthal, *The Rise of the Counter-Establishment*, pp100–1, 106–7.
23 Nigel Ashford, 'Politically Impossible? How Ideas, Not Interests and Circumstances, Determine Public Policies', *Policy*, Autumn, 1997, p25.
24 Krugman, *Peddling Prosperity*, p173.
25 Quoted in Kangas, 'Milton Friedman and the Natural Rate of Unemployment'.
26 Blumenthal, *The Rise of the Counter-Establishment*, p110.
27 *Ibid.*, p117; Kangas, 'Milton Friedman and Monetarism'.
28 Quoted in Blumenthal, *The Rise of the Counter-Establishment*, p264.
29 *Ibid.*, pp120, 264, 275; Kangas, 'Milton Friedman and Monetarism'.
30 Blumenthal, *The Rise of the Counter-Establishment*, pp167–8.
31 Raymond J. Keating, 'A Walk on the Supply Side', *The Freeman*, vol 45, no 5, 1995.
32 Krugman, *Peddling Prosperity*, pp83–6; Blumenthal, *The Rise of the Counter-Establishment*, pp8, 179.
33 Paul Krugman, 'The Dismal Science', *Slate Magazine*, 15 August 1996, http://slate.msn.com/code/story/actions.
34 Blumenthal, *The Rise of the Counter-Establishment*, pp169–70.
35 *Ibid.*, pp169–70.
36 *Ibid.*, p203.
37 Nouriel Roubini, 'Supply Side Economics: Do Tax Rate Cuts Increase Growth and Revenues Reduce Budget Deficits?' Nouriel Roubini, 1997, http://equity.stern.nyu.edu/~nroubini/SUPPLY.HTM; Krugman, *Peddling Prosperity*, pp83–6; Blumenthal, *The Rise of the Counter-Establishment*, pp8, 179.
38 Galbraith, *The Culture of Contentment*, p108.
39 Douglas F. Greer, 'Contestability in Competition Policy: Replacement, Supplement, or Impediment?' in Alan Bollard (ed) *The Influence of United States Economics on*

New Zealand, Wellington, NZ-US Educational Foundation and the New Zealand Institute of Economic Research, 1988, pp40–41.

40 Tom Weyman-Jones, 'Deregulation', in Peter M. Jackson and Catherine M. Price (eds) *Privatisation and Regulation: A Review of the Issues*, London and New York, Longman, 1994, p100.

41 *Ibid.*, pp104–9.

42 Greer, 'Contestability in Competition Policy', p41.

43 *Ibid.*, pp42–3, 60.

44 *Ibid.*, pp56, 61.

45 Quoted in Easton, 'From Reaganomics to Rogernomics', p74.

46 Self, *Government by the Market?* px.

47 Ashford, 'Politically Impossible?', p24; Self, *Government by the Market?* p1.

48 Georgina Murray and Douglas Pacheco, 'Think-tanks in the 1990s', Australian National University, www.anu.edu.au/polsci/marx/interventions/thinktanks.htm accessed 23 January 2001.

49 Cited in Self, *Government by the Market?* pp58–9.

50 *Ibid.*, p4.

51 Roger Kerr, 'Taking Part in the Public Policy Debate in the 1990s', *Independent Business Weekly*, 26 November 1993, p11.

52 Self, *Government by the Market?* p22.

53 *Ibid.*, pp59–62.

54 *Ibid.*, p58.

55 G. Bertram quoted in Jane Kelsey, *Economic Fundamentalism*, London, Pluto Press, 1995, p67.

8

Disseminating Pro-Business Policies

Since the 1980s there has been no serious challenge to the economic philosophy of the free market in the United States. It was then that a free-market orthodoxy established its ascendancy over American public culture... It has gone far towards establishing itself as the unofficial American civil religion.

JOHN GRAY[1]

Joseph Coors, who had made a great deal of money from the beer brewing corporation his grandfather founded, was one of those inspired by the business battle plan in the Powell Memorandum: 'Coors recalls that the Powell memorandum "stirred" him up and convinced him that American business was "ignoring" a crisis.'[2] In 1973 Coors, angry after being found guilty of price fixing, unlawful limitation of competition and other illegal practices by the Federal Trade Commission, invested $250,000 of Coors Corporation money to start the Heritage Foundation. It was to become one of the most influential think tanks in the US, one that, ironically, put much effort into promoting the free market on the grounds that it encouraged competition. Coors spent a further $300,000 on a building to house it, and committed millions of dollars to its ongoing operations.[3] This commitment enabled it to collect further funds from other corporate donors, such as petroleum tycoon Edward Noble.

Coors was on the board of directors of the National Association of Manufacturers (NAM), managed plants where unions were banned, and was a staunch Reagan supporter. UK newspaper *The Guardian* referred to Coors as an 'ultraconservative businessman who, for all practical purposes, bought the White House for Ronald Reagan in 1980'. Coors supported Ronald Reagan from the 1960s and Reagan often visited the Coors' family home. The Coors Corporation sponsored Reagan's radio shows, while the Heritage Foundation supplied him with many of his policy ideas. After Reagan was elected president, 'Joe became a member of his Kitchen Cabinet, offering staffing and policy suggestions ...'.[4]

The initial leadership of the Heritage Foundation was drawn from the youthful staff of conservative politicians in Washington, including Paul Weyrich, who served as the foundation's first president, and Edward Feulner, who has been the foundation's long-term president since 1977. Feulner, who is a member of the Mont Pèlerin Society and was also its president from 1996–98,[5] understands the role of think tanks well. He noted that while intellectuals such as Milton Friedman were necessary to 'articulate' free market ideas, think tanks introduced these ideas into the policy arena, marketed them and sought to change government policy:

> *It takes an institution to help popularise and propagandise an idea – to market an idea. Think tanks are second-hand dealers of ideas ... [that] host conferences, lectures and seminars and publish policy reports, books and monographs to popularise an idea. Through 'outreach' programmes an institution can promote an idea on a continuing basis and cause change. But this takes time.*
>
> *Procter and Gamble does not sell Crest toothpaste by taking out one newspaper ad or running one television commercial. They sell it and resell it every day by keeping the product fresh in the consumer's mind. The institutes I have mentioned sell ideas in much the same manner.*[6]

Feulner cited Supply-side Economics as an example. The Heritage Foundation brought the theory 'to the attention of opinion leaders in Washington' by producing a book, *Essays in Supply Side Economics*, and by hosting a conference attended by 400 congressional aides, members of Congress, bureaucrats, academics and journalists. After the conference copies of the book were sent out, press releases issued, and 'op-ed' columns produced from the book for newspapers all over the US. He noted that in contrast to 'electoral politics', which occur only at election time to persuade voters, 'policy politics', in which think tanks engage, occur all the time and are aimed at setting the policy agenda and influencing public opinion.[7]

Think tanks were part of a larger free market policy push funded by conservative foundations and large corporations. Throughout the 1970s they established and funded 'a veritable constellation of think tanks, pressure groups, special-interest foundations, litigation centers, scholarly research and funding endowments, publishing and TV production houses, media attack operations, political consultancies, polling mills, and public relations operations' that promoted free market ideology and attacked government regulation. They 'developed the social and political networks necessary to tie this nascent empire together. The end product was a tidal wave of money, ideas, and self-promotion that carried the Reaganites to power.'[8]

Oil industry money was invested through business people such as billionaire Republican Richard Mellon Scaife and Mobil Oil. Chemical industry money was invested through foundations such as the Olin Foundation. Lynde and Harry Bradley invested manufacturing money, Smith Richardson invested pharmaceutical money, and the Koch family invested energy money. This influx of money meant not only that conservative think tanks proliferated, but that other think tanks moved towards the right. As Jerome Himmelstein points out in his book *To the Right*: 'The political mobilization of big business in the mid-1970s gave conservatives greater access to money and channels of political influence. These helped turn conservative personnel into political leaders and advisers, and conservative ideas, especially economic ones, into public policy.'[9]

Think tanks or policy institutes have played a major role in disseminating and popularising free market ideas and ideologies in a number of countries. They replaced advertisers and business associations as the new free market missionaries.

UK THINK TANKS

The rise of Thatcherism in Britain can be attributed in large part to the endeavours of two think tanks. The first was the Institute of Economic Affairs (IEA) which promoted a *laissez-faire* libertarian view, keeping the economic fundamentalism 'alive when academic opinion had pronounced it brain-dead'.[10]

Lord Anthony Fisher conceived of the idea of the IEA at the prompting of Friedrich von Hayek in the early 1950s, having visited the Foundation for Economic Education (FEE) in the US. According to Ralph Harris, a director of the IEA and member of the Mont Pèlerin Society, 'The institute started in 1957, you could say the direct result of the Mont Pèlerin Society, of *The Road to Serfdom*, of Hayek's ideas of freedom and competitive enterprise.' It set out to gain wide acceptance for the 'philosophy of the market economy' through communications directed at the opinion leaders such as intellectuals, politicians, business people and journalists. It started as a one-person operation and at its height in the 1980s reached 15 full-time employees with a half-million-pound budget provided mainly by about 250 companies, including large transnational firms.[11]

The IEA began by producing pamphlets based on Hayek and Friedman's ideas, as well as analyses of various policies in the light of those ideas. It promoted Friedman's monetarism by producing summaries of his ideas, inviting him to speak at conferences, and introducing him to leading politicians, including Margaret Thatcher before she was prime minister: 'The IEA effectively networked Friedman in the UK.' The IEA also published articles by public choice theorists such as Buchanan.[12]

During the 1970s, the IEA managed to enrol several academics and influential journalists to promote economic fundamentalism, as well as some prominent MPs, most notably Margaret Thatcher. It had trained young economists at the IEA early in their careers, which helped provide personnel for the free market think tanks established in the 1970s and 1980s.[13]

The Centre for Policy Studies (CPS) was to some extent an outgrowth of the IEA. It was founded in 1974 by Keith Joseph, an active member of the IEA, and Margaret Thatcher, who had also been associated with the IEA. Joseph, a former Tory minister, who is credited with Thatcher's conversion to economic fundamentalism, is reported to have been converted himself when he took a suitcase of IEA-recommended books and pamphlets by Friedman and Hayek on holiday with him. Margaret Thatcher had read Hayek's *Road to Serfdom* while at Oxford and it is said to have 'made a lasting impression on her'. Thatcher also became a member of the Mont Pèlerin Society.[14]

> *In the mid-1970s, not long after becoming Leader, she visited the Conservative Party's research department. ... She reached into her briefcase and pulled out a book. It was Hayek's The Constitution of Liberty. She held it up for all to see. 'This,' she said sternly, 'is what we believe.' She slammed it down on the table and then proceeded to deliver a monologue on the ills of the British economy.*[15]

While the IEA pledged itself to be 'independent of any political party' and therefore did not publish policy recommendations, the CPS was set up to convert the Tory party to economic fundamentalism and formulate policies for the party that were in line with this philosophy. It seldom exceeded seven full-time employees and an annual budget of £150,000.[16]

The IEA and the CPS were small compared to the average US think tank, but effective in the British environment because of the 'extreme centralisation of British political and public life'. This gave easy access to key people within government, the media and the financial sphere. They needed only to concentrate their persuasion on 'a strategic policy-making elite' to be effective.[17]

> *These 'second-hand dealers in ideas' – to use the IEA's own description of its role – were typically not intellectual originators but served to collect, distil and preserve certain strands of ideas and to diffuse them more widely, not least as detailed interventions in current policy debates.*[18]

The CPS, in particular, has been accused of being an 'intellectual jackdaw, gleaning most of its ideas from overseas experiments – and in particular from the US. These were then reworked to fit Britain, packaged in pamphlet form and fired across the media's bows.'[19]

The IEA and the CPS 'provided the ideas that gave intellectual shape to the instincts and energy of Thatcherism' in Britain. They helped to convert the Tory leaders to economic fundamentalism while they were in opposition, and gave the Thatcher government 'a style of politics whose cutting edge was its ideological crusade'. When elected as prime minister in 1979, Thatcher nominated Ralph Harris, head of the IEA, for the House of Lords and wrote to thank him and two of his colleagues: 'It was primarily your foundation work which enabled us to rebuild the philosophy upon which our Party succeeded in the past. The debt we owe you is immense and I am very grateful.'[20]

Once in power, Thatcher set about implementing the economic ideology she had been imbued with, including monetarism, privatization and government spending cuts. Such policies met with much opposition, including within her own Conservative Party, especially as unemployment and business bankruptcies increased. But Thatcher refused to turn away from her fundamentalist path. She famously told a 1980 party conference: 'Turn if you like ... The lady's not for turning.'[21] Before the Falklands War she became the most unpopular prime minister in British polling history. Following the Falklands War, she was re-elected with a landslide.

The Adam Smith Institute (ASI) was established in 1981 with a policy focus. It was chaired by Hayek and published pamphlets by and on Hayek but also specific policy proposals. It was, in its own words, 'part of a worldwide movement towards free markets and free trade'. It still publishes tributes to Hayek and Friedman, and bills itself as 'Britain's leading innovator of market economic policies'.[22]

During the Thatcher reign, the ASI was a driving force behind privatization. It sought to make privatization acceptable to the public by creating interests in favour of it through 'encouraging management buy-outs, cheap or free shares to employees and widespread share ownership among the public'. It organized 'right-wing talk-ins' and distributed pro-privatization literature to councillors, civil servants and the media.[23]

The ASI had a budget of £200,000 in 1988, mainly from business donations. It worked closely with a collection of Tory MPs calling themselves the No Turning Back group, which was 'devoted to renewing the energy of radical Tory ideas and keeping the Government up to the ideological mark'.[24] The ASI attained a reputation for getting radical ideas turned into policy:

> *It is a handy sort of body for the government to have around. It can trample on taboos, shout the unthinkable, sit back and take the flack. In time the hubbub subsides and in the still reflection that follows the idea no longer seems quite so outrageous. Whereupon along comes a minister and polishes off the job.*[25]

As well as the think tanks there were more secret associations such as the Argonauts, 'a "club" of Thatcher's staunchest allies' including Alfred Sherman, head of CPS; Michael Ivens, director of Aims of Industry; Walter Goldsmith, director-general of the Institute of Directors; and representatives of the National Federation of Building Trades Employers and the Association of British Chambers of Commerce.[26]

According to *The Economist*, 'Politicians looked to the think tanks for instant policies, journalists for instant opinions, and people on the make used them for instant connections.'[27] Academic Simon James says:

> *The tiny handful of think tanks operating in Britain have a very mixed track record. The larger and less ideological amongst them have exercised a moderate influence on certain specific public policy issues. As to the smaller and more ideologically zealous think tanks, most have made no impression worth writing about. But one or two have exercised an influence greatly disproportionate to their size, and played a key role in*

> *making Britain in the 1980s to a surprising extent a testing ground for the ideas of the radical right.*[28]

These think tanks, particularly the CPS, played a major role in setting the policy agenda of the Thatcher government, providing it with most of its policy initiatives, including trade union 'reforms,' privatization of public authorities such as water and electricity, and welfare cuts. Thatcher's chief of staff, economic adviser and all four heads of the No 10 Policy Unit were former contributors to the CPS. The Policy Unit served as a conduit for ideas from CPS and other conservative think tanks.[29]

Even after Margaret Thatcher's departure, the ideas of the conservative think tanks continued to influence Prime Minister John Major, and he continued to apply Thatcher's policies. The Tories had managed to blame the poor performance of the British economy on the global economy rather than government incompetence. Richard Cockett, who has charted the rise of conservative think tanks in Britain in his book *Thinking the Unthinkable*, notes that a new consensus, which included keeping government control of industry to a minimum, has been achieved by those think tanks. The free market ideas of think tanks such as the IEA have become the new conventional wisdom so that even the Labour Party in Britain 'employs the language of economic efficiency and choice, albeit reluctantly'.[30]

> *Furthermore, most of the economic liberal agenda that the Conservative Party espoused during the 1980s was duly adopted by the Labour Party in the wake of their 1987 election defeat ... Indeed, by the 1992 election, it became very hard to tell the two main political parties apart on economic policy.*[31]

R. Desai, writing in *New Left Review*, agrees: 'The Labour Party, by the late 1980s, resigned itself to operating within the political parameters laid down by Thatcherism.' However he adds that the think tanks were disappointed that more of their agenda was not taken up and that 'political and electoral convenience' had continued to remain the overriding consideration of the Thatcher government. He also notes that the wider public was never really converted to economic fundamentalism.[32]

The UK think tanks were emulated in other parts of the world. John Blundell, when president of the IEA, boasted:

> *Starting in the mid-'70s, the IEA model began to be copied around the world, and Antony found himself in great demand as a consultant to such fledgling groups. By the late '70s his mailbag was so large that he incorporated the Atlas Economic Research Foundation to be a focal point for intellectual entrepreneurs wishing to establish independent,*

> *public policy institutes. Today, Atlas lists some 50+ institutes in some 30+ countries that it has helped to establish, develop, and mature.*[33]

US THINK TANKS

In the US too, conservative corporate-funded think tanks have been responsible for the transmission and promotion of free market ideas and policies.

> *These bodies provided a vital arena for fusing academic theories with practical policies and for spreading the new gospel among politicians, officials, academics and the media ... The 'policy intellectuals' in the think tanks, private offices of ministers and the large policy staffs which serve President and Congress adapt the original ideas to what they see as political opportunities. The media are enlisted to spread the ideas in the form of simple, often dogmatic assumptions. Bureaucracies are permeated with new policy directions and axioms. A new ideology is created for political consumption.*[34]

In the US 'think tanks and foundations perform the research and advocacy functions that in many other industrial nations would be undertaken by the organized political parties'. The American political parties do not play much role in policy development and do not have policy research units. It has been suggested that American political parties are not only unable to come up with ideas but that they lack any ideological coherence: 'Think tanks have played a crucial role in building and supporting policy consensus and thereby replaced American parties which tend to work rather as electoral coalitions than as places of ideological discussion and policy planning.'[35]

Ricci, in his book *The Transformation of American Politics*, argues that politicians often lack any vision or philosophy or a coherent set of values that would enable them to deal with the mass of information at their disposal; to distinguish between the 'good and bad, significant and insignificant, relevant and irrelevant'. Politicians and government officials therefore look to experts in the think tanks to interpret and make sense of all that information. This gives rise to a set of policy entrepreneurs based in think tanks who usually have the coherent vision that politicians lack, particularly the conservative think tanks that promote the market place as an alternative to big government.[36]

Corporate-funded neoconservative think tanks proliferated and expanded in the US in the 1970s, promoting the free market and campaigning against big government and government regulation. Their explicit political goals caused them to be referred to as advocacy think tanks. These think tanks helped bring Ronald Reagan to power and then influenced his policies when he was elected president in 1980. 'Virtually every major policy initiative proposed by President Reagan percolated to the White House by means of an ideological filtration system.' As in the UK, the relationship was two-way. Reagan gave the free market ideologues position and status, in return they gave his ideas credibility. According to Feulner of the Heritage Foundation, 'Our presence made Reaganism more acceptable.'[37]

Reagan, who had been a travelling salesman of free market ideology for General Electric in the 1950s, found free market think tanks to be aligned with his own ideological position and that they provided a justification for his pro-business policies.[38]

> *In the Reagan years the view that taxes and regulation were a drag on economic growth became a political dogma, treated by conservatives as revealed truth, needing only to be asserted, not demonstrated.*[39]

Reagan's views that 'government is not the solution, it is the problem' and that 'American people today are overtaxed, over-regulated and over-governed' were clearly influenced by the thinking of Friedman, Hayek and other economic fundamentalists. 'One of the major motifs of Reagan's mythology was the battle of the "special interests" against "the people". Other names for the "special interests" were "big government," or merely "Washington".'[40]

Paul Krugman notes in his book *Peddling Prosperity* that there is 'a constant market for doctrines that play to popular prejudices, whether they make sense or not' and this is particularly the case 'in times of economic stress'. Reagan played to popular prejudices with his images of 'welfare queens driving Cadillacs' and 'rooms full of bureaucrats each taking care of a single Indian'. Although these images 'had relatively little to do with reality', they enabled him to portray America as 'overregulated and overtaxed, groaning under the weight of Big Government' at a time when Americans paid less in tax than people in other affluent nations.[41]

> *As the example of Ronald Reagan shows, real political success comes not simply from appealing to the interests that people currently perceive, but from finding ways to redefine their perceived interests, to harness their discontent in favor of changes that you can lead. In the 1980s, conservatives succeeded in defining a vision of what was wrong with America – Big Government, excessive taxes – that resonated with the American public and gave them an extended lease on power . . .*[42]

The Hoover Institution on War, Revolution and Peace was one of the most influential think tanks during the Reagan presidency. Reagan was one of the Honorary Fellows of the Institution along with Hayek and Margaret Thatcher. Friedman has been a Senior Research Fellow there since his retirement from the University of Chicago in 1977. The Hoover Institution is home to Hayek's collected papers as well as Friedman's. It has a long history dating back to 1919 when it was set up to study communism and was later the beneficiary of a $7 million endowment from the William Volker Fund (see Chapter 7), which was worth some $70 million by the turn of the century.[43]

The American Enterprise Institute (AEI) was also said to have played a key role in the free market political shift in the US in the 1970s and to have been 'a major source of policy advice' to Reagan. It was said to operate 'as the most sophisticated public-relations system in the nation for dissemination of political ideas'.[44]

The AEI had started as a very small operation in 1943 with the aim of restoring 'free-market economics in the aftermath of the New Deal'. It was formed 'as an adjunct to the US Chamber of Commerce' by a group of businessmen who were 'horrified' at 'talk of making wartime price and production controls permanent to prevent another Depression'. Early on it brought in Friedman, then a little known economist, as adviser. One White House official told *The Atlantic* that the AEI played a large part in getting Ronald Reagan elected by making 'conservatism intellectually respectable'. Its promotion of deregulated markets found expression in Reagan policies. By 1985, it employed 176 people, boasted 90 adjunct scholars and a budget of $12.6 million, 45 per cent from some 600 major corporations.[45]

The Heritage Foundation was also extremely influential during the Reagan years. It provided information to members of Congress, and most of its policy recommendations, outlined in a document entitled *Mandate for Change*, were adopted by the Reagan administration. Feulner received a Presidential Citizen's Medal from Ronald Reagan for being 'a leader of the conservative movement ... who has helped shape the policy of our Government'. By 1985 the Foundation was almost as large as AEI. It promoted deregulation of industry, an unrestrained free market and privatization. *The Economist*'s *Good Think-Tank Guide* described the foundation's ideology as 'red-blooded, celebratory capitalism'.[46]

For ideas to have impact they have to be marketed, which is what the free enterprise think tanks understood: 'I make no bones about marketing', said William Baroody Jr, head of the AEI, 'We pay as much attention to dissemination of product as to the content.'[47] AEI used ghost writers to produce op-ed articles on behalf of scholars, and sent them to over a hundred 'cooperating' newspapers at the rate of three articles every two weeks. It was also one of the first think tanks to utilize television and radio broadcasts, producing a monthly show screened on over 400 television stations and a weekly talk show programme for over 180 radio stations. It also produced books; legislative analyses; conferences for policy makers; four magazines, including *Regulation* and *Public Opinion*; and seminars for corporate managers.[48]

It was the Heritage Foundation that perfected the art of marketing ideas and forging contacts. Its policy analysts were assigned policy specialities and 'expected to develop contacts' on key congressional committees; to cultivate congressional staff with lunches; and to keep track of the progress of bills in Congress. The foundation spends only 40 per cent of its budget on actual research. More than half its budget goes on marketing and fund raising, including 35–40 per cent of its budget on public relations. All this marketing enables the Foundation to successfully attract mass media coverage for its publications and policy proposals. The Foundation claims that it usually gets 200 or more stories nationwide from each of the position papers it publishes.[49]

The Foundation produces hundreds of publications every year, including books and a quarterly journal, *Policy Review*. Its speciality is its 'backgrounders' or 'bulletins', which are short essays (between 2 and 20 pages) on current issues – 'brief enough to read in a limousine ride from National Airport to Capitol Hill'. These are provided to government officials, employees and journalists without charge, and are usually personally delivered. The Heritage Foundation, like other think tanks, conducts public opinion polls as a means of – as a Foundation employee put it – 'influencing public opinion, not just reflecting it'.[50]

The Foundation aims its publications at government and the media rather than the public:

> *Its most avid consumers are members of the conservative congressional staffs who must brief their bosses and supply them with legislative arguments, pro or con; the conservative appointee in an executive agency who is leery of relying on the expertise of civil service employees and may want to consult with an ideologically compatible expert; and the journalist who wants to balance an article with insights drawn from an authoritative conservative source.*[51]

Like the Heritage Foundation, the Cato Institute was influential during the Reagan years. The Cato Institute was another of the new generation of Washington-based think tanks established with business money in 1977. It was started with $500,000 from Charles Koch, whose father, businessman Fred Koch, had helped to found the John Birch Society. Koch was CEO of oil/chemical conglomerate Koch Industries.[52] Cato campaigns for reduced government and deregulation of the economy. It calls for many government functions to be turned over to the private sector, and the extremity of some of its views has occasionally brought it into ridicule. According to *The Economist*:

> *Cato's vision, taken to its logical extreme (and people at the institute are keen on taking things to their logical extremes), would be an America in which a family does whatever it likes at home; pays virtually no taxes and expects no state provision or support; has its own tank and machine gun for defence; and ignores other countries. In short, an updated version of the Wild West.*[53]

William Niskanen was acting chair of Reagan's Council of Economic Advisers in 1985 when he left to become chair of the Cato Institute. He was previously a director of economics at the Ford Motor Company, a founder of the National Tax Limitation Committee and a defence analyst at the Pentagon.[54]

MECHANISMS OF INFLUENCE

Think tanks in the US are very well-resourced because of the funding they receive from corporations and wealthy foundations. The Heritage Foundation is now the wealthiest Washington-based think tank with an annual budget of around $35 million, thanks to direct corporate donations, and indirect corporate donations through conservative foundations and individuals. Donor corporations include automobile manufacturers, coal, oil, chemical and tobacco companies.[55] Similarly, most of the Cato Institute's annual budget of around $16 million comes from private grants and gifts from foundations, including the Sarah Scaife, Olin and Bradley Foundations; individuals; and corporations, including Philip Morris, American Express, the American Petroleum Institute, Exxon, Shell Oil, Eli Lilly and Pfizer.[56]

The AEI had an annual budget of around $18 million in 2002. Its board of directors is largely made up of the CEOs of large corporations including American Express, Dow Chemical and ExxonMobil. Its major donors include various foundations such as the Olin Foundation, the Scaife Foundation, Lynde and Harry Bradley Foundation and many corporations including General Electric, Ford, General Motors, Eastman Kodak, Proctor & Gamble Fund, and Shell.[57]

To influence government and set the agenda in a variety of policy arenas, think tanks insinuate themselves into the networks of people who are influential in particular areas of policy. They do this by organizing conferences, seminars and workshops and by publishing books, briefing papers, school kits, journals and media releases for policy-makers, journalists and people able to sway those policy-makers. They liaise with bureaucrats, consultants, interest groups, lobbyists and others. They take advantage of informal social networks – clubs, business, family, school/university. They seek to provide advice directly to the government

Table 8.1 *Donations by selected foundations to selected think tanks 1985–2002*

	Hoover Institution	*AEI*	*Heritage Foundation*	*Cato Institute*
Sarah Scaife Foundations[58]	$7.6 million	$4.4 million	$17 million	$1.8 million
Lynde and Harry Bradley Foundations[59]	$1.7 million	$15 million		$13 million
John M. Olin Foundation[60]	$5 million	$7 million	$8 million	$800,000
Koch Family Foundations[61]	$5000	–	$1 million	$12.5 million
Smith Richardson Foundation[62]	$1.3 million	$4 million	–	–
1999 only				
Selected Corporate Foundations[63]	$128,000	$1.6 million	$341,000	$241,000

Source: Media Transparency, 'The Strategic Philanthropy of Conservative Foundations', www.mediatransparency.org/movement.htm; G. W. Domhoff. *Who Rules America? Power and Politics*, 4th edn. McGraw Hill, New York, 2002, p83

officials in policy networks and to government agencies and committees through consultancies or through testimony at hearings. Ultimately, think tank employees become policy-makers themselves, having established their credentials as a vital part of the relevant issue network.

In the US, think tanks participate directly in policy-making because policy-makers seek advice from them. One survey published in 1982 found that most 'officials in the Department of State, the Central Intelligence Agency, the National Security Council, and the Department of Defense' were more influenced in the long-term by think tanks than by public opinion or special-interest groups, and many were more influenced by think tanks than by the media or interaction with members of Congress. A more recent survey of congressional staff and journalists covering government affairs found that over 90 per cent of them believed think tanks were still influential in American politics.[64]

In their efforts to influence and become part of the policy-making process, think tanks have more in common with interest groups or pressure groups than academic institutions. Nevertheless, employees of think tanks are treated by the media as independent experts and are often preferred to experts from universities or interest groups as a source of expert opinion because they are articulate and trained to perfect the TV sound bite and give quotable quotes for newspapers. When they appear as experts on television shows or are quoted in the newspapers they have more credibility than a company expert or a representative of a business association, even though they may be pushing the same line.[65] They regularly write newspaper opinion pieces and give newspaper interviews. Many write their own newspaper columns.

More important, however, than their ability to shape individual policies, has been the ability of the conservative think tanks to move the whole policy agenda to the right.

> *First, they help to set the agenda of the political debate. They inject arguments (neatly packaged for a copy-hungry media) into the public arena before they are raised by politicians. This both softens up public opinion and pushes the consensus farther to the right.*[66]

An additional function that think tanks provide in the US, which is often done by the political party in other countries, is facilitation of 'elite transfer'. In countries such as Britain and Australia, Cabinet ministers are chosen from the elected members of government. In the US this is not necessarily the case. Additionally, the American system allows each new administration to appoint its own senior bureaucrats, including the staff of government departments, heads of departments and advisory councils. These are not necessarily selected from the public service, as was once the case in other countries.[67]

This means that when a new government is elected, top-level personnel in the administrative arm of government are changed for people whose ideology is more suited to the incoming government. Think tanks provide a source of such personnel. Whereas once administrations had been staffed with businessmen and party officials, presidents from Jimmy Carter through to George W. Bush have made wide use of think tank personnel to fill high-level government positions. Reagan chose people from the think tanks and free market policy networks to staff his administration along with the businessmen and party officials. Some 150 of his administration came from the Heritage Foundation, the Hoover Institution and the AEI alone.[68]

Think tanks provide a fast track to a political career and a public profile in the policy arena. They also provide a place for discarded government officials to go when there is a change of government, where they can be employed until 'their' government is re-elected while still having some influence over public policy while they are waiting. They form a sort of informal shadow government.[69] AEI played host to several members of the Ford administration when Gerald Ford left office – including Ford himself, who also became a resident fellow there – and also to members of the Reagan administration when Reagan left office. Describing this process as a 'carousel of power', *The Economist* said:

> *Now that Mr Reagan has left power, many of his appointees, such as Jeane Kirkpatrick and Richard Perle, are working at AEI. Every American think tank director has a dream and a nightmare. The dream is to house the next administration; the nightmare is to house the last one. AEI seems to have managed both in the course of a decade.*[70]

The circulation of personnel suits the think tanks well. Employing ex-government officials gives a think tank access to politicians and others in government and attracts the funds of corporations who want access. When a think tank's employees are taken up by a new administration, the think tank has its best chance to have its ideas and agenda accepted by the government and to influence policy. Those employees are then able to recommend others in the think tank for government positions.

With an eye to the revolving door between think tanks and government positions, the Heritage Foundation and the Cato Institute have sought to nurture a new generation of conservative leaders within their ranks by sponsoring college students and promising junior bureaucrats and providing them with a place to meet and socialize. The Heritage Foundation also promotes a 'talent bank' of potential candidates for official positions in government administrations on the premise that its policies will be more influential if its people are in positions of influence.[71]

> *In the past two decades, the most important function served by the network of conservative think tanks has not been the germination of new ideas, but the creation of a 'new cadre' of professionals ... Not only have the dozens of conservative think tanks created a framework*

> *for disseminating ideas that exist largely outside the established infrastructure of academic journals, university presses, and commercial publishing ... they have also designed career vehicles for conservative activists and thinkers.*[72]

Think tanks have become essential vehicles of business propaganda and policy marketing. Rather than just react to proposed government policies, in the 1970s, US corporations began to initiate policies more actively and shepherd them through the policy-making process till they became government policy. Think tanks enabled them to do this. The more government was attacked and its role reduced, the more freedom and opportunities were provided to business.

NOTES

1 John Gray, *False Dawn: The Delusions of Global Capitalism*, London, Granta Books, 2002, pp103–4.
2 Lee Edwards, *et al.*, *The Power of Ideas: The Heritage Foundation at 25 Years*, Jameson Books, 1998.
3 Dan Baum, *Citizen Coors: A Grand Family Saga of Politics, Business, and Beer*, New York, Perennial, 2001, p105.
4 'Joseph Coors', Dkosopedia, www.dkosopedia.com/index.php/Joseph_Coors accessed 18 December 2004; Harold Jackson, 'Joseph Coors: The Man Who Bought the White House for Ronald Reagan', *The Guardian*, 19 March 2003; Edwin J. Feulner, 'Coors, R.I.P'. *National Review*, 18 March 2003, www.nationalreview.com/comment/comment-feulner031803.asp.
5 www.montpelerin.org/pastpresidents.html.
6 Edwin J. Feulner, 'Ideas, Think-Tanks and Governments: Away from the Power Elite, Back to the People', *Quadrant*, November, 1985, p22.
7 *Ibid.*, pp22–3; Feulner cited in Alex Carey, 'Conspiracy or Groundswell?' in Ken Coghill (ed) *The New Right's Australian Fantasy*, Fitzroy, Victoria, McPhee Gribble and Penguin Books, 1987, p14.
8 Jerry M. Landay, 'The Powell Manifesto', Mediatransparency.org, 20 August 2002, www.mediatransparency.org/stories/powell.htm; Eric Alterman, 'Fighting Smart', *Mother Jones*, vol 19, no 4, 1994, p59.
9 Kirkpatrick Sale, *The Green Revolution: The American Environmental Movement, 1962–1992*, Hill and Wang, New York, 1993, p49; Landay, 'The Powell Manifesto'; Jerome L. Himmelstein, *To the Right: The Transformation of American Conservatism*, Berkeley, California, University of California Press, 1990, pp129, 146.
10 R. Desai, 'Second-Hand Dealers in Ideas: Think-Tanks and Thatcherite Hegemony', *New Left Review*, vol 203, no Jan–Feb, 1994, p29; 'Of Policy and Pedigree', *The Economist*, 6 May 1989, p53.
11 Greg Lindsay, 'The CIS at Twenty: Greg Lindsay Talks to Andrew Norton', *Policy*, Winter, 1996, www.cis.org.au/glint.htm, p18; Disinfopedia, 'Antony Fisher', Center for Media & Democracy, 3 July 2004, www.disinfopedia.or/wiki.phtml?title=Antony_

Fisher; William Cran and Daniel Yergin, 'The Commanding Heights: The Battle for the World Economy', Public Broadcasting Service, 2002, www.pbs.org/wgbh/commandingheights/; Richard Cockett, *Thinking the Unthinkable: Think-Tanks and the Economic Counter-Revolution 1931–1983*, Harper Collins, 1994; Desai, 'Second-Hand Dealers in Ideas', p140; Desai, 'Second-Hand Dealers in Ideas', p29.

12 Nigel Ashford, 'Politically Impossible? How Ideas, Not Interests and Circumstances, Determine Public Policies', *Policy*, Autumn, 1997, p22; Peter Self, *Government by the Market? The Politics of Public Choice*, Hampshire and London, Macmillan, 1993, p65.

13 Cockett, *Thinking the Unthinkable*; Desai, 'Second-Hand Dealers in Ideas', pp29, 183–4, 188–9.

14 Ashford, 'Politically Impossible?', p23; Daniel Yergin and Joseph Stanislaw, *The Commanding Heights: The Battle between Government and the Marketplace That Is Remaking the World*, New York, Simon & Schuster, 1998, pp92–105; Susan George, 'How to Win the War of Ideas', *Dissent*, vol 44, no 3, 1997.

15 Yergin and Stanislaw, *The Commanding Heights*, pp105–110.

16 Cockett, *Thinking the Unthinkable*; Desai, 'Second-Hand Dealers in Ideas', p30; Simon James, 'The Idea Brokers: The Impact of Think Tanks on British Government', *Public Administration*, vol 71, no Winter, 1993, pp132, 182–3, 237.

17 Desai, 'Second-Hand Dealers in Ideas'.

18 *Ibid.*

19 Daniel Butler, 'Radicals without Reins', *Accountancy*, vol 116, no 1224, 1995.

20 Desai, 'Second-Hand Dealers in Ideas', p31; James, 'The Idea Brokers', p497; Thatcher quoted in Cockett, *Thinking the Unthinkable*, p173.

21 Quoted in Yergin and Stanislaw, *The Commanding Heights*.

22 Dexter Whitfield, *Making It Public: Evidence and Action against Privatisation*, London, Pluto Press, 1983, p47; Adam Smith Institute, 'The Adam Smith Institute', Adam Smith Institute, www.adamsmith.org.uk/ accessed 7 May 2001.

23 Ashford, 'Politically Impossible?', p24; Whitfield, *Making It Public*, p46.

24 Robin Oakley, 'Privatized Policy-Making for the Tory Right', *The Times*, 17 February 1989; Alan Rusbridger, 'A Thought for Tomorrow', *The Guardian*, 22 December 1987.

25 Rusbridger, 'A Thought for Tomorrow'.

26 Whitfield, *Making It Public*, p47.

27 'The Good Think-Tank Guide', *The Economist*, vol 321, no 7738, 1992.

28 James, 'The Idea Brokers', p492.

29 Desai, 'Second-Hand Dealers in Ideas', pp32, 34; James, 'The Idea Brokers', pp322, 497, 501.

30 Gray, *False Dawn*, p33; Cockett, *Thinking the Unthinkable*.

31 Cockett, *Thinking the Unthinkable*, p322.

32 Desai, 'Second-Hand Dealers in Ideas', p60.

33 John Blundell, 'Waging the War of Ideas: Why There Are No Shortcuts', Atlas Economic Research Foundation, January, 1990, www.atlasusa.org/toolkit/waging_war.php.

34 Self, *Government by the Market?* pp65, 69.

35 William Greider, *Who Will Tell the People: The Betrayal of American Democracy*, New York, Simon & Schuster, 1992, p52; Winand Gellner, 'The Politics of Policy "Political Think Tanks" and Their Markets in the US Institutional Environment', *Presidential Studies Quarterly*, vol 25, no 3, 1995, p505.
36 David Ricci, *The Transformation of American Politics: The New Washington and the Rise of Think Tanks*, New Haven, Yale University Press, 1993, pp41–49.
37 Sidney Blumenthal, *The Rise of the Counter-Establishment: From Conservative Ideology to Political Power*, New York, Time Books, 1986, pp8, 36.
38 *Ibid.*, p250.
39 Paul Krugman, *Peddling Prosperity: Economic Sense and Nonsense in the Age of Diminished Expectations*, New York, W.W. Norton, 1994, p65.
40 Reagan quoted in Marian Sawer, 'Political Manifestations of Australian Libertarianism', in Marian Sawer (ed) *Australia and the New Right*, North Sydney, George Allen & Unwin, 1982, p14; Blumenthal, *The Rise of the Counter-Establishment*, p9.
41 Krugman, *Peddling Prosperity*, ppxiii, 6–7.
42 *Ibid.*, p7.
43 Sawer, 'Political Manifestations of Australian Libertarianism', p14; George, 'How to Win the War of Ideas'; Jane Knoerle, 'Local Family Endows Chair at Hoover Institution', *The Almanac*, 26 June 2002, www.almanacnews.com/morgue/2002/2002_06_26.hoover.html.
44 Mark T. Berger, *The Battle for Asia: From Decolonization to Globalization*, New York, RoutledgeCurzon, 2004, p150; Bette Moore and Gary Carpenter, 'Main Players', in Ken Coghill (ed) *The New Right's Australian Fantasy*, Fitzroy, Victoria, McPhee Gribble and Penguin Books, 1987, p146.
45 G. William Domhoff, *Who Rules America? Power and Politics*, 4th edn, New York, McGraw Hill, 2002, p79; Blumenthal, *The Rise of the Counter-Establishment*, pp32–42; AEI, 'AEI's Diamond Jubilee, 1943–2003', American Enterprise Institute for Public Policy Research, 2004, www.aei.org/about/contentID.20031212154735838/default.asp.
46 James A. Smith, *The Idea Brokers: Think Tanks and the Rise of the New Policy Elite*, New York, Free Press, 1991, pp200, 286; 'The Good Think-Tank Guide'; Ricci, *The Transformation of American Politics*; John S. Saloma, *Ominous Politics: The New Conservative Labyrinth*, New York, Hill and Wang, 1984, p29.
47 Quoted in Blumenthal, *The Rise of the Counter-Establishment*, p43.
48 *Ibid.*, p44.
49 *Ibid.*, p48; Gellner, 'The Politics of Policy "Political Think Tanks"', p502; Christopher Georges, 'Conservative Heritage Foundation Finds Recipe for Influence: Ideas Plus Marketing Equal Clout', *Wall Street Journal*, August 10 1995; R. Kent Weaver, 'The Changing World of Think Tanks', *PS: Political Science and Politics*, vol 22, no September, 1989, p572; Smith, *The Idea Brokers*, p287.
50 Bencivenga cited in Donald E. Abelson, 'From Policy Research to Political Advocacy: The Changing Role of Think Tanks in American Politics', *Canadian Review of American Studies*, vol 25, no 1, 1995, p106; Jeffrey L. Katz, 'The Conservative Idea Machine', *Governing*, February, 1992; Weaver, 'The Changing World of Think Tanks', pp161–2.
51 Smith, *The Idea Brokers*.
52 People for the American Way, 'Right Wing Organizations: Cato Institute', People for the American Way, March, 2003, www.pfaw.org/pfaw/general/default.aspx?oid=9261;

'Koch Industries', Wikipedia: the Free Encyclopedia, 16 November 2004, http://en.wikipedia.org/wiki/Koch_Industries.

53 'The Good Think-Tank Guide'.

54 William A. Niskanen, 'Cato Institute', Cato Institute, 1995, www.cato.org/people/niskanen.html 1995; 'The Good Think-Tank Guide'.

55 People for the American Way, 'Right Wing Organizations: Heritage Foundation', People for the American Way, September, 2002, www.pfaw.org/pfaw/general/default.aspx?oid=4287; Sharon Beder, *Global Spin: The Corporate Assault on Environmentalism*, 2nd edn, Devon, Green Books, 2002, p79; Heritage Foundation, 'Consolidated Financial Statements and Supplemental Schedules of Functional Expenses for the Years Ended December 31, 2003 and 2002, and Independent Auditors Report', Washington, DC, Heritage Foundation, 2004, p12.

56 People for the American Way, 'Right Wing Organizations: Cato Institute'.

57 AEI, 'Finances', American Enterprise Institute for Public Policy Research, 2004, www.aei.org/about/contentID.20021215114 15722/default.asp; People for the American Way, 'Right Wing Organizations: American Enterprise Institute', People for the American Way, September, 2002, www.pfaw.org/pfaw/general/default.aspx?oid=4456.

58 www.mediatransparency.org/search_results/recipientsoffunder.php?providerID=3.

59 www.mediatransparency.org/search_results/recipientsoffunder.php?providerID=1.

60 www.mediatransparency.org/search_results/display_recipients_by_olin_total.htm.

61 www.mediatransparency.org/search_results/kochaggregate.php.

62 www.mediatransparency.org/search_results/recipientsoffunder.php?providerID=6.

63 Domhoff, *Who Rules America?* p83.

64 Cited in Ricci, *The Transformation of American Politics*, p2 and Strobe Talbott, 'The Brookings Institution: How a Think Tank Works', *US Foreign Policy Agenda*, vol 7, no 3, 2002.

65 Gellner, 'The Politics of Policy "Political Think Tanks"', p505; Ricci, *The Transformation of American Politics*, p162.

66 'Of Policy and Pedigree', p54.

67 'Think-Tanks: The Carousels of Power', *The Economist*, 1991; Abelson, 'From Policy Research to Political Advocacy: The Changing Role of Think Tanks in American Politics'; Gellner, 'The Politics of Policy "Political Think Tanks"', p499; Smith, *The Idea Brokers*, pxv; Weaver, 'The Changing World of Think Tanks', pp570–1.

68 Blumenthal, *The Rise of the Counter-Establishment*, p33; Richard N. Haass, 'Think Tanks and US Foreign Policy: A Policy-Maker's Perspective', *US Foreign Policy Agenda*, vol 7, no 3, 2002.

69 Abelson, 'From Policy Research to Political Advocacy: The Changing Role of Think Tanks in American Politics'; Smith, *The Idea Brokers*, pp206–7; Weaver, 'The Changing World of Think Tanks', pp569, 571; Haass, 'Think Tanks and US Foreign Policy'.

70 'Think-Tanks: The Carousels of Power'.

71 Gellner, 'The Politics of Policy "Political Think Tanks"', p500; David Stoesz, 'Policy Gambit: Conservative Think Tanks Take on the Welfare State', *Journal of Sociology and Social Welfare*, vol 14, no 4, 1987; Smith, *The Idea Brokers*, p207.

72 Smith, *The Idea Brokers*, p206.

9

Think Tanks Down Under

[N]o one can doubt the tremendous success that the 'New Right' American and British policy organisations and think tanks have had in cloning themselves in Australia, and then in reorganising the public policy agenda along Anglo-American 'free' market lines – continental European social democratic experience is excluded almost to the point of invisibility.

MICHAEL PUSEY[1]

The Liberal Prime Minister Malcolm Fraser invited economists Friedrich von Hayek and Milton Friedman (see Chapter 7) to Australia after he was elected in 1975 and they 'had numerous meetings with businessmen, central bankers, government officials, especially those concerned with economic policy, and faculties and students at universities'. Their visits 'inspired the formation of several right-wing think tanks, the most influential of which were the Centre for Independent Studies in Sydney and the Centre for Policy Studies in Melbourne'. These think tanks promoted a free market economic rationalist agenda in Australia and were the leading 'ideas factories' in the 1980s.[2]

The Centre for Independent Studies (CIS) was established on a small basis in 1976 under the leadership of Greg Lindsay. Lindsay still heads CIS today and is on the board of directors of the Mont Pèlerin Society. CIS's inspiration was said to be the UK Institute of Economic Affairs (IEA) and Lindsay recalls meeting with Anthony Fisher, head of the IEA, to discuss his plans to set up an Australian think tank along the lines of the IEA. He was encouraged in this by various business leaders from Broken Hill Proprietary Co. (BHP), Conzinc Riotinto Australia (CRA), Western Mining Corporation and Shell. Lindsay had been influenced by reading Ayn Rand, Hayek, Friedman and Ludwig von Mises and attracted by the value they placed on the individual. CIS's early Council of Advisers included Hayek as well as Australian economics professors, sociologists and philosopher Lauchlan Chipman, whom Lindsay had also consulted about the setting up of his think tank.[3]

Lindsay had been active in the Workers' Party, which had been formed the year before by advertising man John Singleton and others. Despite its name, it sought to promote Friedman's economic views and libertarian political philosophy. Singleton published a book, *Rip Van Australia*, with the co-founder of the Workers'

Party, Bob Howard. The book had a foreword by mining magnate Lang Hancock and espoused the 'philosophy of absolute freedom, absolute capitalism'.[4] It said of government bureaucracy that it:

> *... is a gigantic Wettex soaking up human energy, ideas, wealth, initiative, creativity and time ... Modern bureaucracies ... trade in privilege, power, influence, status, votes and, a distant last in most cases, public service ... They are, in the true sense of the word, parasites. They hinder and feed off the productive efforts of others.*[5]

Using the argument of public choice (see Chapter 7), without referring to the theory, the book explains how the State deals in privilege, with the various special-interest groups from big companies to welfare lobbies, women's lobbies, Aboriginal lobbies, all 'vigorously jostling one another for a position at the public trough'.[6] 'Politicians buy the votes of vested interests... by distributing privilege.'[7]

The book extolled a pure form of capitalism, one described by the Austrian school of economics and people such as von Mises and Hayek, but which has never actually existed: 'A proper free market is consistent with individual freedom.'[8] Actual free markets have always been distorted by government intervention. The market, according to the book, is more important than democracy, which, is 'inherently immoral' because it means majority rule, that is coercion of people by a majority.[9]

With the help of Singleton, the Workers' Party achieved wide media coverage. It fielded candidates in the 1975 federal election under the slogan 'less tax, less government, more freedom', and again in the 1977 federal election, gaining up to 18.6 per cent of the vote in one electorate. In 1979 it changed its name in most states to the Progress Party. It pushed for deregulation and a flat uniform tax of 20 per cent, and was against minimum wage laws. It faded out in the 1980s but not before the major parties had taken on some of its policies, such as less taxation.[10]

Other organizations formed at this time included the Society for Individual Liberty, the Foundation for Economic Education, the Society for the Development of Austrian Economics and the Adam Smith Club.[11]

In 1979, when CIS was still a part-time hobby of Lindsay's, he approached Hugh Morgan, CEO of Western Mining Corporation (now WMC), one of the world's largest mining companies, for support. Morgan, whose father had been managing director of Western Mining before him, was described in the *Sydney Morning Herald* in 1985 as 'the most important conservative figure in Australia. He is not merely an outspoken captain of industry, he is at the centre of a large and growing network of activists who are seeking to reshape the political agenda in this country.'[12]

Morgan also played leadership roles in the mining industry, including formal roles in the Australian Mining Industry Council and the Western Australian Chamber of Mines, and it is said that 'Morgan serves as a public affairs icebreaker for industry in general and the mining industry in particular.'[13] Morgan was a major supporter of market-oriented think tanks. He identified four targets that he and his networks were concentrating on: the education system, the growth of the public sector, the power of trade unions and the arbitration system. He was also critical of sectors of the church establishment for focusing on wealth distribution rather than wealth creation.[14] Morgan, now retired from WMC, is head of the Business Council of Australia.

Morgan recognized that you can't just change public opinion on one issue. Rather it has to be 'over a wide front through a broadly-based campaign'. He chaired the Australian Lecture Foundation (ALF) which provided funds and organizational resources for bringing prominent free market speakers to Australia from the US and the UK during the 1980s. These speakers would be featured by various think tanks. This was considered to be a very economical way to get exposure for free market ideas. Morgan told *Herald* journalist Paul Sheehan that the corporate funding of think tanks was also a way to 'reshape the political agenda ... Politicians can only accept what is in public opinion polls, so we have to change public opinion.'[15]

Following the approach from Lindsay, Morgan rang around his business colleagues and got a funding commitment of $40,000 per year for the following five years for CIS from WMC, CRA, BHP, Shell, Santos and *The Advertiser*. This enabled Lindsay to become its full-time director and CIS to have an office in St Leonards. Today CIS has offices in Sydney and Wellington, NZ. It runs seminars, workshops and conferences, and publishes books and monographs as well as a journal entitled *Policy*. It runs free weekend seminars for students 'who are committed to learning and exchanging ideas about classical liberalism'.[16]

Although it claims to be independent, the CIS gets two-thirds of its funding from foundations and businesses[17] and its work is shaped by its free market philosophy. Greg Lindsay is, in fact, a vice president of the Mont Pèlerin Society; in the 1980s CIS organized the Pacific Regional Meeting of the Mont Pèlerin Society. CIS is committed to 'an economy based on free and competitive markets' and 'individual liberty and choice', including 'the right to property'. It claims government decision-making should be turned over to the market and that the market and its automatic pricing mechanism should be used to allocate resources. It has strong links with the Washington-based Cato Institute (see Chapter 8).[18]

CIS deals with 'practical public policy issues' as well as 'more intellectual issues focusing on the way societies work and the importance of liberty in securing prosperity both economically and socially'. It publishes the work of various conservatives, including media baron Rupert Murdoch; economists such as Hayek and Friedman; conservative US law professor and 'takings' expert, Richard Epstein; Nick Greiner, a former premier of New South Wales; and various think tank scholars from the US and the UK. 'We are the retailers and wholesalers of ideas' says Lindsay.[19]

HATCHING ECONOMIC RATIONALISM

Businessmen played a central role in setting up, funding and promoting CIS and other free-market organizations that flourished in the 1970s and 1980s, and staffing their boards. These organizations imported US free-market think tank material into Australia – for example from the Cato Institute, the Reason Foundation and the Foundation for Economic Education (FEE – see Chapter 4). Other businessmen involved include media mogul Rupert Murdoch, Elders IXL's John Elliott, and former head of the Australian Stock Exchange, Ian Roach. Mining and resources companies have been prominent funders including WMC, Santos, Shell Australia, CRA and BHP.[20]

The growth of these conservative business-financed think tanks contributed to the 'new prominence of neo-conservative ideas in economic debate in Australia', which was labelled the 'New Right'.[21] However, economic policy advisers and civil servants also played a vital role in both Australia and New Zealand, as did 'a network of well-funded research institutions, staffed mostly by market-oriented economists', including 'the Industries Assistance Commission, the research arms of the Treasury and the Department of Finance, the Bureau of Agricultural Economics, Industry Economics and Labour Market Research'.[22]

In Australia the free market ideology promoted by these think tanks came to be known as economic rationalism.[23] It embodied a belief that 'economic resources are better allocated through market forces than by government intervention' or, alternatively, 'a doctrine that seeks to extend market principles to as many aspects of human life as possible'. Kenneth Davidson, the economics editor of *The Age* and an exception amongst economics journalists, noted in 1992:

> *Economic rationalism dominates the universities, the central or coordinating bureaucracies, the privately endowed think tanks, the business lobbies, and the media.*[24]

For critics the ideology was anything but rational but for vested interests, particularly business interests; it was entirely rational. In operation it meant that 'considerations of economic cooperation and social justice' were subordinated to 'the principles of the free market, private enterprise' and individual incentives. Government functions and services were judged by narrow economic criteria rather than their responsiveness to social needs.[25]

Another reason for labelling the new policies as economic rationalism, pointed out by political economist Frank Stilwell, was that it was based on theoretical reasoning rather than practical experience: 'Markets are efficient. There is inefficiency in Australian industry. Ergo, market forces must be given freer rein . . .'.[26] The policy agenda of those who subscribed to 'a hard-line free-market approach', included freeing up the labour market through lowering youth wages, decentralizing wage fixing, repealing the arbitration system and individual labour agreements. It also included deregulation to promote efficiency, competition and productivity, privatization of government authorities, and reducing the size of government by cutting back government functions and spending, reducing taxation and welfare and contracting out public service functions to the private sector.[27]

Since the late 1970s, think tanks have proliferated in Australia and to a lesser extent in New Zealand. This has been especially so during the 1990s. In 1990 there were 15, by 1993 there were 75. Most of them were pro-market and opposed to government intervention. As in the US and UK, their inspiration came from economists such as Hayek and Friedman. They constantly reiterated the unbreakable 'connection between economic and political freedom', and 'their long-term aim is to re-define the terms of debate on political and social issues in ways favourable' to the corporations that fund them.[28]

These think tanks particularly targeted elite opinion.[29] Writing in the *Australian Financial Review* in 1990, Tom Dusevic observed:

> *... the plethora of think tanks which has emerged in recent times ... have sought to set the agenda, influence government policies and get their doctrines into the mainstream.*
>
> *To do this they have waged what has amounted to the greatest propaganda exercise outside wartime. Their targets are the intellectual elites in politics, the bureaucracy, business and the media.*[30]

The think tanks provided research and data to support the corporate push for the economic rationalist agenda, and fed the media and the school system with specially tailored information. At the time, Australia was facing some economic problems such as high inflation and low economic growth, and these think tanks represented the situation as an economic crisis caused by a failure of the welfare state. They attacked government and union power and spending and praised the virtues of free and unimpeded enterprise.[31]

Although these corporate-funded pro-market think tanks still used the 'old boys networks' of 'the club, the state, the media, the university, etc.', they 'developed new ways of operating, for example, the conference circuit, and the journal' as well as the submission, the report, and the consultancy; all used to apply 'focused pressure on target bodies'.[32] A number of Australian think tanks are modelled on US think tanks and have close ties with some of them, including the Heritage Foundation, the Cato Institute and the American Enterprise Institute.[33] Millions of dollars were being channelled into these organizations each year for the promotion of conservative, market-oriented ideas.[34]

PROLIFERATING THINK TANKS

The Centre for Policy Studies (CPS), based at Monash University, was founded and headed by Professor Michael Porter, a member of the Mont Pèlerin Society. It was set up with money from the US Ford Foundation and critics suggested it was little more than 'a conduit for US neo-classical debate, rather than an initiator of new areas of inquiry and technique', and was 'too little concerned with real-world obstacles to reform'. Although underwritten by the university, the centre attracted corporate funds from bodies such as the Australian Mining Industry Council and Alcoa Australia. The centre was committed to deregulation and the substitution of government intervention by market forces. It argued for reduced government spending but received a $500,000 a year subsidy from the government. Both CIS and CPS hosted seminars by Friedman when he came to Australia in 1981.[35]

Porter established high-level relationships in New Zealand (NZ), forming a friendship with Roger Douglas while he was still in opposition, and a strong relationship with NZ Treasury officials. When Labour came to power in NZ there was a regular interchange between CPS and Treasury with visits back and forth.[36]

CPS did 'high-level research' for the Australian and NZ governments as well as government authorities and private companies, particularly on privatization and making electricity and telecommunications provision competitive. Porter espoused public choice theory. He argued that government enterprises 'are captured by interest groups'; for example, that the Department of Aviation was run for airlines.[37]

CPS received government funding until 1987. It was also paid $1.5 million over three years by the Business Council of Australia (BCA), the Confederation of Australian Industry, the Australian Small Business Association, the Australian Chamber of Commerce and the Australian Employers' Federation for a research project entitled the National Priorities Project. The project was to examine government spending and taxation, a key priority area being the promotion of a flat tax system.[38]

Centre 2000, a smaller, more short-lived think tank, was established in 1979 to support economic and individual liberty and argue the case for the free market. It mobilized support amongst disaffected farmers in rural areas, and it sponsored student competitions and donated text books advocating free markets to schools and universities (see Chapter 6). Rather than carrying out its own research, it marketed free market ideas, using street theatre, publications and pubic relations.[39]

Crossroads was a discussion group formed in 1977 by John Hyde, former Liberal politician and leader of the economic rationalists or 'dries' in the Fraser Liberal government. It started off as the core of the Liberal Party 'dries' and expanded to include politicians, businessmen and academics including Andrew Hay, Rod and David Kemp, Hugh Morgan, Michael Porter, John Stone, Nick

Greiner and Ian McLachlan of the National Farmers' Federation, as well as NZ Business Roundtable members and NZ politicians, including Ruth Richardson. It held its first conference in 1980 and met twice a year until at least 1997. The group became 'a network, a political cell for market policies, a talkfest, a lobby group'.[40]

> *[T]hose who joined later became, with some exceptions, the nucleus of the 'free market' counter-establishment of the 1980s. Those who stuck gave their careers, minds, or money to the cause. Within the decade, the Crossroads core group and its ideas had taken control of non-Labor politics in Australia.*[41]

Crossroads produced no written documents and was referred to by Porter as a 'secret society'. It created front groups for particular campaigns, such as the Car Owners' Association, which placed large anti-tariff advertisements. Porter admits that Crossroads plotted and schemed but 'only for the benefit of the country'. Crossroads was said to have been behind the formation of the H. R. Nicholls Society.[42]

The H. R. Nicholls Society was set up in 1986 to attack union power and the arbitration system and advocate a deregulated labour market. Its members included industrial lawyers, politicians, employers, farmers and business people, as well as academics. Mining companies were particularly well represented, as was the National Farmers' Federation. Founders included Michael Porter, John Stone and Peter Costello. Hugh Morgan's personal assistant, Ray Evans, a member of the Mont Pèlerin Society, also played a major role in the formation of the society and became its president.[43] At its first meeting, Hugh Morgan, chair of Western Mining (WMC) presented a paper entitled *The Nature of Trade Union Power*. He says of the society: 'The advent of the H R Nicholls Society will, I am confident, rank in Australia's history with the discovery of a major orebody, and tonight's book launching compares with the production of the first refined metal.'[44]

Porter set up a private think tank, the Tasman Economic Research Institute – now the Tasman Institute – in 1990, with the backing of businessmen including Hugh Morgan, Rupert Murdoch, John Elliott and Dick Pratt. Former NZ finance minister Roger Douglas was its deputy chair. Tasman was set up with $50,000 contributions from six different corporations and $100,000 from Porter himself. By 1991 it had 38 corporate members including Arthur Andersen, the Australian Coal Association, the Australian Mining Industry Council, BHP, BP, Shell, CRA, Esso, Western Mining Corporation, ICI, News Limited, the New Zealand Business Roundtable, and the Electricity Corporation of New Zealand. It worked closely with the NZ Business Roundtable and awarded the inaugural Tasman Medal for 'services to economic reform' to Roger Kerr, director of the Roundtable. The second recipient of the Tasman Medal was Ray Evans (see above).[45]

The Tasman Institute, like CPS, is heavily influenced by US neoconservative thinking. Its Research Council includes several US professors. Tasman also has considerable NZ links. Of particular note is the presence and influence of New Zealanders Rod Deane on the Advisory Council (1991), Roger Douglas, as co-founder and co-chairman in 1991, and John Fernyhough as director in 1991.[46]

Another prominent Australian conservative think tank, and the oldest, is the Institute of Public Affairs (IPA). It was set up in 1943 by a group of Melbourne businessmen concerned that the use of government intervention to regulate Australian society during the war might be extended into peacetime. The IPA's mission was to oppose the Australian Labor Party (ALP) and assist with the establishment of the Liberal Party and the development of policies for it.[47] Branches were formed in other states.

The IPA began publishing *Review* in 1947. According to David Kemp – whose father Charles 'Ref' Kemp was a founding member and director of the IPA – and who became a minister of the Liberal government (1997–2004), this publication 'has been perhaps the single most influential private source of liberal economic analysis over the years, both within the Liberal Party and beyond'.[48] (David Kemp was influential, as a speech writer for Malcolm Fraser. Whilst Fraser implemented few free-market policies, under the influence of Kemp he read Hayek and was said to be inspired by him. It was Fraser who promoted free market ideologue John Stone to the permanent head of the Treasury.[49])

In its early years, the IPA drew on both Keynes and Hayek. However, from the late 1970s to the mid-1980s, under the direction of Rod Kemp, David's brother and currently a Liberal Party senator and minister, the IPA enjoyed a corporate-fed revival. Kemp was approached to be director of the IPA by Sir James Balderstone, who sat on the boards of BHP, Westpac Bank and AMP Insurance, and the IPA was relaunched with Morgan, Balderstone and other business leaders on its board. Morgan became treasurer of the IPA in 1982 and John Stone was appointed as senior fellow in 1984. Corporate membership of IPA, although always considerable, increased from 350 in 1985 to 980 in 1987.[50]

IPA renewed its 'faith in old-style competitive capitalism, the free market and the social and political values which match them'. Despite its early origins, the IPA embraced economic rationalism, advocating, among other things, 'less regulation and smaller government generally', privatization, free trade and 'rational economic policies'. It ran conferences in conjunction with the American Enterprise Institute (see Chapter 8). The NSW IPA referred favourably to the reforms in Chile, where the Chicago School economists had introduced free market reforms at great social cost (see Chapter 10).[51]

In 1990, more than a year before the free market Kennett government was elected, 13 business organizations commissioned the Tasman Institute and the IPA to establish Project Victoria to design a privatization strategy. These organizations included the Australian Chamber of Manufacturers, the BCA, the State Chamber of Commerce and Industry, the Victorian Employers' Federation and the Victorian

Farmers' Federation. The Tasman Institute, as Porter pointed out, 'provided most of the policy expertise, particularly for infrastructure issues, for Project Victoria'.[52]

Project Victoria was far reaching. It covered water, ports, electricity and public transport, and the Kennett government used this basis to extend variations of privatization to roads, hospitals, prisons and schools. Tasman and IPA prepared a number of reports and strategies between 1991 and 1993. 'Project Victoria's reform agenda underlay many of the economic reforms of Victoria.'[53] The Kennett government implemented most of Project Victoria recommendations after it was elected, and in some cases went further, slashing the public service workforce by more than three times the 1991 report recommendations.[54]

The Tasman Institute also advised the NSW government on corporatization of water authorities. Its clients have included CRA, BHP, NZ Business Roundtable, NZ Treasury, North Limited, Shell Australia, Victorian Employers' Chamber of Commerce and Industry, Victorian Treasury, Western Mining and the World Bank.[55]

The Australian Institute of Public Policy (AIPP) was set up in 1983 with seed money from the US-based Atlas Foundation and later support from mining companies CRA and WMC. The AIPP modelled itself on the Heritage Foundation in the US as well as the British IEA. Its first executive director was John Hyde. It, too, pushed privatization, deregulation, and market solutions for almost everything. In the 1980s it published *Mandate to Govern*, modelled after the Heritage Foundation's *Mandate for Leadership*. It amalgamated with the IPA in 1991 and John Hyde became director of the new IPA.[56]

Almost one-third of IPA's $1.5 million annual budget comes from mining and manufacturing companies. Its council has included Rupert Murdoch, as well as other conservative business leaders. Like many of the US conservative think tanks, the IPA has good connections in the media via right-wing commentators with regular columns in major newspapers. It also has good political connections.[57] As well as Rod and David Kemp both being ministers in the Howard government, current Finance Minister Peter Costello was also a member of the IPA.

In 1990 the executive director of the IPA, Peter Kerr, who had been adviser to two Liberal Party leaders, told the *Australian Financial Review*: 'My experience with politicians is that unless someone is out there and constantly monitoring them and pushing agendas, then you don't get change.'[58]

The Sydney Institute is a breakaway group from the IPA, headed by Gerard Henderson, formerly director of IPA NSW and chief of staff for John Howard (currently Liberal prime minister of Australia). It set up a Centre for Commercial Freedom and labelled itself 'Australia's most influential, privately funded think tank'. It was backed by businessmen such as Phil Scanlan from Coca-Cola Amatil and Rodney Adler from FAI, who was sentenced to 4½ years' jail in 2005 for 'criminal behaviour against the interests of shareholders' as a director of failed HIH Insurance.[59] The Sydney Institute boasts of 'links with similar institutes around the world, including the American Enterprise Institute (Washington), the Manhattan

Institute (New York), the European Policy Forum (London), Keidanren (Tokyo) and the Centre for Strategic & International Studies (Jakarta)'.[60]

The Sydney Institute is very small but influential, centred around Henderson and his wife Anne Henderson. It calls itself a 'privately funded current affairs forum' and promotes free market ideas. It holds weekly forums and international conferences as well as publishing a journal, *The Sydney Papers*, and a magazine.[61] Gerard Henderson writes a weekly column for major newspapers in Sydney (*Herald*), Melbourne (*Age*), Brisbane and Tasmania.

The Committee for Economic Development in Australia (CEDA) was originally modelled on the US Committee for Economic Development, and in 1984 it made a conscious decision to move towards an American Enterprise Institute (AEI) model. It promotes conservative ideologies and policies. It publishes reports, articles and pamphlets that are widely distributed, organizes conferences and seminars, and holds 'regular private briefings with key financial journalists, and regular luncheons with editors of newspapers and executives of TV and radio stations'.[62]

LINKAGES AND OVERLAPS

Table 9.1 shows the extent to which there is a crossover of membership and association between various Australian think tanks (and also links to the international Mont Pèlerin Society and the Liberal Party of Australia). It shows that these think tanks have close ties and similar ideological stances, but also that the sheer number of think tanks does not necessarily indicate wide membership or broad community support. *National Times* reporters noted the incestuous relationship between them in 1985:

> *However strenuously they deny the connection, those within the inner circle of the movement are linked. With the exception of Rod Kemp, who says he hasn't been asked yet, the leaders of the think tanks write for each other's publications, attend and give seminars and present papers at each other's conferences.*[63]

Ian Marsh, who has published several reviews of think tanks in Australia, and was a research director in the Liberal Party, views think tanks as the 'springboard for the new right in Australia', influencing both major parties, and championing in the wider community 'a range of new issues to the political agenda – privatisation, deregulation, microeconomic reform, labour market reform, trade liberalisation'.[64] Their output is massive, despite their limited funding compared with US think tanks. During the 1990s, more than 80 think tanks employed about 1600 people and each year published about 900 reports and discussion papers and held 600 conferences and symposia.[65]

Table 9.1 *Some key people and their published connections – past and present*

Organization	*IPA*	*Liberal Party*	*Mont Pelerin Society*	*CIS*	*Cross-Roads*	*Centre 2000*	*AIPP*	*H.R. Nicholls Society*	*Tasman Inst.*
Founded	1943	1945	1947	1976	1977	1979	1983	1986	1990
John Elliott[66] Elders IXL		■		■					■
Ray Evans[67] Western Mining	■	■	■					■	
Andrew Hay[68] Fed. of Employers		■			■		■	■	
Gerard Henderson[69] Liberal Party	■	■						■	
John Hyde[70] ex Liberal Minister	■	■		■	■	■	■	■	
Wolfgang Kasper[71] Academic			■	■	■		■		
Bert Kelly[72] ex Liberal Minister		■		■	■		■	■	
David Kemp[73] Liberal Minister	■	■		■	■		■	■	
Rod Kemp[74] Liberal Minister	■	■			■		■	■	
Leonie Kramer[75] Academic	■					■			■
Greg Lindsay[76] Director, CIS		■	■	■	■				
Ian McLachlan[77] Farmers' Federation		■			■		■	■	
Hugh Morgan[78] Western Mining	■	■		■	■	■	■	■	■
Michael Porter[79] Academic			■		■			■	■
John Stone[80] ex Treasury	■				■	■		■	

Key: ■ past or present connection

Marsh argues that think tanks have been 'spectacularly successful' in achieving reduced government expenditure, reduced government intervention, weakened trade unions and a 'level-playing field' industry policy. In 1996 he noted that having 'done their job on privatization, deregulation and competition policy' they were moving onto the 'social agenda' to tackle issues such as welfare.[81] In their wake, economic advisers and management consultants such as ACIL Economics, Allen Consulting, Access Economics and the Centre for International Economics, took over the role of influencing government behind the scenes on 'economic' policy as well as providing the detailed technical advice necessary for implementation of free market policies.[82]

The Tasman Institute has kept up with the trend away from think tanks by transforming itself into a consultancy. In 2000 it merged with London Economics (Australia) to form Tasman Economics. London Economics claims to have 'played a key role in UK privatisation'[83] and was one of the leading consultants on the deregulation of Australia's government enterprises from 1989 to 1992. It worked with various state governments and had 'a strong influence on the utility reform process in Australia'. It was a consultant for the restructuring of the State Electricity Commission of Victoria (SECV), Melbourne Water and the Victorian Gas and Fuel Corporation. It advised the Queensland government on the sale of electricity generation and led Queensland's Electricity Industry Structure Task Force from 1996–98. It also advised the NSW government on privatization of the electricity industry in 1997 and advised the Industry Commission on electricity market reform in NSW in 1998.[84]

London Economics has also been involved in electricity and water industry restructuring in a number of other countries, including India (investigation for the World Bank), Malaysia, Thailand, Indonesia and New Zealand. It has advised companies in France, Germany, Italy and Spain on the impact of deregulation. The Tasman Institute also advised Asian countries on privatization.[85] In 2002 Tasman Economics merged with ACIL Consulting to form ACIL Tasman.

Jan McMahon, secretary of the Australian Public Service Association, argues that the main reason governments employ consultants to restructure public services, rather than doing it themselves, is to ensure their work can be kept 'commercial-in-confidence' to prevent it being made public through freedom of information requests and public inquiries.[86] Consultants and advisers, particularly those from think tanks, have played a dual role; first promoting privatization as a scheme that will benefit everyone, and then reaping a good share of the benefits themselves in fees for advising on how to do it. Having been successful at this in Australia, some of them are now repeating their 'successes' in developing countries.

During the 1980s think tanks, through their expostulation of free market ideologies, provided not only legitimation to business activities and the priority of profits and economic considerations over all other social considerations, but they provided a legitimation for the falling wages and growing inequalities that were occurring in Australia and NZ. They also coordinated and united businesses that might otherwise have competed on particular issues, into a united pro-market campaign.[87]

NOTES

1 Michael Pusey, *Economic Rationalism in Canberra*, Cambridge, Cambridge University Press, 1991, p27.
2 Christopher Sheil, *Water's Fall: Running the Risks with Economic Rationalism*, Annandale, NSW, Pluto Press, 2000, p30; Diane Stone, 'Old Guard Versus New Partisans: Think Tanks in Transition', *Australian Journal of Political Science*, vol 26, no 2, 1991, p203; Tim Duncan and Anthony McAdam, 'New Right: Where It Stands and What It Means', *The Bulletin*, 10 December 1985, p44.
3 Marian Sawer, 'Political Manifestations of Australian Libertarianism', in Marian Sawer (ed) *Australia and the New Right*, North Sydney, George Allen & Unwin, 1982, pp7–8; Greg Lindsay, 'The CIS at Twenty: Greg Lindsay Talks to Andrew Norton', *Policy*, Winter, 1996, www.cis.org.au/glint.htm, p18; Paul Kelly, *The End of Uncertainty: The Story of the 1980s*, St Leonards, NSW, Allen & Unwin, 1992, p47; Georgina Murray and Douglas Pacheco, 'Think Tanks in the 1990s', Australian National University, www.anu.edu.au/polsci/marx/interventions/thinktanks.htm accessed 23 January 2001.
4 John Singleton and Bob Howard, *Rip Van Australia*, Cassell, 1977.
5 *Ibid.*, pp24–5.
6 *Ibid.*, p26.
7 *Ibid.*, p79.
8 *Ibid.*, pp31–3.
9 *Ibid.*, p77.
10 Lindsay, 'The CIS at Twenty', p17; Singleton and Howard, *Rip Van Australia*, back cover; Sawer, 'Political Manifestations of Australian Libertarianism', pp2–6; Andrew Clark, 'In Their Own Image', *Australian Financial Review Magazine*, March 2001, p32.
11 Sawer, 'Political Manifestations of Australian Libertarianism', p7.
12 Clark, 'In Their Own Image', p34; Paul Sheehan, 'The Right Strikes Back', *Sydney Morning Herald*, 2 March 1985, p37.
13 Tim Duncan, 'Western Mining's Messiahs of the New Right', *The Bulletin*, 2 July, 1985, p70.
14 Sheehan, 'The Right Strikes Back', p37.
15 Duncan, 'Western Mining's Messiahs of the New Right', p69; Bette Moore and Gary Carpenter, 'Main Players', in Ken Coghill (ed) *The New Right's Australian Fantasy*, Fitzroy, Victoria, McPhee Gribble and Penguin Books, 1987, p150; Christopher Jay, 'New Right Policy Moves out of the Politician's Hand', *Australian Financial Review*, 11 February, 1986, p17; Morgan quoted in Sheehan, 'The Right Strikes Back', p37.
16 Kelly, *The End of Uncertainty*, p47; Lindsay, 'The CIS at Twenty', p19; Helen Noyes, 'Economic Rationalism', Bachelor of Economics (Social Science) Honours, University of Sydney, 1995, p20; CIS flyer, Liberty & Society Scholarships 1995, 1996.
17 Greg Lindsay interviewed on *Counter Point*, ABC Radio National, 12 July 2005.

18 www.montpelerin.org/officers.html; Moore and Carpenter, 'Main Players', p149; Alex Carey, *Taking the Risk out of Democracy*, ed Andrew Lohrey, Sydney, UNSW Press, 1995, p227; Greg Lindsay, 'The Centre for Independent Studies', Centre for Independent Studies, 1995, www.cis.org.au/oldindex.html; Noyes, 'Economic Rationalism', p20.

19 Lindsay, 'The Centre for Independent Studies'; Carey, *Taking the Risk out of Democracy*; CIS, 'Publications', Centre for Independent Studies, 1995, www.cis.org.au/bklist.html; Lindsay, 'The CIS at Twenty', p20.

20 Tom Dusevic, 'The Idea Factories', *Australian Financial Review*, 25 May 1990, p3; Sawer, 'Political Manifestations of Australian Libertarianism', p2; Marianne Carey and Tina Powis, 'The New Right Thinktanks', *National Times*, 13–19 September, 1985, p15; Wilson Da Silva, 'The New Social Focus', *Australian Financial Review Magazine*, May, 1996, p24.

21 Noyes, 'Economic Rationalism', p16.

22 Duncan and McAdam, 'New Right', p38.

23 A term popularized by Michael Pusey who defined economic rationalism as 'the dogma which says that markets and money can *always* do *everything* better than governments, bureaucracy and the law'. Quoted in Greg Whitwell, 'Economic Ideas and Economic Policy: The Rise of Economic Rationalism in Australia', *Australian Economic History Review*, vol 33, no 2, 1993, p8.

24 Kenneth Davidson, 'Defrocking the Priests', in Donald Horne (ed) *The Trouble with Economic Rationalism*, Newham, Victoria, Scribe, 1992, p58.

25 Frank Stilwell, 'Economic Rationalism: Sound Foundations for Policy?' in Stuart Rees, Gordon Rodley and Frank Stilwell (eds) *Beyond the Market: Alternatives to Economic Rationalism*, Leichhardt, NSW, Pluto Press, 1993, pp27–8; Emy and Hughes cited in Tim Battin, 'What Is This Thing Called Economic Rationalism?' *Australian Journal of Social Issues*, vol 26, no 4, 1991, p295; Elaine Thompson, 'Where Is the Economy?' in Donald Horne (ed) *The Trouble with Economic Rationalism*, Newham, Victoria, Scribe, 1992, p15.

26 Stilwell, 'Economic Rationalism', p33.

27 Clark, 'In Their Own Image', p34; Duncan and McAdam, 'New Right', pp41–2.

28 Murray and Pacheco, 'Think Tanks in the 1990s'; Susan Oliver, 'Where Do Governments Get Their Advice – Lobby Groups, Think Tanks, the Universities and the Media', *Canberra Bulletin of Public Administration*, December, 1993; Bernie Taft, 'The New Right in Practice', in Ken Coghill (ed) *The New Right's Australian Fantasy*, Fitzroy, Victoria, McPhee Gribble and Penguin Books, 1987, pp28–9.

29 Dusevic, 'The Idea Factories'.

30 *Ibid.*, p1.

31 Noyes, 'Economic Rationalism', p16; Stone, 'Old Guard Versus New Partisans' p211.

32 See Michael Porter's comment in interview with Jane Kelsey re 'It's mates, mates always mates' Jane Kelsey, *Reclaiming the Future: New Zealand and the Global Economy*, Wellington, Bridget Williams Books, 1999, p63; Murray and Pacheco, 'Think Tanks in the 1990s'.

33 Moore and Carpenter, 'Main Players', p146.

34 Carey, *Taking the Risk out of Democracy*, pp101–2.

35 Duncan and McAdam, 'New Right', p44; Jay, 'New Right Policy Moves out of the Politician's Hand', p17; Kelsey, *Reclaiming the Future*, p64; David Clark, 'Direct the Public Subsidies to Left and Right – Then Let the Arrows Fly', *Australian Financial Review*, 15 December 1986, p16; Sawer, 'Political Manifestations of Australian Libertarianism', pp8–9; Carey and Powis, 'The New Right Thinktanks', p14.

36 Kelsey, *Reclaiming the Future*, p64.

37 Tim Duncan, 'Mark of Cain in Attack on New Right Academics', *The Bulletin*, 14 October 1986, p26; Kelsey, *Reclaiming the Future*, p64; Jay, 'New Right Policy Moves out of the Politician's Hand'.

38 Peter Self, *Government by the Market? The Politics of Public Choice*, Hampshire and London, Macmillan, 1993, p67; Duncan, 'Mark of Cain in Attack on New Right Academics', p26; Moore and Carpenter, 'Main Players', p158.

39 Noyes, 'Economic Rationalism', p19; Duncan and McAdam, 'New Right' p45; Carey and Powis, 'The New Right Thinktanks'.

40 Duncan, 'Mark of Cain in Attack on New Right Academics', p27; Moore and Carpenter, 'Main Players', p155; Kelly, *The End of Uncertainty*, p42; Kelsey, *Reclaiming the Future*, p65.

41 Kelly, *The End of Uncertainty*, p41.

42 Kelsey, *Reclaiming the Future*, p65; Tasman Institute, 'Tasman Institute Annual Review', Melbourne, Tasman Institute Pty Ltd, Tasman Economic Research Pty Ltd, December 1997, pp66–7.

43 Trevor Matthews, 'Employers' Associations, Corporatism and the Accord: The Politics of Industrial Relations', in Stephen Bell and Brian Head (eds) *State, Economy and Public Policy*, Melbourne, Oxford University Press, 1994, p211; Moore and Carpenter, 'Main Players', p154; Kelly, *The End of Uncertainty*, p46; H. R. Nicholls Society, 'Contributors', www.hrnicholls.com.au/nicholls/nichvo12/vol12pro.htm accessed 1 June 2005.

44 John Stone, "Repairing Australia", H. R. Nicholls Society, 1986 www.hrnicholls.com.au/nicholls/nichvol1/vol1repa.htm 2000.

45 Dusevic, 'The Idea Factories', p3; Kelsey, *Reclaiming the Future*, p65; Tasman Institute, 'Tasman Institute Annual Review', Melbourne, Tasman Institute Pty Ltd. and Tasman Economic Research Pty Ltd, December 1991l *Tasman Update* February 1997 p1.

46 Tasman Institute, 'Tasman Institute Annual Review'; *Tasman Annual Reviews* 1991–1998.

47 David Kemp, 'Liberalism and Conservatism in Australia since 1944', in Brian Head and James Walter (eds) *Intellectual Movements and Australian Society*, Melbourne, Oxford University Press, 1988, p328.; Noyes, 'Economic Rationalism'; Stone, 'Old Guard Versus New Partisans: Think Tanks in Transition', p209.

48 Kemp, 'Liberalism and Conservatism in Australia since 1944', p329.

49 Sawer, 'Political Manifestations of Australian Libertarianism', p9.

50 Duncan and McAdam, 'New Right', p44; Kelly, *The End of Uncertainty*, p48; Bob Burton, 'Right Wing Think Tanks Go Environmental', *Chain Reaction*, no 73–74, 1995, p27.

51 IPA Report, Institute of Public Affairs Ltd, 1991, p1; Marion Simms, *A Liberal Nation: The Liberal Party & Australian Politics*, Sydney, Hale & Iremonger, 1982, pp153–6; Moore and Carpenter, 'Main Players', p148.

52 Des Moore and Michael Porter (eds) *Victoria: An Agenda for Change*, Melbourne, the Tasman Institute and the Institute of Public Affairs for Project Victoria, 1991, preface; Tasman Institute, 'About Us/Projects', Tasman Institute, www.tasman.com.au/main/a_nz.html accessed 20 July 2001.
53 Tasman Institute, 'About Us/Projects'.
54 Alan Kohler, 'The Radical Right Wing Speeds the Kennett Revolution', *The Age*, 14 February 1997, p15.
55 Da Silva, 'The New Social Focus', p26; John Lyons, 'Think-Tank Commanders', *Sydney Morning Herald*, 9 March 1991, p43; Tasman Institute, 'Clients', Tasman Institute, www.tasman.com.au/main/clients.html accessed 6 April 2001.
56 Stone, 'Old Guard Versus New Partisans', p204; Jay, 'New Right Policy Moves out of the Politician's Hand', p17; Kelly, *The End of Uncertainty*, p47; Noyes, 'Economic Rationalism', p22; Moore and Carpenter, 'Main Players', p149.
57 Burton, 'Right Wing Think Tanks Go Environmental'; Pusey, *Economic Rationalism in Canberra*, pp27, 227; IPA Report, Institute of Public Affairs Ltd, 1991, pp1–3.
58 Dusevic, 'The Idea Factories', p3.
59 *Ibid.*, p3; ASIC, 'Rodney Adler Sentenced to Four-and-a-Half Years' Jail', Australian Securities & Investment Commission, 14 April 2005.
60 The Sydney Institute, 'Welcome to the Sydney Institute', Sydney Institute, www.sydneyins.org.au/home.html accessed 6 April 2001.
61 *Ibid*, accessed 7 June 2005.
62 Carey, *Taking the Risk out of Democracy*; Lindsay, 'The Centre for Independent Studies', pp100–101,122; Andrew Rowell, *Green Backlash: Global Subversion of the Environment Movement*, London and New York, Routledge, 1996, p243.
63 Carey and Powis, 'The New Right Thinktanks', p14.
64 Quoted in Dusevic, 'The Idea Factories', p3.
65 Marsh cited in Murray and Pacheco, 'Think Tanks in the 1990s'.
66 Dusevic, 'The Idea Factories'; Tasman Institute, 'Tasman Institute Annual Review'; David McKnight, 'The New Right: A Consumer's Guide', *Sydney Morning Herald*, 9 June 1986.
67 Greg Lindsay, 'Threats to Freedom Then and Now', *Policy*, Autumn, 1997, www.cis.org.au/Policy/mps.html; Moore and Carpenter, 'Main Players'; Murray and Pacheco, 'Think Tanks in the 1990s'.
68 Moore and Carpenter, 'Main Players'.
69 *Ibid.*; Dusevic, 'The Idea Factories'; Tasman Institute, 'Tasman Institute Annual Review'.
70 Moore and Carpenter, 'Main Players'; Lindsay, 'The CIS at Twenty'.
71 Lindsay, 'Threats to Freedom Then and Now'; CIS, 'Staff and Contact Details', Centre for Independent Studies, www.cis.org.au/mainpages/staff.html accessed 6 April 2001; Kelly, *The End of Uncertainty*, pp42, 46, 47.
72 Moore and Carpenter, 'Main Players'; CIS, 'The Bert Kelly Lecture', Centre for Independent Studies, www.cis.org.au/mainpages/events.html accessed 6 April 2001.
73 Kelly, *The End of Uncertainty*, pp42, 46, 47.
74 Moore and Carpenter, 'Main Players'.
75 *Ibid.*; McKnight, 'The New Right'; Dusevic, 'The Idea Factories'; Tasman Institute, 'Tasman Institute Annual Review'.

76 Lindsay, 'Threats to Freedom Then and Now'; Moore and Carpenter, 'Main Players'; Clark, 'In Their Own Image'; Kelly, *The End of Uncertainty*, pp42, 46, 47.

77 Moore and Carpenter, 'Main Players'; Doug McEachern, *Business Mates: The Power and Politics of the Hawke Era*, Sydney, Prentice Hall, 1991, p95.

78 Moore and Carpenter, 'Main Players'; CIS, 'Staff and Contact Details'; Dusevic, 'The Idea Factories'; Tasman Institute, 'Tasman Institute Annual Review'; Kelly, *The End of Uncertainty*, pp42, 46, 47.

79 Lindsay, 'Threats to Freedom Then and Now'; Moore and Carpenter, 'Main Players'; Dusevic, 'The Idea Factories'; Tasman Institute, 'Tasman Institute Annual Review'.

80 Moore and Carpenter, 'Main Players'.

81 Quoted in Da Silva, 'The New Social Focus', p21.

82 Personal communication between Truda Gray and Clive Hamilton, 8th August 2000.

83 Tasman Economics, 'Our Founders', Tasman Economics, www.tasman.com.au/founders/founders.htm accessed 26 June 2002.

84 Tasman Economics, 'About Us', Tasman Economics, www.tasman.com.au/aboutus/abt_london.htm accessed 26 June 2002; Tasman Economics, 'Our Founders'.

85 Tasman Economics, 'Our Founders'; Kohler, 'The Radical Right Wing Speeds the Kennett Revolution', p15.

86 Miles Kemp, 'Out of Service', *The Advertiser*, 29 July 2000, p65.

87 Murray and Pacheco, 'Think Tanks in the 1990s'.

10

Economic Advisers

It is, of course, quite appropriate – and indeed necessary – to be sceptical about government 'intervention'. The trouble is that they then put their faith in the metaphor of 'the market', and they turn this faith into a mystique which they then pursue without any scepticism at all.

DONALD HORNE[1]

When General Pinochet ousted the democratically elected socialist government of Salvador Allende in 1973 he put the economy into the hands of a group of some 30 Chilean economists, known as the 'Chicago Boys' because many had studied economics at the University of Chicago with Milton Friedman. Friedman visited Chile in 1975, when military dictator Pinochet asked for help with his economic policy,[2] and gave a number of lectures there advising what should be done to fix the Chilean economy. This is ironic given that Friedman, in his book *Capitalism and Freedom*, argued for the necessary relationship between 'political freedom and a free market'. What Chile under Pinochet unequivocally demonstrated was that free market economic policies could be implemented in a decidedly anti-liberal political system.

As instruments of the military regime, the Chicago Boys were able to implement Friedman's policies, and other free market policies, without compromise for 16 years from 1973 to 1989. They were able to impose austerity measures without fear of a political backlash from people put out of work and unable to afford food and shelter. Their policies included drastic government spending cuts, the privatization of state-owned businesses, the lifting of all restrictions on foreign investment and the decimation of business regulations.[3]

Although Friedman chose to portray the Chilean experience as an economic miracle and a model for other developing countries, as did the World Bank and the International Monetary Fund (IMF), the benefits of this so-called miracle went to the wealthy and to foreign corporations, while the poor suffered. Chile experienced major fluctuations, oscillating between recessions and boom times, while employment levels fell and bankruptcies soared. Between 1972 and 1987 Chile's per capita GNP (Gross National Product) fell 6.4 per cent, and unemployment averaged around 16 per cent, a performance that was worse than most other Latin American nations. Those who objected 'disappeared' or were assassinated or imprisoned.[4]

Workers were worse off than they had been before the Pinochet coup, with the share of national income going to workers declining from 52.5 per cent in 1970 to 30.7 per cent in 1989. During the same period, the share of wealth enjoyed by the top 20 per cent of the population increased dramatically so that by 1989, they enjoyed 54.6 per cent of household consumption. Industries became concentrated in the hands of a few firms; 600 miles of roads in Santiago remained unpaved through lack of government spending; and pollution levels soared, particularly in the cities, because of a lack of government regulation.[5]

Things would have been even worse if Pinochet had not reversed some of the policies of the Chicago Boys when 'Chile's industry keeled over and died' with a drop in GDP (Gross Domestic Product) of 19 per cent in 1982–83. The population rioted despite the threat of being shot. Pinochet reinstated a minimum wage and union rights, instituted a government programme that created 500,000 public service jobs, and regulated the flow of foreign capital.[6]

Nevertheless, the same failed free market policy prescription was actively promoted by the World Bank and IMF, not only in Latin America, but in all parts of the world from the mid-1980s.[7] It was the driving force behind the structural adjustment programmes being imposed on all indebted developing nations. World Bank and IMF loans became conditional upon the adoption of policies such as privatization, outsourcing, downsizing of public service workforces, reducing barriers to foreign investors and redirecting government spending away from public services and publicly-owned enterprises into debt servicing.

Both the World Bank and the IMF underwent a policy shift during the 1980s. They took on the free market policy prescription being advanced by corporate-funded think tanks in the US and the UK at the time and, helped by a change of personnel, became missionaries of free market dogma.

The influence of US free market thinking on the IMF and the World Bank is reinforced by the dominance of economists in those organizations. More than 80 per cent of the World Bank's economists, who are far more influential than the social scientists employed by the bank, were trained in either Britain or North America: 'In the 1980s and early 1990s, their outlook, and that of virtually all of the remaining 20 per cent, was increasingly based on the assumptions and methodologies of neo-classical economics.' These people in turn hired people of like mind so that economists of other persuasions were unlikely to be employed at the bank. There is also a well-worn revolving door between these multilateral banks and international financial firms such as Chase Manhattan, Deutsche Bank and JP Morgan; something that is encouraged by the World Bank.[8]

The IMF had not started off with these free market policies. It was originally established to maintain economic stability, based on a Keynesian understanding of how this would be achieved. As noted in Chapter 7, Keynes argued that economic downturns could be remedied by governments increasing aggregate demand and stimulating the economy. The IMF could help poor countries to do this by loaning them money raised from the taxes of wealthier countries. The former chief economist of the World Bank, Joseph Stiglitz, says of the IMF:

> *Founded on the belief that markets often work badly, it now champions market supremacy with ideological fervor. Founded on the belief that there is a need for international pressure on countries to have more expansionary economic policies – such as increasing expenditures, reducing taxes, or lowering interest rates to stimulate the economy – today the IMF typically provides funds only if countries engage in policies like cutting deficits, raising taxes, or raising interest rates, that lead to a contraction of the economy.*[9]

Similarly, there was a shift in emphasis at the World Bank. In the 1970s the dominant economic consensus had been that government debt in poor countries was not a problem because it was necessary for governments to invest in the infrastructure and services necessary for national economic growth. Walden Bello and Shea Cunningham argue that economic growth in developing countries until the 1980s was facilitated by an 'activist state or public sector', which assisted development in the absence of a strong private sector:

> *Contrary to doctrinaire conservative interpretations, the prominence of the state in post-colonial economic development did not stem from a usurpation of the role of private enterprise; rather it was a response to the weakness of private industrial interests.*[10]

However, in the 1980s, the World Bank shifted from project lending to enable governments to invest in developing their public sector, to loans that were conditional upon governments implementing free market policies, and encouraging the private sector to take over public services. World Bank policies now ignore the positive role of State intervention in favour of allowing the market to reign.

Other influential nations tend to go along with free market policy prescriptions because nations are represented on the IMF by their finance ministers and central banks, and these tend to represent the financial communities and be staffed by people who have had careers, or hope to, with private financial firms and banks. In addition, economists in the bureaucracies of many countries have been trained in neo-classical theory as orthodoxy.

Even in the mid-1980s, the Chicago School represented a minority economic opinion in the US. One survey of 200 industrial economists found 68 per cent were opposed to the Reagan government policies that had been promoted by the Chicago School.[11] Nevertheless, this doctrine was taught in some of the most elite US universities and the graduates of these, particularly the 'high-flying graduates from elite US universities such as Stanford, Harvard, and Chicago', then went on to get government positions and became senior advisers around the world (as in Chile): part of an 'influential network of strategically placed individuals'.[12]

> *Many of the most powerful economic policy-makers in emerging market countries received their training from one of the few top-notch business training grounds for executives in the US. For instance, Guillermo Ortiz, Mexico's renowned finance minister and later governor of the central bank, did his graduate work at Stanford's Business School ... Thailand's Minister of Finance, Tarrin Nimmanahaeminda, received his BA from Harvard and obtained an MBA in finance at Stanford as well ...*[13]

THE WASHINGTON CONSENSUS AND STRUCTURAL ADJUSTMENT

In 1990 John Williamson, an economist with experience working for the World Bank, the IMF, and the UK Treasury, compiled a list of free market policies that were being pressed onto Latin American nations 'by the powers-that-be in Washington'. He called this package of economic 'reforms' the 'Washington Consensus'.[14] The World Bank calls it the 'market-friendly view'. His list covered:

- *Fiscal Discipline*: Reduced budget deficits at all levels of government (after taking account of debt).
- *Public Expenditure Priorities*: Redirecting government expenditure from areas of public demand that provide little economic return to areas with 'high economic returns and the potential to improve income distribution, such as primary health and education, and infrastructure'.
- *Tax Reform*: Broadening the tax base and cutting marginal tax rates to provide more incentive to high income earners to invest their money.
- *Financial Liberalization*: Aiming towards market-determined interest rates and the abolition of preferential interest rates for privileged borrowers.
- *Exchange Rates*: Setting exchange 'to induce a rapid growth in nontraditional exports', as well as to ensure exporters remain competitive.
- *Trade Liberalization*: Reduction of tariffs and trade restrictions.
- *Foreign Direct Investment*: Abolition of barriers to investment by foreign firms and foreign firms to be treated on the same basis as local firms.
- *Privatization*: Privatizing government businesses and assets.
- *Deregulation*: Abolition of regulations that impede investment or restrict competition, and requirement that all regulations be justified 'by such criteria as safety, environmental protection, or prudential supervision of financial institutions'.
- *Property Rights*: Securing property rights without excessive costs.[15]

These measures, a codified version of the Chicago School prescriptions, were measures that would expand business opportunities, reduce the cost of doing business and minimize the regulations that business would have to abide by. They were the policies being promoted by corporate-funded think tanks in the US and the UK. The 'Washington Consensus' was pushed by Washington policy networks supported by large corporations and international financial interests and incorporated into an economic reform agenda for most countries in the world.

Williamson recognized the role of economic advisers in achieving the Washington Consensus. He used the term 'technopols' to describe the 'burgeoning breed of economic technocrats who assume positions of political responsibility'.[16] These people were not only 'able to judge what institutions and policies are needed in specific circumstances in order to further economic objectives' but also had the political skills and ability to persuade others to adopt those policies.[17]

Technopols, like corporate-funded think tanks, played a key role in ensuring business-friendly measures were adopted in affluent countries by governments of many different political persuasions during the 1980s, including the conservative governments of Margaret Thatcher in Britain, Ronald Reagan in the US and Brian Mulroney in Canada, and labour/social democratic governments in Australia and New Zealand. By the end of the 1980s, most Western countries were moving towards smaller government and market deregulation.[18] This was not because of the power of the free market ideas themselves, or the efficacy of the policies in meeting their stated purposes. Rather, it was because of the power of those who backed these ideas, the corporations. International financial markets also played a key role in disciplining governments that strayed from the free market path by sending their share markets plummeting.[19]

The Washington Consensus was a policy prescription that benefited transnational corporations, large companies and international financial institutions, often at the expense of small local businesses, and always at the expense of the poor. It placed an 'exaggerated faith in market mechanisms' for solving economic problems and it gave economic goals priority over social goals, destroying socially beneficial traditions and desirable aspects of cultures in the process. Progressive taxation systems were dismantled and government social services decimated. In the extreme, governments were to be reduced to being responsible for little more than law and order and national defence.[20]

As a result of Thatcher's free market policies, inequality increased in Britain faster than any other industrialized country apart from New Zealand, where the free market formula was being applied even more zealously (see below). The tax burden for the majority of households was increased and the poorest no longer benefited from the nation's economic growth. Between 1977 and 1990 the percentage of the population earning less than average income in Britain trebled.[21]

Union power in Britain was reduced. One rationale behind this attack on trade unions was that they were 'intermediary institutions standing between workers and the market'. The goal was to create an American-style labour market 'with its high levels of mobility, downward flexibility on wages and low costs for employers'. Indeed, the combination of weakened union powers, deregulation of labour laws and the downsizing of the workforces of private and public organizations ensured that many full-time, permanent jobs disappeared for good or were replaced by part-time and/or contract positions. Even those in full-time jobs were often paid less than what was needed to support a family. 'The diseases of poverty – TB, rickets, and others – returned.'[22]

Those forced into unemployment found that welfare had also been subjected to fundamentalist policies that included reduced entitlements and other 'incentives' to ensure the unemployed would accept any job that was offered, no matter how poorly paid. The government goal of full employment that had been thought to be necessary for social stability and cohesion was abandoned in the name of Friedman's theory of a natural rate of unemployment (see Chapter 7).[23]

Free market policies were bad enough for affluent nations like Britain. Imposing such conditions on poor nations was devastating. Yet they were imposed on the most vulnerable nations by the multilateral development banks and the IMF, beginning with Mexico in 1982 when the Mexican government threatened to default on its $80 billion debt.

Mexico had adhered to the Washington consensus, reducing government expenditure, controlling wages and prices, and privatizing State-owned enterprises. As in other countries where the formula was implemented, the rich got richer, the poor got poorer and the middle-class shrank. Mexico was transformed 'from an exceptionally stable Latin American country to one facing a highly problematic future' and the promised gain of economic growth was not realized.[24]

When Mexico again threatened to default on its international loans in 1994, the US government facilitated a rescue package that included $20 billion worth of loan guarantees from the US and an emergency IMF loan of $18 billion. It was the most expensive rescue that had ever been carried out. It was considered necessary to prevent stock market crashes in other Latin American countries; to protect US investments in Mexico; to protect the North American Free Trade Agreement (NAFTA); and most importantly to prevent the collapse of one of the showcases of free market reforms:[25]

> *It was the prime site for the American project of engineering the free market through the world. Since the early 1980s it had a political elite obedient to the transnational financial organizations in which American free-market doctrines were institutionalised.*[26]

In fact, many of the nations following the World Bank/IMF prescriptions did not prosper: 'the majority of those nations that have followed the IMF's advice have experienced profound economic crises: low or even declining growth, much larger foreign debts and the stagnation that perpetuates systemic poverty'. Some countries that had declined the IMF's 'enhanced structural adjustment' loans were in contrast better off.[27]

In the two decades before the introduction of the Washington Consensus, when government spending and welfare schemes were looked on with approval (1960–1980), the income per person grew by 73 per cent in Latin America and 34 per cent in Africa. In the following two decades, as the Washington consensus was implemented, incomes in Africa declined by 23 per cent and the Latin American economies have only grown by 6 per cent.[28]

In developing countries life expectancy has dropped. The gap between rich and poor has increased. Forty-four per cent of people in developing nations live in poverty and unemployment has doubled in the last decade.[29] Even the IMF admits that 'in recent decades, nearly one-fifth of the world population have regressed'.[30] This is most evident to the populations of developing countries:

> *A popular and political groundswell is building from the Andes to Argentina against the decade-old experiment with free-market capitalism. The reforms that have shrunk the state and opened markets to foreign competition, many believe, have enriched corrupt officials and faceless multinationals, and failed to better their lives.*[31]

In countries with a tradition of strong unions, union power has been diminished through labour market deregulation, workplace restructuring and the restructuring of wage-setting systems. The State no longer intervenes to protect the weaker members of society and to ensure equity. Economic efficiency, growth and competition are now paramount. Nevertheless, despite these goals, the end result of the reforms has not been better economic performance: 'what purports to be a recipe for the revitalisation of industry is more a device for redistribution from poor to rich'.[32]

The Washington Consensus was clearly in the interests of big business and it is a powerful constituency. Theories-turned-ideologies provided a means for disguising and legitimizing vested interests. They supported the argument 'that state regulation and aid were destroying the essence of an 'enterprise culture' and that this could only be rectified by reducing that regulation and providing big incentives to business people. 'Conversely, it was necessary to rebut the concept of "social justice" as an illusory ideal which triggered an endless growth of the state and led to wasteful schemes of redistribution to placate particular interests.'[33] Middle-class guilt over the poor was countered with arguments that compassion led to laziness and destroyed enterprise.

The setting aside of equity is presented by free market economists as a simplifying device:

> *... we will not be concerned with the equity or otherwise of the distribution of the economy's wealth in general, or a given industry's social surplus in particular. Our only criterion of economic welfare will be the sum of consumer and producer surplus however distributed. While this assumption removes what many political observers might regard as*

> *a critical issue, it has the advantage of allowing us to concentrate solely on questions of economic efficiency.*[34]

Economic theories that set aside equity in this way, unsurprisingly, have been used to promote policies that are inequitable. 'In the past economic life has been constrained by the need to maintain social cohesion.' The free market formula seeks to separate markets from social needs. Economic efficiency is very narrowly defined and usually not in terms of the efficient provision of social or non-economic goals. Efficiency is seen as a non-political, objective goal, while politics is to be avoided because it is a manifestation of interest-group activity that distorts efficiency. It is argued that economic efficiency is a matter of economic calculation not political nor ethical judgement.[35]

Many developed countries voluntarily adopted the pro-business free market policies prescribed by the Washington Consensus, mainly because of the influence of business lobbies and their free market missionaries, the think tanks and economic advisers, as well as international financial markets and institutions. During the 1980s, Australia and New Zealand 'embarked on programmes of economic and social transformation arguably more comprehensive in scope and intensity than anywhere else in the Western World'. These programmes of market 'liberalization', undertaken by labour/social democratic governments, 'cut away many of the key mechanisms employed to achieve traditional social democratic objectives' and destroyed 'the ethos and institutional pillars on which Labor's support had always been based'.[36]

Advisers in New Zealand

In New Zealand (NZ) the free market formula was applied in a more uncompromising way than in other countries. Every major social institution was 'reformed' and restructured leaving it the closest thing there was 'to the pure neo-liberal model of lean government and a free-market economy'.[37] The 'reforms' were supported by international institutions such as the World Bank, the IMF and the OECD (Organisation for Economic Co-operation and Development), which saw NZ 'as an important test case for reform in a Western developed country'.[38]

The prime moving force for change was Minister for Finance Roger Douglas. Douglas was trained as an accountant and had been a businessman. While in opposition Douglas, a reformed interventionist, received his advice from businessmen and from Treasury economists seconded to the Opposition Research Unit. He was heavily influenced by their free market approach. As early as 1980 he published a book setting out his free market philosophy entitled *There's Got to be a Better Way!* which, together with an alternative budget he published the same year, got him fired from the Shadow Cabinet.[39]

After the 1981 election, which Labour lost, 'Douglas, assisted by a handful of other Labour MPs, several businessmen, an economist in the Opposition Research Unit and a Treasury official seconded to his office, set about preparing an economic blueprint for Labour's re-election.' The blueprint sought to reduce the role of government and facilitate the operation of the market. It was the blueprint used by the Labour Party when it was elected in 1984 and the programme of restructuring that resulted was dubbed 'Rogernomics' (after Roger Douglas).[40]

Once elected, Douglas's power in Cabinet was supplemented by two senior politicians of like mind who were made associate ministers of finance – David Caygill and Richard Prebble. These three ministers worked as a team on policy development and strategy, and dominated the Cabinet's Policy Committee. The team was also represented on all the other policy-making committees. The cabinet was mainly made up of young professionals rather than old-time trade unionists, and Prime Minister David Lange, a lawyer, had little interest in, or knowledge of, economics. Lange accepted his minister's assurance that the new programme of reforms would deliver social equity as well as economic growth.[41]

Douglas was recognized for his efforts by the Mont Pèlerin Society in 1989 when it met in NZ. At the time, the partnership between Douglas and Lange had fallen apart over Douglas's proposal to implement a 23 per cent flat tax. Douglas's reforms had already resulted in 7.5 per cent unemployment, high interest rates and economic growth of only 1.5 per cent.[42]

Nevertheless, the Labour Party managed to win the 1987 election, in part because it had gained middle-class supporters through measures such as tax cuts. The government also had strong media support and had earned loyalty from some voters through some fairly progressive policies in areas such as Maori rights, women's affairs and employment equity. Its popular banning of US ships with nuclear weapons from NZ ports fired up nationalistic feelings, and this nationalism was further fuelled by the bombing of the Greenpeace vessel, *Rainbow Warrior*, in Auckland harbour by the French secret service.[43]

Most significantly, the main opposition, the National Party, offered no real alternative as it was adopting the same free market agenda. The struggles within the National Party to reach this position had been aided by international alliances and local business influence. The party had been networking with neoconservative parties in other parts of the world, especially the Republicans in the US and the Tories in the UK, exchanging information and discussing techniques, strategies and restructuring.[44]

Nevertheless, the changes introduced in the Labour government's second term of office were so unpopular that it lost office to the Nationals in 1990. Ruth Richardson, the new minister for finance (and also member of the Mont Pèlerin Society), agreed with free market policies and was just as determined to implement them. What is more, she had more Cabinet support than Douglas had had, with many Cabinet members being 'free market ideologues'. The National government undertook the reforms that Labour had neglected, cutting back the remnants of the welfare state, including income support for the poor, and 'removing legislative protections in industrial relations.'[45]

The NZ Treasury was very powerful in successive governments as it provided economic advice to the government as well as controlling finances. It also employed nearly all the government's economists and provided other departments with economic advice. Although the earlier National government had not always listened to the Treasury, the Labour government did. Treasury economists 'were heavily influenced' by the free market economic thinking coming from 'certain US universities' and by OECD economists and policy makers who were in turn influenced by American free market economics.[46]

The US influence came in part because, as in Chile, many key NZ economists had received post-graduate training at US universities such as Harvard and Rochester, but also because the Treasury used US economists as policy consultants. Additionally, many Reserve Bank officials had spent time working for the World Bank and the IMF, and new Treasury recruits were sponsored to study at US universities. Visits by American economists to NZ, and by key NZ economists to the US, were another major source of influence.[47]

Treasury and Reserve Bank economists portrayed their views as representing the new consensus amongst the international economics profession. And while this was not actually the case, it was emerging as the consensus in English-speaking international policy circles, such as the OECD, IMF, and the General Agreement on Tariffs and Trade (GATT) – all heavily influenced by US economists – and amongst the most influential policy-makers in the UK and Australian governments.[48]

NZ economists outside of the Treasury had little influence, especially those critical of the government's programme of reform. The influence of US economists did not seem to permeate the university economics departments in the same way it did in Australia, and the theories justifying Rogernomics were seldom taught in universities.[49]

The Treasury 'had a coherent internal position and was impatient with dissenting views'. After the Labour government was elected in 1984, Treasury economists produced a briefing outlining the forthcoming reforms, entitled 'Economic Management'. It signalled a major shift in government policy orientation from stability and equity to efficiency and competitiveness, and its policy prescriptions were all carried out in the following decade.[50]

Untried policies being promoted by US economists were implemented in NZ with little adaptation for local circumstances. Chicago School theories about labour market deregulation were applied despite the huge differences in geographical, institutional and cultural aspects of the labour markets. Similarly, when Chicago School welfare policies were adopted in NZ, the traditional concern with equity and social well-being went out the window. Kelsey notes that US economic theories were 'implemented in almost undiluted form' in NZ, even theories that had never been tried as policy in the US.[51]

A 1985 meeting of the NZ Association of Economists criticized the Treasury for putting too much faith in theoretical models, saying it was 'in danger of misleading the political masters into believing that the facile solutions ... which are attainable in neoclassical models are characteristic of the real world with which they have to deal'.[52]

Government restructuring in NZ ensured that all departmental proposals and policies with economic or financial implications had to be endorsed by the Treasury, with no right of appeal if the Treasury decided to oppose a policy. This gave it final say on almost all government activity. The Reserve Bank of NZ, which administered monetary policy, was also converted to free market economics early on and was influential with government as well as the wider economics profession. It produced a number of influential reports promoting deregulation of financial markets and other free market reforms to the financial sector. In 1989 it became independent of government.[53]

There were also key individuals who performed the role of change agents, moving from job to job in the public service. These individuals usually had connections with conservative think tanks and the corporate world, particularly the NZ Business Roundtable (see Table 10.1 for some examples). Economists in the Treasury were also moved around to facilitate reforms.[54] Some individuals moved around between Australia and NZ.

Newly restructured agencies and departments were headed by people appointed by the new government who could be trusted to implement market-based reforms and run the new organizations along commercial, managerialist lines. Roderick Deane, who was appointed CEO of the Electricity Corporation (ECNZ) is an example. He had financial management experience at the Reserve Bank and as head of the State Services Commission (SSC). In turn, he appointed senior managers who had 'extensive private sector experience in critical areas such as finance, treasury, industrial relations and marketing'.[55] Elected representatives on boards (for example, local health and electricity supply) were replaced with ministerial appointees.[56]

ADVISERS IN AUSTRALIA

Unlike NZ, there was a much more wholesale conversion of the economic profession in Australia to a market-oriented approach to the discipline and ensuing policy recommendations.[57] Economists trained at the Australian National University (ANU) and other university economics departments, who were too young to remember the Depression and had no experience of the real world of business and production, 'ingested rationalist economic theory from their professors as if it were God-given revelation, the pure and only truth'. They then moved into the public service where their faith 'insulated them from reality'.[58]

Table 10.1 *Some New Zealand change agents and their connections*

	Positions	*Business connections*	*Think tank connections*
Rod Deane	IMF Deputy Governor, Reserve Bank Head of SSC CEO, Electricorp CEO, Telecom	Business Roundtable, Fletcher Challenge Board	Trustee of the CIS[59] Tasman Institute[60]
Roger Kerr	Foreign Affairs Treasury Electricorp Board Close to Douglas	Director, Business Roundtable	
Sir Ron Trotter (knighted in 1985 by Labour)	Economic adviser Reserve Bank Board Chair, Telecom Health system restructure	Chair, Business Roundtable Managing Director, Chair, Fletcher Challenge	Trustee of CIS
Alan Gibbs	Chair, Forestcorp Board Health services review Telecom Board	Business Roundtable	CIS Board[61]
Wayne Gilbert	CEO, Mercury Energy South East Queensland Electricity Board, Maritime Services Board of NSW	Business Roundtable Carlton & United Breweries. Tooth & Co.	H. R. Nicholls Project Victoria[62]

Adapted from: Jane Kelsey, *Economic Fundamentalism*, London, Pluto Press, 1995, pp47–48

> *The phenomenon of the 1980s reflected the worldwide policy consensus expressed in treasuries around the globe, notably in Canberra, and articulated forcefully within forums of the IMF and the OECD. The international brotherhood of economic advisers was a dominant intellectual force throughout the decade.*[63]

The concern of Australian Treasury officials with financial matters ensured that they were more sympathetic to free market policies than other public servants and they led the push for economic 'reform' in government. However, it was not till the Australian Labor Party (ALP) was elected to government in 1983, with Paul Keating as Treasurer, that they found a sympathetic conduit for their advice and senior Treasury officials moved into the newly formed office of Prime Minister and Cabinet (PMC).[64]

According to journalist Paul Kelly, Prime Minister Bob Hawke and his treasurer, Paul Keating, 'chose to elevate belief in the market forces to an article of faith for their government and the ALP – an historic step'. Change, and the move away from traditional Labor values and goals, which had been nationalistic and in favour of government intervention, was more gradual than in NZ but the direction was clear. Hawke and Keating forged a consensus between business and organized labour based on the premise that improved economic performance depended on greater reliance on the market and less government.[65]

> *... the issue at the centre of Australia's politics ceased to be: how can government intervene in economic life to create desirable social outcomes? By the 1990s it had been reformulated as: how can governments create competitive market situations to ensure world-best practice is pursued and international standards are achieved?*[66]

The shift in the ALP government approach was such that, although elected in 1983 on promises of an expanded budget 'to increase demand and commence the arduous task of sustained economic recovery', the Treasury view prevailed and by 1984 the prime minister was promising not to raise taxes nor increase the deficit as a proportion of GDP. In fact, over the following seven years, the deficit fell from 28.9 per cent to 23.7 per cent of GDP. Similarly, prior to the election, Labor had been critical of a proposal for deregulation of the financial sector. However, once in government it accepted advice from a committee of economists from the financial sector, the Treasury and the Reserve Bank, which recommended financial deregulation. And this was swiftly implemented.[67]

Paul Keating, as treasurer in the Labor government, was a prime mover towards market-oriented policies. He was not an economist but 'was a very quick learner of a very particular and partial story fed to him by his advisers', particularly those in the Treasury. Prime Minister Hawke had a limited personal vision for reform and 'no deep policy commitment'. He followed policy advice from the Treasury and his own personal advisers.[68] Garnaut, as one of those advisers, states: 'Hawke and Keating's preferment of technocratic advisers with interests in market-oriented reform assisted in the government articulation of a wide-ranging programme of reform in the early years of the government.'[69]

After it was elected, the Labor Cabinet adopted a principle of solidarity that aided the changes. All ministers had to publicly support Cabinet decisions.[70] This meant that it was easier for Hawke and Keating to carry the day without fear of being criticized publicly by members of Cabinet.

A struggle within the opposition Liberal Party during the 1980s between the 'dries', who promoted free market policies, and the 'wets', who argued that the government should regulate against the excesses of the market, was won by the dries. Several key people in the Liberal Party had come through the Melbourne University Liberal Club in the 1960s when Hayek's book *The Constitution of Liberty* was the hot topic in discussion groups, as was material from the London-based Institute of Economic Affairs (IEA – see Chapter 8) and the New York-based Foundation for Economic Education (FEE – see Chapter 4).[71] 'The Liberal embrace of free-market economics became a virtually undisputed position. The policies of small government, industry deregulation, labour market deregulation, cutting the tax burden and renewing the fight against inflation were largely accepted.'[72]

The winning over of the Liberal Party ensured that there was little mainstream opposition to ALP government reforms. 'Sceptics and critics [of the market-based reforms] have, since the early 1980s, been confined to the margins of political debate.'[73] While the Labor government was never able to deregulate the labour market to the extent that ideologues required, the incoming Liberal government in 1996 had no such qualms, although it was thwarted by the Senate until it won control of both Houses of Parliament in 2004.

The public service was restructured in Australia as it had been in other countries so as to implement free market policies. Ministerial advisers took over some of the duties of senior public servants and were very influential in determining policy, enabling ministers' offices to take the lead in policy formation. The ALP had been concerned that after eight years of Liberal Party rule the bureaucracy had been captured by their way of thinking. For this reason, government departments were required to use external experts and consultants. Consultants 'contributed policy advice, policy analysis and policy development'. The government relied more on external policy advice and was therefore more vulnerable to business influence.[74]

The flexibility in appointment and removal of departmental secretaries enabled people to be appointed from outside the public service to key senior positions, and for the government to remove those who were not following the correct ideological line without having to give a reason. Whereas once this appointment process was supposed to be independent of the government of the day, now appointments had to be by the Governor-General on the basis of advice and a recommendation from the prime minister.

Fixed-term appointments replaced tenure. Almost half the senior public service was replaced between 1984 and 1990.[75] 'The bewildering whirl of "musical chairs" among departmental heads has continued, with some appointments of people without the slightest experience in any aspect of their new department's operations.'[76]

The creation of a Senior Executive Service that was subject to political appointments followed the tradition in Canada and the US. A Senior Executive Service was also created at the state level. In fact, Victoria did it before the federal government. In the state of NSW, the Senior Executive Service now consists of hundreds of public officials employed on contracts. Continuing appointment depends on 'yearly appraisals made by a private firm of consultants..'.[77]

In a study of the Commonwealth Senior Executive Service (SES), sociologist Michael Pusey found that they were predominantly conservative in their political views, tending to emphasize individualism and small government and free market economics. He argued that they 'tend to see the world in terms that neutralize and then reduce the norms of public policy to those of private enterprise ...'[78]

> *Certainly the evidence suggests that structured inequalities in the classification of SES officers across the different categories of departments, combined with the actual operation of the promotion system, has given a cumulatively disproportionate power to the younger economic rationalists in the central agency departments of Treasury, Finance and the Prime Minister and Cabinet who now comprise some 70 per cent of the Senior Executive Service population of these departments.*[79]

The conservatism of the Senior Executive Service resulted from a selection process that favoured people with private school backgrounds and training in university economics departments where the philosophy of market economics prevails (see Chapter 6).[80] Former US Treasurer Alan Greenspan has claimed that 'what is being taught in the universities today will determine national economic policy 10 years from now'. Pusey observed this to be true in Australia: 'it is through the power of a particular university economics curriculum that the recent past has had the strongest hand in casting the nations' future'. Pusey was referring to a neoclassical economics curriculum 'that swept through the economics departments of Australian universities from about 1947 onwards'. In the 1980s there were very few sizeable groups of university economists willing to challenge the neoclassical paradigm.[81]

Public sector economists had, according to Pusey, 'close relations with economists in peak business groups, the private sector economists in the finance sector, and with the staff of the economic "think tanks" and the "research" centres that have been set up by the New Right private-sector interest groups to feed ready-made economic "advice" into the top end of Canberra'. Pusey also found in his interviews with public sector economists that their overseas experience with organizations such as IMF, the OECD, the World Bank, the GATT and economics departments of US universities were most likely to influence the way they did their work.[82]

The restructuring of the public service was aimed at giving greater control to the Cabinet and 'an enhanced emphasis on the government's policy priorities'. Prime Minister Bob Hawke said the restructuring was 'to ensure that the public service is not a stumbling block for broader, economy-wide change; indeed, that the public service becomes where possible an effective instrument for the achievement of that change'.[83]

As in NZ, some key public servants have played a central role in advancing the free market policy agenda, particularly at the state level. In NSW Gary Sturgess played a key role. Sturgess was a member of the Mont Pèlerin Society and the CIS (see Table 10.2). When Nick Greiner was elected NSW Premier in 1988, Sturgess became director-general of the newly-formed Cabinet Office.[84] Sturgess has since referred to 'the trust which developed between the heads of government and their immediate advisers' as one of the most important factors that contributed to achieving free market reforms in Australia.[85]

Cabinet papers show that Sturgess had enormous power. Every policy proposal from government departments and ministers was filtered and commented on by Sturgess before it got to the premier. Sturgess, although virtually unknown to the public, was said to have more power than even Cabinet members, having better access to and influence over Premier Greiner: 'No decisions of substance are made without him.' He wrote many party policy documents before the Liberals came to power, and then was responsible for their implementation once in government. He was said to be the one providing the ideological depth to Greiner and to be at 'the core of government philosophy'. This philosophy came from free market economists in the US and the UK.[86]

Many MPs resented Sturgess's power, and the *Sydney Morning Herald* reported that several believed 'that Sturgess is an ideologue who lives behind locked doors treating NSW as his own personal New Right political experiment, oblivious to the reactions of real people, to the problems caused by some of the change he has fostered'. In particular, the rate of implementation, set by Greiner and Sturgess for corporatization of large government agencies such as electricity, water and banking, was much too fast for the Cabinet.[87]

When the Liberal Party suffered a massive decline in support at the 1991 NSW elections, Sturgess was blamed as being at the heart of the overly ideological approach to government that had caused so much community resentment. He had to make 'a strategic withdrawal from cabinet meetings', attending only those parts that dealt with policy. When Greiner was forced to step down in 1991, Sturgess also resigned as the new premier sought 'to distance his administration from the unpopular Greiner government'. Sturgess became a private consultant.[88]

Ken Baxter is another example of a prime mover in public sector reform and privatization. As an increasingly well-paid public servant, he moved back and forth between NSW and Victoria supervizing government reforms (see Table 10.2). 'In Victoria, Baxter presided over massive cuts to services, more than 200 school closures and extensive privatisation and contracting out. He slashed more than 40,000 public-sector jobs and introduced individual contracts.' [89]

The hold of economic advisors is still strong in Canberra. Lindy Edwards, a former economic adviser herself, notes that ambitious government bureaucrats still 'flock to economics courses at the Australian National University or the University of Canberra' to ensure their career advancement, even as school-leaver enrolments in economics have been falling off: 'Those with the right economic credentials were promoted and those without them stood by as they were leap-frogged by young up-and-comers with the "correct" worldview.'[90]

At the federal level of government, the Department of Prime Minister and Cabinet, the Treasury, and the Department of Finance and Administration, are the most powerful as they 'control the whole government agenda and the purse strings'.

Table 10.2 *Some Australian change agents and their connections*

	Positions	*Business connections*	*Think tank connections*
John Stone[91]	Head of Treasury IMF, World Bank Boards Queensland Senator Shadow Minister of Finance	Company director: Peko-Wallsend Sperry Ltd J.T. Campbell & Co. Syndicated newspaper column	Senior fellow, IPA Visiting Prof., CPS Founder, H. R. Nicholls Society Crossroads Centre 2000
Gary Sturgess	Director-General, NSW Cabinet Principle adviser to Premier Greiner Consultant to govt	Investment analyst for MIM Holdings Serco Group Board Consultant to industry	Mont Pèlerin Society[92] CIS[93] Crossroads[94]
Michael Roux	Executive Director, Office of State Owned Enterprises Deputy Secretary, Treasury CEO, Vic. Office Trade & Invest. Man. Director, Accident Compensation Comm. CEO, Transport Accident Comm. Man. Dir., Road Traffic Auth. Chair, Motor Accident Board Chair, Housing Employee Auth. Dir-Gen, Vic. Dept. Employment & Training; Chair, Vic. Superannuation Board	Chair of Roux Int., Aust. Developmt Fund, VicSuper P/L, RBZ Group Director, Vic. Funds Managemt Corp. Director, Deutsche Funds Management; Adviser to the Deutsche Bank Group in Australia; and to the Frank Russell Company	Honorary Trustee of CEDA Chairman of the Australian Davos Connection, World Economic Forum
Max Moore-Wilton	Dep. Sec. Commonwealth Dept of Primary Industries Head of NSW Roads and Traffic Authority Head, NSW Dept of Transport Head, NSW Maritime Serv. Bd Man. Dir., Aust. National Line Gen. Manager, Aust. Wheat Bd Secretary, Dept PM and Cabinet	Formerly a national director and acting head of Australian Stock Exchange CEO, Sydney Airports Corp.	

Table 10.2 *continued*

	Positions	*Business connections*	*Think tank connections*
Ken Baxter	Dir-Gen, Victorian Cabinet office Director, NSW Premier's Dept Head, NSW Office of Public Management, Chair, Australian Dairy Corp. Chair, Council of Aust. Govts Electricity Reform Committee Chair, NSW Rail Reform Task Force	A director of Pan Pharmaceuticals Ltd, VRI Biomedical, KPMG Consulting, Thai Dairy Industry	
Paul Barratt	Head of Defence Head of Primary Ind. & Energy Other senior posts: Dept of Minerals & Energy; Dept of Trade; Dept of Foreign Affairs and Trade	Former head of Business Council Principal, CEO Collegiate	Institute of Applied Economics and Social Research

Their ministers are also the most powerful in the government. Any submission from the other departments goes to the central departments for comment and these central agencies usually discuss it over the phone to come up with a united position on it to ensure their ministers all get the same advice about it.[95]

Because the central agencies are not familiar with the complexities of the real-life problems the other departments are trying to deal with, and because they don't have to deal directly with constituents and interested parties, they base their judgements and decisions on ideological grounds. They use economic rationalism to make assumptions to fill in gaps in their knowledge and as a filter to discard policies and actions that do not fit with their goals.[96]

> *As people become more powerful they make more and more decisions in a day. As a result, they make their decisions on the basis of less and less information. In the vacuum of detailed information assumptions fill the gaps. In the absence of evidence to the contrary, people assume the world works according to their prejudice. Their ideology slips into gear.*[97]

These elite bureaucrats don't have much contact with the community. They work and socialize with each other, confirming their shared ideology. Over time the other departments learn what sort of policies and proposals are likely to be approved by the central agencies and start applying those criteria when developing policies. They seek to employ bureaucrats from the central agencies to help them tailor their own policies for success. As a result, alternative policies get squashed at inception.[98] Even ministers bow to the supposed expertize of the bureaucracy in economic matters.

> *When all the heavy weights are imbued with the 'economic wisdom', most up-and-comers conform to the economic framework for fear of being labelled 'soft' or 'not educated enough'. They become groupies of the dominant culture.*[99]

The traditional system of policy advice in Australia, NZ and Britain, where the Civil Service was supposed to be peopled by professionals providing disinterested policy analysis and advice in the public interest, has been replaced by one where there is much more opportunity for outsiders with ideological and financial interests to influence policy. What is more, the power of particular sectors of the public service, the central and coordinating departments such as Finance, Prime Minister and Cabinet and Treasury have become more powerful than other departments, enabling neoclassically trained economists within the public service to become more influential. It was these departments that were often the driving force behind public sector reforms as well as the broader free market programme.[100]

OUTCOMES

These free market reforms were supported heavily outside Australia and NZ. The international finance community was so pleased with the NZ free market direction that it voted Roger Douglas top finance minister of the year in 1986 in *Banker* magazine. Treasurer Paul Keating was named International Finance Minister of the Year in 1987 by *The Economist* for his reforms.[101]

As a result of the 'reforms', NZ shifted from being one of the most regulated OECD countries to one of the least regulated.[102] By 1995, despite the heavy social costs the 'experiment' was exacting, international institutions and the business media were hailing the experiment as a model for the rest of the world. Moody's Investors Services described: 'The reorientation of New Zealand economic policy after 1984 represented one of the most ambitious and comprehensive structural reforms undertaken by any OECD country.' But it nevertheless noted: 'As it turned out, the reform process has proved somewhat tortuous and quite painful for many segments of New Zealand society ...'.[103]

Inequality grew in NZ, which had prided itself on being an egalitarian society, faster than in any other industrialized country. Although American commentators blamed a growing underclass on an overly generous welfare system, there was no underclass in NZ until welfare was cut and citizens subjected to the rigours of the free market.[104]

Yet the pain suffered by the one in six New Zealanders who found themselves below the poverty line by 1993 could not be defended as an unfortunate effect of rapid economic growth. According to Jane Kelsey, who analysed the NZ experiment in her book *Economic Fundamentalism*: 'Between 1985 and 1992 total growth across OECD economies averaged 20 per cent; New Zealand's economy shrank by 1 per cent over the same period' despite an increasing population. At the same time productivity was static, unemployment skyrocketed, inflation soared (around 9 per cent per year), investment halved, overseas debt quadrupled and interest rates remained high. People left NZ in droves.[105]

The new pro-market, pro-business agenda was so alien to the ideals of the NZ Labour Party that membership dropped from 100,000 in 1984 to 10,000 in 1988. The gap between the government and the party also widened, with the government not even being bound by the party's Policy Council decisions which were supposed to set party policy.[106]

The 'success' being acclaimed by foreign commentators can be seen, not in social or economic terms, but in ideological terms. Kelsey wrote:

> *What the self-authorised attestors of success – the major industrial powers, the self-interested players in the capital markets, the evangelical libertarian intellectuals and free-market economists, the financial journalists of trans-national media, the credit rating agencies with their own vested interests, and the like – were really applauding was the unimpeded imposition of a particular ideological model to which they adhered, notwithstanding its economic and social consequences . . . Constant repetition and mutual reinforcement helped elevate the rhetoric beyond effective critique.*[107]

As in NZ, there is little evidence that the Australian public supported free market reforms. John Carroll claims: 'The unfortunate nation had become split between virtually the entire people on one side, and a narrow tripartite elite consensus on the other, made up of the leadership of both major political parties and the top echelons of the key policy-making bureaucracy.'[108] Australian people were told there was no choice, economic rationalism was necessary to be able to compete in a globalized world.[109]

The reinvigoration of the Australian manufacturing sector that was supposed to result from economic restructuring never occurred. The extra money generated in the 1980s by lower corporate taxes, voluntary union wage restraint, higher profits and deregulation was supposed to provide investment incentives to business, but it was seldom reinvested in productivity. Rather, it was squandered on 'increased executive salaries, increased luxury consumption and a mass of unproductive investment, seeking wealth through shuffling paper, takeover bids and counter-bids'.[110]

The wages' share of the economy declined from 62 per cent in 1975 to 53 per cent in the late 1980s, where it has remained. In the meantime, profits have risen from 16 per cent of GDP in 1975 to 27 per cent today.[111] As in NZ, Australia's reputation for egalitarianism and equitable distribution of income was destroyed as inequities in Australia began to rival and exceed other countries.

For most of Australia's history there had been an unwritten social compact aimed at 'building a workers' paradise'. Manufacturing industries were protected so that they could pay good wages. A minimum wage was set that would be sufficient to support a family.[112] There was also a view that those who were disadvantaged and vulnerable should be given a helping hand, that mates should help mates, that we were all in this together and should cooperate and pull together; that friendship and family and community and health and environment were just as important, if not more, to quality of life as wealth. In this view, government had a clear role, which included protecting the weak from exploitation by large powerful commercial interests; ensuring that the economy delivered benefits to the majority of people; and maintaining the egalitarian society that Australians had come to expect.

NOTES

1 Donald Horne, 'It's Time for a Think', in Donald Horne (ed) *The Trouble with Economic Rationalism*, Newham, Victoria, Scribe, 1992, p8.

2 José Piñera, 'Chile', in John Williamson (ed) *The Political Economy of Policy Reform*, Washington, DC, Institute for International Economics, 1994, p225; Sidney Blumenthal, *The Rise of the Counter-Establishment: From Conservative Ideology to Political Power*, New York, Time Books, 1986, p112.

3 Piñera, 'Chile', p225; Steve Kangas, 'Chile: The Laboratory Test', Liberalism Resurgent, www.huppi.com/kangaroo/L-chichile.htm accessed 15 August 2004.

4 Kangas, 'Chile'; Blumenthal, *The Rise of the Counter-Establishment*, pp113–114.

5 Kangas, 'Chile'.

6 Greg Palast, *The Best Democracy Money Can Buy*, London, Pluto Press, 2002, p73.

7 Joseph E. Stiglitz, *Globalization and Its Discontents*, New York, W. W. Norton & Co., 2002, p16.

8 Mary Ann Haley, *Freedom and Finance: Democratization and Institutional Investors in Developing Countries*, New York, Palgrave, 2001, p69; Mark T. Berger, *The Battle for Asia: From Decolonization to Globalization*, New York, RoutledgeCurzon, 2004, p154; Haley, *Freedom and Finance*, p108.

9 Stiglitz, *Globalization and Its Discontents*, pp12–13.

10 John Weeks, 'Credit Where Discredit Is Due', *Third World Resurgence*, April, 1994, p32; Walden Bello and Shea Cunningham, 'The World Bank & the IMF', *Z Magazine*, July, 1994, www.zmag.org/zmag/articles/july94bello.htm.

11 Cited in Brian Easton, 'From Reaganomics to Rogernomics', in Alan Bollard (ed) *The Influence of United States Economics on New Zealand*, Wellington, NZ-US Educational Foundation and the New Zealand Institute of Economic Research, 1988, p75.

12 Stiglitz, *Globalization and Its Discontents*, p19; John Carroll, 'Economic Rationalism and Its Consequences', in John Carroll and Robert Manne (eds) *Shutdown: The Failure of Economic Rationalism and How to Rescue Australia*, Melbourne, The Text Publishing Company, 1992, p9; Jane Kelsey, *Reclaiming the Future: New Zealand and the Global Economy*, Wellington, Bridget Williams Books, 1999, pp63–4.
13 Haley, *Freedom and Finance*, p69.
14 John Williamson, 'In Search of a Manual for Technopols', in John Williamson (ed) *The Political Economy of Policy Reform*, Washington, Institute for International Economics, DC, 1994, p17; Institute for International Economics, 'About the Institute for International Economics', IIE, www.iie.com/ADMINIST/aboutiie.htm accessed 6 January 2001.
15 Williamson, 'In Search of a Manual for Technopols', pp26–8.
16 *Ibid.*, p11.
17 *Ibid.*, p12.
18 Peter Self, *Government by the Market? The Politics of Public Choice*, Hampshire and London, Macmillan, 1993, p70.
19 Sharon Beder, *Suiting Themselves: How Corporations Drive the Global Agenda*, London, Earthscan, 2006, Chapter 3.
20 Frank Stilwell, 'Economic Rationalism: Sound Foundations for Policy?' in Stuart Rees, Gordon Rodley and Frank Stilwell (eds) *Beyond the Market: Alternatives to Economic Rationalism*, Leichhardt, NSW, Pluto Press, 1993, p36; Williamson, 'In Search of a Manual for Technopols', p17.
21 John Gray, *False Dawn: The Delusions of Global Capitalism*, London, Granta Books, 2002, pp25–6, 29, 32 .
22 *Ibid.*, pp25–6, 29.
23 *Ibid.*, pp28–9.
24 *Ibid.*, pp48–50, 53.
25 *Ibid.*, pp45–6.
26 *Ibid.*, p46.
27 Gabriel Kolko, 'Ravaging the Poor: IMF Indicted by Its Own Data', *Multinational Monitor*, June, 1998, p21.
28 Palast, *The Best Democracy Money Can Buy*, p48.
29 Paul Blustein, 'IMF's "Consensus" Policies Fraying', *Washington Post*, 26 September 2002, pE01; Richard Lapper, 'Piling on the Pressure', *Financial Times*, 5 October 2002, p1; Juan Forero, 'Still Poor, Latin Americans Protest Push for Open Markets', *New York Times*, 19 July 2002, pA-1.
30 Quoted in Palast, *The Best Democracy Money Can Buy*, p50.
31 Forero, 'Still Poor, Latin Americans Protest Push for Open Markets', pA-1.
32 Stilwell, 'Economic Rationalism' p35.
33 Self, *Government by the Market?* p72.
34 Tom Weyman-Jones, 'Deregulation', in Peter M. Jackson and Catherine M. Price (eds) *Privatisation and Regulation: A Review of the Issues*, London and New York, Longman, 1994, p99.
35 Gray, *False Dawn*, p1; Tim Battin, 'What Is This Thing Called Economic Rationalism?' *Australian Journal of Social Issues*, vol 26, no 4, 1991, pp301–3.
36 Francis G. Castles, Rolf Gerritsen and Jack Vowles (eds) *The Great Experiment: Labour Parties and Public Policy Transformation in Australia and New Zealand*, Sydney, Allen

& Unwin, 1996, ppix, 18; Paul Kelly, *The End of Uncertainty: The Story of the 1980s*, Allen & Unwin, St Leonards, NSW, 1992, p15.

37 Gray, *False Dawn*, pp39–40.

38 Allan Bollard, 'New Zealand', in John Williamson (ed) *The Political Economy of Policy Reform*, Washington, DC, Institute for International Economics, 1994, p92.

39 Patrick Massey, *New Zealand: Market Liberalization in a Developed Economy*, New York, St Martin's Press, 1995, pp66–9; Bollard, 'New Zealand', p89; Massey, *New Zealand*, p65.

40 Jane Kelsey, *Economic Fundamentalism*, London, Pluto Press, 1995, pp30–1; Bollard, 'New Zealand', p89.

41 Jonathan Boston and John Uhr, 'Reshaping the Mechanics of Government', in Castles, *et al.* (eds) *The Great Experiment: Labour Parties and Public Policy Transformation in Australia and New Zealand*, p52; Massey, *New Zealand*, p69; Bollard, 'New Zealand', p90.

42 Tim W. Ferguson, 'New Zealand's Unfinished Economic Experiment', *Wall Street Journal*, 1 December 1989.

43 Bollard, 'New Zealand', p93; Chris Eichbaum, 'Market Liberalisation in New Zealand: Fightback! In Practice?' in Peter Vintila, John Phillimore and Peter Newman (eds) *Markets, Morals & Manifestos: Fightback! & the Politics of Economic Rationalism in the 1990s*, Murdoch, WA, Institute for Science and Technology Policy, Murdoch University, 1992, p225; Castles, *et al.* (eds) *The Great Experiment*, p16; Massey, *New Zealand*, p74.

44 Kelsey, *Economic Fundamentalism*, p39.

45 Greg Lindsay, 'Threats to Freedom Then and Now', *Policy*, Autumn, 1997, www.cis.org.au/Policy/mps.html; Massey, *New Zealand*, p74; Kelsey, *Economic Fundamentalism*, p41; Brian Easton, 'From Rogernomics to Ruthanasia: New Right Economics in New Zealand', in Stuart Rees, Gordon Rodley and Frank Stilwell (eds) *Beyond the Market: Alternatives to Economic Rationalism*, Leichhardt, NSW, Pluto Press, 1993, p150.

46 Bollard, 'New Zealand', p90; Boston and Uhr, 'Reshaping the Mechnics of Government', p52; Easton, 'From Reaganomics to Rogernomics', p71.

47 Bollard, 'New Zealand', p91; Kelsey, *Economic Fundamentalism*, p54; Easton, 'From Reaganomics to Rogernomics', p72.

48 Kelsey, *Economic Fundamentalism*, pp53–4.

49 Easton, 'From Reaganomics to Rogernomics', p72.

50 Bollard, 'New Zealand', pp91, 94.

51 *Ibid.*, p91; Easton, 'From Reaganomics to Rogernomics', pp86–8; Kelsey, *Economic Fundamentalism*, p55.

52 Quoted in Kelsey, *Economic Fundamentalism*, p65.

53 *Ibid.*, pp49–53; Bollard, 'New Zealand', p91.

54 Bollard, 'New Zealand', p92.

55 Barry Spicer, *et al.*, *Transforming Government Enterprises: Managing Radical Organisational Change in Deregulated Environments*, St Leonards, NSW, Centre for Independent Studies, 1996, p77.

56 Kelsey, *Economic Fundamentalism*, p52.

57 Rolf Gerritsen, 'Microeconomic Reform', in Stephen Bell and Brian Head (eds) *State, Economy and Public Policy*, Melbourne, Oxford University Press, 1994, p272.

58 Carroll, 'Economic Rationalism and Its Consequences', p13.
59 CIS, 'Staff and Contact Details', Centre for Independent Studies, www.cis.org.au/mainpages/staff.html accessed 6 April 2001.
60 Tasman Institute, 'Tasman Institute Annual Review', Melbourne, Tasman Institute Pty Ltd and Tasman Economic Research Pty Ltd, December 1991.
61 CIS, 'Staff and Contact Details'.
62 Tasman Institute, 'Tasman Institute Annual Review', p11.
63 Kelly, *The End of Uncertainty*, p31.
64 Greg Whitwell, 'Economic Ideas and Economic Policy: The Rise of Economic Rationalism in Australia', *Australian Economic History Review*, vol 33, no 2, 1993, p21.
65 Bob Catley, *Globalising Australian Capitalism*, Cambridge, 1996, Cambridge University Press, p66; Whitwell, 'Economic Ideas and Economic Policy', p12.
66 Catley, *Globalising Australian Capitalism*, p65.
67 John Langmore, 'The Labor Government in a De-Regulatory Era', in Brian Galligan and Gwynneth Singleton (eds) *Business and Government under Labor*, Melbourne, Longman Cheshire, 1991, pp79–83.
68 Carroll, 'Economic Rationalism and Its Consequences', p10; Stilwell, 'Economic Rationalism' p32; Kelly, *The End of Uncertainty: The Story of the 1980s*, p55.
60 Ross Garnaut, 'Australia', in John Williamson (ed) *The Political Economy of Policy Reform*, Washington, DC, Institute for International Economics, 1994, p70.
70 Kelly, *The End of Uncertainty*, p30.
71 David Kemp, 'Liberalism and Conservatism in Australia since 1944', in Brian Head and James Walter (eds) *Intellectual Movements and Australian Society*, Melbourne, Oxford University Press, 1988, p337.
72 Kelly, *The End of Uncertainty: The Story of the 1980s*, p402.
73 Belinda Probert, 'Globalisation, Economic Restructuring and the State', in Stephen Bell and Brian Head (eds) *State, Economy and Public Policy*, Melbourne, Oxford University Press, 1994, p99.
74 John W. Holmes and Thomas A. Wileman, 'Reform in the Australian Public Service 1983–1996', Office of the Auditor General of Canada, www.oag-bvg.gc.ca/domino/other.nsf/html/aus.html accessed 29 June 2001; R. S. Parker and J. R. Nethercote, 'The Administrative Vocation in the 1990s', in S. S. Richardson (ed) *Public Administration under Scrutiny: Essays in Honour of Roger Wettenhall*, Canberra, Centre for Research in Public Sector Management, University of Canberra and Institute of Public Administration Australia, 1996, p105; Boston and Uhr, 'Reshaping the Mechanics of Government', p56; John Halligan and John Power, *Political Management in the 1990s*, Oxford, Oxford University Press, 1992, pp79, 84.
75 Holmes and Wileman, 'Reform in the Australian Public Service 1983–1996'; Parker and Nethercote, 'The Administrative Vocation in the 1990s', p100; Elizabeth Harman, 'The Impact of Public Sector Reforms on Australian Government', in Patrick Weller, John Forster and Glyn Davis (eds) *Reforming the Public Service: Lessons from Recent Experience*, South Melbourne, Macmillan Education Australia, 1993, p27.
76 Parker and Nethercote, 'The Administrative Vocation in the 1990s', p101.
77 Halligan and Power, *Political Management in the 1990s*, p107; Michael Pusey, *Economic Rationalism in Canberra*, Cambridge, Cambridge University Press, 1991, p297.

78 Pusey, *Economic Rationalism in Canberra*, p8.
79 *Ibid.*, p8.
80 *Ibid.*; Michael Pusey, 'Canberra Changes Its Mind: The New Mandarins', in John Carroll and Robert Manne (eds) *Shutdown: The Failure of Economic Rationalism and How to Rescue Australia*, Melbourne, The Text Publishing Company, 1992, p39.
81 Greenspan quoted in APEE, 'The Association of Private Enterprise Education', Association of Private Enterprise Education, www.apee.org/about/main.html accessed 6 December 2001; Pusey, *Economic Rationalism in Canberra*, pp5–6; Aynsley Kellow, 'Changing Conceptions of Responsiblity in Government', in John Porter (ed) *Public Administration in Australia: A Watershed*, Sydney, Hale & Iremonger, 1990, p69.
82 Pusey, *Economic Rationalism in Canberra*, p133.
83 Michael Keating, 'Mega-Departments: The Theory, Objectives and Outcomes of the 1987 Reforms', in Patrick Weller, John Forster and Glyn Davis (eds) *Reforming the Public Service: Lessons from Recent Experience*, South Melbourne, Macmillan Education Australia, 1993, p2.
84 Bernard Logan, 'Power Behind the Premier's Throne', *Sydney Morning Herald*, 3 April 2000, p6; Matthew Moore, 'Greiner's Muscle Man Toughs It Out', *Sydney Morning Herald*, 18 August 1990.
85 Gary L. Sturgess, 'Microeconomic Reform: An Overview', in Brian Galligan, Bob Lim and Kim Lovegrove (eds) *Managing Microeconomic Reform*, Canberra, Federalism Research Centre, ANU, 1993, p9.
86 Logan, 'Power Behind the Premier's Throne', p6; Moore, 'Greiner's Muscle Man Toughs It Out'; Editorial, 'Exit Architect of Greinerism', *Sydney Morning Herald*, 26 September 1992, p24; Mark Coultran, 'Greiner Steps Back from the Precipice', *Sydney Morning Herald*, 28 March 1992, p26.
87 Moore, 'Greiner's Muscle Man Toughs It Out'; Logan, 'Power Behind the Premier's Throne', p6.
88 Editorial, 'Exit Architect of Greinerism', p24; Matthew Moore, 'Greiner Adviser Blamed', *Sydney Morning Herald*, 29 June 1991, p4; Tim Dodd, 'Greiner's Top Man Quits to Become Policy Consultant', *Sydney Morning Herald*, 25 September 1992, p5.
89 Chris Spindler, 'Carr Government Takes Conservative Lead', *Green Left Weekly*, 1995, http://jinx.sistm.unsw.edu.au/~greenlft/1995/206/206p6.htm, p6.
90 Lindy Edwards, *How to Argue with an Economist: Reopening Political Debate in Australia*, Cambridge, Cambridge University Press, 2002, p7.
91 Peter Blazey, 'Now It's Stirrer Stone, Company Director', *The Bulletin*, 27 August 1985.
92 Lindsay, 'Threats to Freedom Then and Now'.
93 Tom Burton, 'How We Packaged Nick', *Sydney Morning Herald*, 26 March 1988, p65.
94 Kelly, *The End of Uncertainty*, p42.
95 *Ibid.*, pp21–3.
96 *Ibid.*, p24.
97 *Ibid.*, p24.
98 *Ibid.*, p26.
99 *Ibid.*, p26.

100 Patrick Weller, 'Reforming the Public Service: What Has Been Achieved and How Can It Be Evaluated?' in Patrick Weller, John Forster and Glyn Davis (eds) *Reforming the Public Service: Lessons from Recent Experience*, South Melbourne, Macmillan Education Australia, 1993, p233.
101 Edwards, *How to Argue with an Economist*, p13.
102 Castles, *et al.* (eds) *The Great Experiment*, p16.
103 Quoted in Kelsey, *Economic Fundamentalism*, p7.
104 Gray, *False Dawn*, p42.
105 Kelsey, *Economic Fundamentalism*, p9.
106 Bollard, 'New Zealand', p94; Castles, *et al.* (eds) *The Great Experiment*, p13.
107 Kelsey, *Economic Fundamentalism*, p11.
108 Carroll, 'Economic Rationalism and Its Consequences', p11.
109 Edwards, *How to Argue with an Economist*, p92.
110 Doug McEachern, *Business Mates: The Power and Politics of the Hawke Era*, Sydney, Prentice Hall, 1991, p80.
111 Matt Wade and Jamie Freed, 'BHP Hits Jackpot of a Lifetime', *Sydney Morning Herald*, 25 August 2005, p1.
112 Elaine Thompson, 'Where Is the Economy?' in Donald Horne (ed) *The Trouble with Economic Rationalism*, Newham, Victoria, Scribe, 1992, p16; Edwards, *How to Argue with an Economist*, p11.

11

People's Capitalism

If the Beatles were still together, they would probably be singing about day traders, not day trippers. RONALD BROWNSTEIN[1]

Empower America was founded in 1993 by corporate lobbyist Vin Weber and three high-flying Republicans: Jack Kemp, a Distinguished Fellow of the Heritage Foundation, had been Secretary of Housing and Urban Development for President George Bush Senior; Jeanne Kilpatrick had been US ambassador to the United Nations (UN); and William Bennet had been Secretary of Education for President Ronald Reagan. Empower America funders included the Scaife and Olin foundations. It was chaired until 1996 by Steve Forbes of the business magazine *Forbes*, and Donald Rumsfeld, current Secretary for Defense, was on the founding board.[2]

Empower America described itself as 'bridging the gap between the array of think-thanks that produce white papers on the public-policy debate and the actual enactment of policy'. In 2004 it merged with an anti-regulation corporate front group, Citizens for a Sound Economy, to form FreedomWorks which 'fights for lower taxes, less government and more economic freedom'. A key issue for Empower America and subsequently FreedomWorks is the replacement of social security by a scheme whereby each worker can invest a portion of their taxation deductions in the stock market to pay for their retirement.[3]

This is something President George W. Bush is now promoting as a way of partially privatizing social security. He has pledged 'to add a private, market-based component to retirement security through "personal retirement accounts"'. Following his re-election in 2004 he set about implementing this programme. The idea is for a portion of the payroll taxes that are used to pay for social security to be diverted into private investment accounts, and it will grow according to the value of the shares, property or bank accounts it is invested in. In this way the money available to people when they retire will be based on the market growth of their investment, which advocates say will be more than they would receive through social security. Since these taxes are currently used to fund present-day retirees, the government has to borrow trillions of dollars to pay for the scheme over ten years.[4]

In one of its background briefing papers, entitled 'How to Fix Social Security', the Heritage Foundation argues that personal retirement accounts are 'the only solution that will give future retirees the opportunity to receive an improved standard of living in retirement. These accounts would give them more control over how to structure their income and allow them to build a nest egg…'.[5]

The logic of the reforms is difficult to understand. The rationale is that in 40 years or so, social security may not have the funds to cover people's pensions. Funds invested in the stock market, however, are presumed to grow much faster than social security funds invested in Treasury bonds, and therefore will make up the shortfall. However, social security funds are invested in low-yielding Treasury bonds because they are safe and the income is guaranteed. The stock market, on the other hand, is volatile and highly risky. Otherwise, 'the government could erase Social Security's entire projected deficit by selling bonds at 3 per cent and buying stocks that yield 7 per cent'. Economist and *New York Times'* columnist, Paul Krugman, notes that, in effect, what the government is proposing to do is 'borrow heavily and put the money in the stock market' via private retirement accounts. That is, the privatization of social security involves the 'government borrowing to speculate on stocks'.[6]

Because this is an idea that does not have popular support, and few people believe that social security is facing a future crisis, the Bush camp is 'raising millions of dollars for an election-style campaign' to promote it in what is expected to be 'the most expensive and extensive public policy debate since the 1993 fight over the Clinton administration's failed health-care plan'. However, this time, business is on the side of the president. The National Association of Manufacturers (NAM) is 'leading the charge for business interests' with an Alliance for Worker Retirement Security, consisting of 40 NAM members headed by Derrick Max, to back the president's social security privatization plan.[7]

Another business coalition, which includes NAM and is also being coordinated by Derrick Max, is the Coalition for the Modernization and Protection of America's Social Security (Compass). Compass is an umbrella group that includes other business groups such as The Business Roundtable, the Financial Services Forum and the National Restaurant Association. It spent $5 million in 2001–2 making the case that social security would face a funding crisis in the future. Now it says its members are backing the president on this plan because they are concerned that he would otherwise use payroll taxes to make up the predicted social security shortfall. Bush denies that this will happen. Nevertheless, Compass is preparing to spend $5million to help the campaign for private accounts.[8]

Various conservative groups are adding their own resources. Progress for America has budgeted $9 million for the campaign and intends to raise more. Club for Growth is hoping to raise $15 million for the campaign.[9]

The privatization of social security, and the financial support it is garnering in the business community, cannot be understood in terms of direct vested interests. Only the financial services companies, such as stockbrokers and investment firms, stand to gain directly from the plan. The push is better understood in terms of a hidden political agenda. Bush presents the reforms as part of his vision of an 'ownership society': 'When people have a stake in something', Treasury Secretary John W. Snow explained, 'it makes the whole social system work better.' Also, if social security is privatized and everyone has their own accounts, then they are no longer dependent on government for their retirement and this is supposed to change people's relationship with government so that they take more personal responsibility for their future.[10]

A stronger, yet unstated motivation, is to involve millions of Americans in the stock market. This becomes clear when we consider the rationale Kemp used to push the scheme:

> *Everyone should be free to experience the miracle of the markets. ... In other words, imagine America not just as a constitutional republic but as a vibrant shareholder democracy where everyone not only has a vote but also owns property ... In a democratic capitalist system that succeeds in giving people access to capital, owners of capital and workers are not different people, but the very same people at different stages of their lives ... I can't think of a better way to directly move capital from Wall Street to Main Street, and from the government to the people, than to allow each worker to become a saver, an owner, and indeed, a capitalist – with personal retirement accounts.*[11]

Kemp claims that in the New Economy 'almost half of all American adults are now participating in the new prosperity as shareholders of stocks and bonds or through their pension funds'. Rather than being the territory of elites, as they once were, he sees 'record numbers of women and young people and minorities' involved in the share market: 'Main Street is taking over Wall Street. It's exciting.... And when people have more than just their own paycheck – when they own a stake in something bigger than themselves – what they really own is a stake in America.'[12]

THINKING LIKE CAPITALISTS

People in business circles see wider share ownership as essential for increasing the popular support for corporate-friendly free market government policies, since more people would then have an interest in seeing the stock market increase in value. This is a key reason for the corporate push for spreading share ownership, particularly through pensions and employee share-ownership schemes. Once people's savings are invested in mutual funds and their pensions are dependent on stock market movements, they become much more concerned about the stock market.

Grover George, president of the American Shareholders Association (ASA) claims:

> *When a wage worker enters the investor class through a work-based 401(k) [retirement accounts that can be invested in the stock market]... his opinions on vouchers, free trade, and entitlement privatization are no likelier to change overnight than his party affiliation. But as his plan assets grow, so do his expectations for their performance. ... over time, he actively seeks sources of information that will maximize his efficiency in his new vocation: that of a capitalist. It is this pursuit that changes his opinions on a variety of partisan and policy questions to favor market-based solutions and their political advocates.*[13]

Kemp points out that if everyone owned stock they would all demand policies from government that encouraged economic growth and business opportunities. The *Australian Financial Review* similarly argued that the new generation of 'worker shareholders' has a 'reason to scour the stock exchange tables every morning' and 'will inject a powerful dose of support for market capitalism, free markets, minimal government, internationalisation and efficient management into the body politic'.[14]

As more people own shares, particularly through pensions and mutual funds, so the readership of business papers and magazines has increased dramatically. By 1997 the *Wall Street Journal* had become the daily paper with the highest circulation, and magazines such as *Money*, *Business Week*, *Forbes* and *Fortune* were likewise doing very well.

Likewise, in Australia a couple of years later, as the number of Australian shareholders increased, the ABC news had replaced its sports anchorperson with a business reporter, and the best-selling book was *Rich Dad, Poor Dad*, which was about how to make money through investment. John Budd, ABC's national editor, called business and finance 'the main participation sport for most Australians'.[15] In addition, finance programmes were increasingly featured on popular television channels.[16] Adele Horin in the *Sydney Morning Herald* noted:

> *The spread of share ownership to the middle class is changing how we spend our time, what we talk about, celebrate, worry about. It has even changed what we watch on television ... The perspective of a shareholder is different from that of a citizen without a portfolio. Mesmerised shareholders can begin to believe rising unemployment is good because it boosts share prices, and applaud a tax system that continues to treat shares and dividends far more favourably than wages. Support for socially responsible corporate behaviour – let alone progressive policies such as a 36-hour working week or paid maternity leave – can evaporate under threat of a sliding share price.*[17]

In the US, in an article entitled 'Your Politics vs. Your Portfolio', Dennis Fox observed:

> *It now matters to more people whether the Dow is up or down, whether the Nasdaq's latest slide is just temporary … it's hard to maintain an anti-corporate political stance when your computer keeps a running tab of your ever-changing net worth.*[18]

Richard Nadler did a study for the neoconservative think tank the Cato Institute, entitled *The Rise of Worker Capitalism.* It included a commissioned survey showing that people who invested in shares were more likely to identify as Republicans than non-investors; this was true even of minorities and single women – not traditionally strong Republican supporters. This meant, he argued, that the rise of share ownership, even when through pension funds, had shifted the political balance in favour of pro-business policies: 'Hypothetically, as workers accumulate capital, their support for free-market and pro-growth policy reforms will increase. The available evidence suggests that this is precisely the case.'[19]

The *Wall Street Journal* claims that the 1980s' criticism of greed, shown in Oliver Stone's movie *Wall Street*, had disappeared by the 1990s as everyone indulged in share ownership:

> *Today, even our lowest earners see that the Decade of Greed and its blockbuster sequel, the 1990s, have benefited just about everyone. Workers nowadays don't have time to hate Gekko, or his 1990s equivalents … They are busy puffing their own stogies and mounting their own shareholder revolution.*[20]

Shawn Tully argued in *Fortune* magazine in 1987 that privatization, 'the hot new trend in business … sweeping Europe', was 'creating a people's capitalism that will almost certainly change ordinary citizens' attitudes toward government and business. As share owners, Europeans will be more likely to support the free-market policies that so many governments have shifted to in recent years. The new capitalists may be even more understanding when managers use their new flexibility to cut costs and, sometimes, jobs.'[21]

Similarly, Padraic McGuinness, an Australian free market ideologue, argued in his weekly newspaper column that 'both the ideological and organisational underpinnings of Labor are being undermined by the spread of people's capitalism … it is certain that the already moribund notion of "them against us", capitalists versus workers, will be thoroughly dead and buried within the next few years … As share ownership spreads there will be more and more questioning of taxes … Share-owning employees also will become more determined than others in their companies to pull their weight, and that abuse of work practices and overmanning should cease.'[22]

A survey commissioned by the ASA found that 'mass ownership of financial assets has midwifed a new birth of freemarket opinion'. It found that Republican affiliation correlated with the length of time that a person had been in a retirement plan. After 10 years those in a 401(k) plan were 7 per cent more likely to support a corporate tax cut, 9 per cent more like to oppose a minimum wage, 10 per cent more likely to support school vouchers, and 17 per cent more likely to support social security privatization than non-investors. They were also more likely to support free trade, death-tax reduction and market-based energy policies. Those owning stocks directly, as opposed to indirectly via pension funds, developed a capitalist ideology even more rapidly.[23]

A Gallup poll in 1999 found that shareowners were more likely to support cuts in capital gains tax, as did Rasmussen Research, which found that the result held for all demographic groups. Similarly, a Pew Research Center survey of attitudes found in 1999 that middle-income share investors were slightly more sceptical of government spending and regulation than other middle-income non-investors.[24] 'It is this educating tendency of capital ownership that the GOP has been slow to grasp', according to Nadler, who urges the Republican Party 'to nurture the movement toward worker capitalism' for this reason. He argues:

> *A young worker starts his 401(k) account not because he identifies with the political Right, but because he wants to save for retirement. Yet by deferring some consumption in favor of savings and investment, he has in fact become a capitalist. The return on his broad-based mutual funds will depend on policy decisions that unite him with more experienced capitalists, whose interests may differ from his more in quantity than in kind. And to the extent that his portfolio becomes important in the life of his family, that unity will increase.*[25]

Peter Du Pont, a former governor of Delaware and policy chairman of the National Center for Policy Analysis claims:

> *The implications of our emerging democratic capitalism are enormous. Once-impossible dreams of 'every man a capitalist' now appear attainable. If most workers and retirees become heavily invested in American business, the political fallout will begin with termination of class-warfare rhetoric and politicians who rely on such demagoguery.*[26]

In Western Europe, a growing 'shareholder culture' is also 'beginning to change the politics', according to George Melloan in the *Wall Street Journal.* He argues that while corporations were once regarded as 'national champions' to be regulated so that they would serve the public interest, now their managers are free to 'resist such pressures on grounds that their primary duty is to shareholders'.[27]

People's capitalism will demand that politicians consider the interest of shareholders, rather than focusing on the presumed needs of pressure groups. The power of unions is already slipping as a new generation of more individualistic Europeans comes on the scene.[28]

Similarly, in the US, Melloan argues that 'the advent of people's capitalism fulfils what for many years has been a Wall Street dream, an era when most Americans would have a stake in American business and would thus be sympathetic to the needs of a capitalist system'. He suggests that this was reflected in US politics in Clinton's attempt to 'co-opt the free market ideals of the Republican Revolution'.[29]

EMPLOYEE SHARE OWNERSHIP

The ownership of shares has long been seen to be a way to get working people to identify with the aims and interests of employers. In 1939 a number of industrial companies testified to a Senate Finance Committee hearing about the value of profit-sharing and how employee ownership of shares enabled the interests of workers and management to be reconciled and union conflict and political class struggle to be diminished.[30]

Various employers also attested to the value of profit sharing in the US in the 1950s. It was aimed at not only ensuring employee loyalty, but also enhancing the idea that the worker and the employer were in partnership to produce profits. In this way, workers would be in favour of any measures aimed at increasing productivity and would identify more closely with employers. 'In other words: if you feel like an owner of the company you'll do what the boss wants without being asked/told.'[31]

Profit sharing in the form of stock options is still promoted today as a way of ensuring that workers have a stake in company profitability. Between 5 and 10 per cent of US companies offer stock options to all employees, even manual workers. Many more offer stock options to executives. Stock options give the employee the right to buy shares some time in the future at a price set in the present (often at a discount to current market value). The more the share price goes up the more the options are worth because the difference between the set buying price and the sale price is more.

Stock options are used to align the interests of employees with those of share holders and to motivate employees to work hard for company success. *HR Magazine* argued that stock options 'help to create a company-wide "ownership culture" by focusing employees' attention on the employers' financial performance'.[32]

It has been found that, since 1992, companies with 'employee ownership' plans outperformed others in terms of productivity and share value increase in the UK, the US and France, and employee share ownership schemes cause workers to be more committed to their company and to be more likely to identify with it. This seems to be independent of the amount of shares owned. However, it has also been found that being able to participate in management decisions is even more important for motivation and commitment, but firms are generally unwilling to go that far.[33]

If workers stand to gain from their shares then there is less need to reward them directly for productivity gains with higher wages. In fact, they will better understand how such wage increases might adversely affect share prices and will make fewer demands to see the productivity gains in their wage packets. In a 1998 consultation paper the UK government argued: 'employees who are also shareholders may better understand the risks faced by the company and its investors, which in turn can encourage recognition of the case for pay responsibility'.[34] 'Pay responsibility' in this case refers to the willingness of employees to forgo pay rises – not to demand pay rises – in the hope of ensuring that company profits and share value will rise. By the end of the 1990s 'the myth of the wage/stock tradeoff was so widely accepted that its truest believers were able to present it as a historical principle'.[35]

Schemes that allow employees to buy shares in the company at discounted prices – or give them to employees as part of bonuses or salary packages – are also aimed at aligning employee interests with those of shareholders. In the UK over 500 companies run Approved Employee Share Plans for some 3.5 million employees. In the US there are between 17 and 20 million workers in large share ownership plans and other schemes that hold employer stock including pension schemes. One in five employees has stock in the company they work for, outside of stock option plans. However, in most cases, employees own a small minority of their company's stock.[36]

The UK government provides tax breaks for approved stock plans as an incentive to encourage them. Chancellor Gordon Brown has argued that employee share schemes 'encourage the new enterprise culture of team work in which everyone contributes and everyone benefits from success ... Britain can and must become a democracy of enterprise, that gives all who create wealth a greater stake in the wealth they create.' He argued that 'Employee share ownership is a milestone in removing once and for all the old "them and us" culture in industry.'[37]

Such views come straight from the propaganda kit of the business lobbies. George Cox, director-general of the UK Institute of Directors (IOD), has argued that employee share plans are a way 'of engaging all employees in the commercial success of the enterprise' and thereby for the UK to 'create a genuine enterprise culture'. Similarly Digby Jones, director-general of the Confederation of British Industry (CBI) has said they are 'an invaluable tool for giving employees a direct stake in the business'.[38]

The UK group ProShare promotes employee share ownership. It evolved out of the Wider Share Ownership Council, and was founded by the UK Treasury, the London Stock Exchange (LSE) and a consortium of major companies, with the aim of encouraging share ownership. It is now independent of government and funded by donations from over 180 companies and grants from LSE and various charities and foundations. It has initiated some 10,000 investment clubs, carries out research and lobbies government to ensure government policies are in the interests of investors.[39] It argues that there is plenty of research to show 'a clear link between employee ownership and improved corporate performance' when employees are encouraged to feel like part owners of the corporation. It also runs 12 different training courses for industry on employee share plans and hopes to develop an externally accredited qualification in the area.[40]

The British Financial Secretary, Stephen Timms, argued in 2000 that employee share ownership 'is a cornerstone of the drive to tackle the productivity gap and promote a high investment Britain, a Britain where we reward enterprise and provide fairness for all'. He said that it would create 'a community of interest between workers and owners'. The government's Share Incentive Plan (SIP) provides tax breaks for firms and employees when employees buy or receive shares in the company they work for. The aim of SIP was to 'foster a community of interest between management and workers so as to contribute to the general well-being of the business'. It hoped to increase the number of shareholders in Britain by 2.5 million over 3 to 5 years at a cost to the government of about £400 million a year.[41]

The Employee Share Alliance (ESA) is a British alliance of business and union groups, including the Trades Union Congress (TUC), the CBI, and the IOD, which aims to promote and publicize SIP. In addition, ProShare organized 14 road shows in conjunction with the Inland Revenue department, to promote SIP in 2002.[42]

Another UK group promoting wider share ownership is the group Job Ownership Ltd (JOL) which 'has been researching, lobbying and advising on employee ownership for over twenty years both in the UK and around the world'. JOL is funded by a group of UK companies that call themselves 'leading employee-owned companies', suggesting that employee stock holders are the company owners. JOL argues that employee share ownership schemes are supported by all political parties. For Conservatives they are a 'way to spread property ownership to a wider constituency, turning them into capitalists' while for the Labour Party they are a form of social ownership.[43]

The National Center for Employee Ownership (NCEO), based in California, encourages companies to create an 'ownership culture' amongst their employees. It claims to be the 'main publisher and research source in the field' of employee ownership.[44] Ownership Associates of Cambridge, Massachusetts, periodically publishes *The Ownership Culture Report*. Defining ownership culture, it states: 'An ownership culture exists in a company where employees think and act like owners.' It argues that employee share ownership schemes encourage workers to act in the company's interest by creating an ownership culture. However, since workers might perceive ownership differently from managers, 'company leaders must work with and, where necessary, challenge employee interpretations of ownership'.[45]

David Wray, from the Profit Sharing/401(k) Council of America, says 'Stock ownership by employees aligns the interests of employees and employers. It reduces the "we versus they" perspective.' Another US-based organization that seeks to create an ownership culture is the Foundation for Enterprise Development (FED) which is 'dedicated to advancing the use of enterprise employee ownership nationally and internationally, in both the public and private sectors'. It argues that share ownership gives employees 'a financial and psychological stake' in the company they work for, 'and therefore a personal stake' which will 'align the interests of employees with the strategic goals of the company'.[46]

In Australia an inquiry was held into share ownership in Australian enterprises in 1999. It was chaired by Liberal MP Brendan Nelson. Witnesses to the hearings told the parliamentary committee that share plans were 'a means of aligning the interests of business and employees so as to achieve better business results'; a way of rewarding employees for their efforts in a 'tax-effective' manner; a method of encouraging savings and 'a means of "democratising" capital: that is, spreading capital ownership and access to capital more widely within the community'.[47]

Nelson argued that 'employee share plans bind people more closely to the activities of their fellow citizens who work within a particular organization' and 'create a more inclusive workplace'.[48]

Shann Turbull, a founding member of the Australian Employee Ownership Association, and author of *Democratising the Wealth of Nations*, argued that corporations misused employee share ownership schemes as a way of legitimizing excessive payments to top executives by offering shares to all employees: 'I am suggesting that we want to see beyond that to get not just a mandate within a corporation, but a mandate within the whole voting constituency of Australia, so that all people have an inclusive vested interest in property ownership.'[49]

The Business Council of Australia (BCA) also support employee share ownership plans because they give large numbers of people a financial stake in the company they work for and therefore an incentive to contribute to its success: 'Shared ownership can create an environment of common goals and shared interest between employees and management.'[50] Eighty per cent of its members listed on the stock exchange had such plans. It cited the Australian Gas Light Company, which stated:

> *... we believe it is important for our employees not only to think like Proprietors, but also to participate in the benefits of improvements in the Company ... linking the employees with the Company as Proprietors has indeed helped focus priorities.*

It also cited Woodside Petroleum, which said its plan 'has been shown to contribute to employee alignment with Company goals'.[51]

Similarly, Workplace Relations Minister Peter Reith was encouraging employee share ownership because, according to *The Bulletin*:

> *By becoming part-owners, staff would hopefully come to better appreciate matters such as costs, profits and the impact of wage rates. They would be less bolshie and more understanding of what management and owners are trying to achieve, as they would all be rewarded along similar lines.*[52]

In its submission, BHP told the same inquiry that employees owned shares or options worth 7.6 per cent of the company's capital and that its motivation in providing this opportunity was to help wage earners to understand and experience private enterprise; to justify 'the profit motive in terms of risk return for investors'; and to encourage 'employees to take a more active interest as co-owners of the company and for them to look beyond their local domain'.[53]

Rob Donkersley, Employee Relations Director for Coca-Cola Amatil, told the inquiry about his company's employee share ownership plan:

> *We feel we have captured the minds of our employees through this plan. We have provided a good vehicle for them to link themselves with the fortunes of the company and take a wider perspective than their individual role in their individual operation could allow ... We believe, although we cannot prove it, there is this beneficial effect in terms of getting the productivity levels that we want and the commitment that we want from employees throughout the enterprise ... Our objective is to have it available in all countries over time.*[54]

However, corporate executives are loath to share any power with the new owners. In the US in the mid-1990s when employees owned an average of 13 per cent of 562 publicly listed companies, employees had a seat on the board of less than 12 of them. Although employee share owners expected a say in corporate decisions, in many cases employees did not even have normal shareholder rights.[55] This was especially the case when shares were held in a mutual fund, or a trust held on behalf of employees, because in such cases fund managers exercised share voting rights (see next chapter). The same was true of share ownership via pension and 401(k) funds.

PENSION FUNDS AND SOCIAL SECURITY

There has been a rapid growth in share ownership in the US over the last two decades (see Figure 11.1) due to the increasing role of shares in pension plans from the 1980s and the rise of mutual funds in the early 1990s (see Figure 11.2). However, these new shareholders hold their shares only indirectly. When people invest in mutual funds they invest in a managed portfolio of various investments including stocks. The same is true of pension funds. It is the fund mangers who have the voting rights at shareholders' meetings.

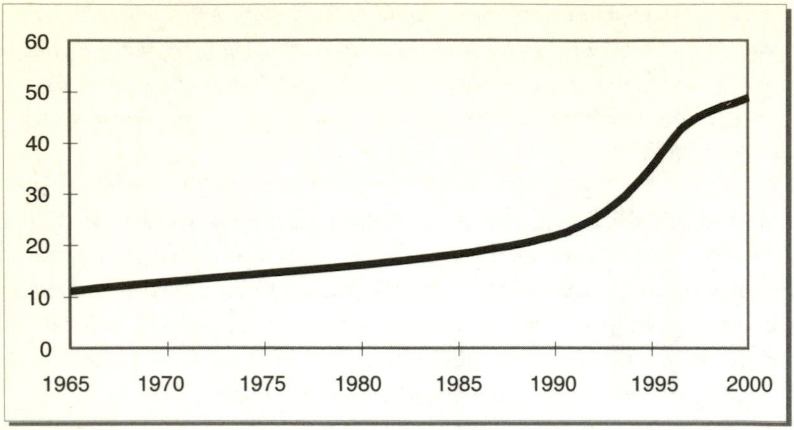

Figure 11.1 *Percentage of householders owning shares in the USA*

Source: Richard Nadler, 'Stocks Populi', *National Review,* 9 March 1998, pp36–9.

People were attracted to mutual funds though the 1990s because of the high returns compared with bank interest, fuelled by rapidly increasing share prices on the stock market which in turn was fed, in part, by the growth of investment by mutual funds. Mutual funds held $3 trillion worth of bonds and stock in 1999 compared to little more than $100 million in 1985. Two-thirds of the holdings of mutual funds represented household investment.[56]

During the 1980s the nature of pension plans changed in the US, with the encouragement of the Reagan administration. 'Defined benefit' plans that paid pensions according to an individual's salary and years of service, gave way to 'defined contribution' plans, referred to as 401(k) accounts, that paid pensions according to the investment growth of set contributions (usually from both employer and employee) which was often invested in stocks. This meant that pensions grew faster when the stock market boomed but could also lose value when it went down. The risk associated with losses to the pension fund moved from the employer to the employee.[57]

'Defined contribution' pension plans were a way of ensuring wider share awareness among workers, even though the ownership was indirect. The Chicago-based magazine *Pensions & Investment Age* argued that the growth of stock-holding pension plans had a role to play in the rise of 'People's Capitalism'. They would ensure that employees would 'assume more responsibility for their corporate assets' and 'come to better understand free enterprise'.[58]

By 1998 55 million workers owned shares through their pension funds. The *Wall Street Journal* suggested the development represented an 'emancipation' of workers 'from the paternalism' of defined benefit plans; an emancipation that

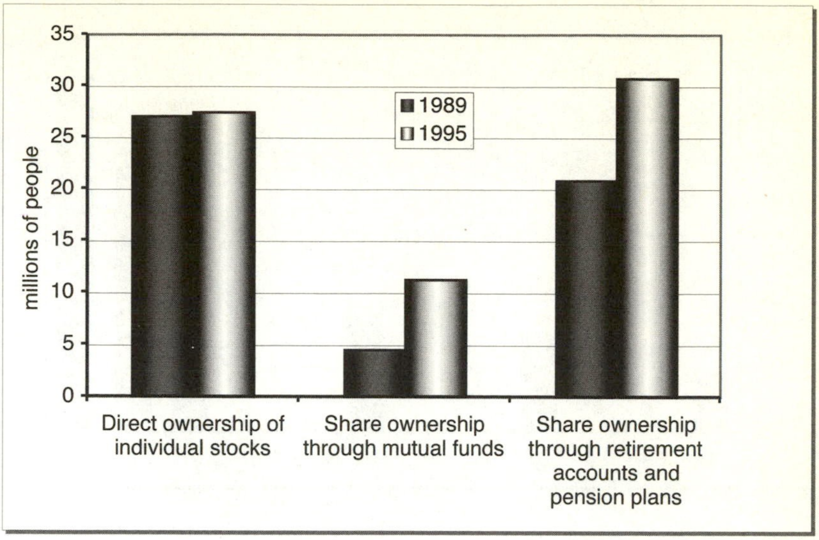

Figure 11.2 *Increasing share ownership in US 1989-1995*

Source: Richard Nadler, 'The Rise of Worker Capitalism', *Policy Analysis,* 1 November 1999, p4.

enabled them to 'become risk-taking capitalists'. Jeffrey Garten, the dean of the Yale School of Management, portrayed it as 'a culture where people invest in markets rather than relying on government support' and John Hood made similar claims in his book *Investor Politics*. Hood is president of the John Locke Foundation, a Visiting Fellow at the Heritage Foundation and a regular media commentator. He argued that 'the goal should be to replace government entitlement programmes with a system that exempts savings and investment from taxation' so as to 'allow individuals and families to invest their own money, rather than expecting the government to "invest" it for them ...'.[59]

Despite the preponderance of indirect share holding, conservatives hailed the development as a confirmation of the legitimacy and widespread beneficence of capitalism. According to Richard Nadler, chair of the Republican Ideas Political Committee and executive director of the American Shareholders Association: 'This resulted in the greatest dispersion of capital ownership in human history.'[60]

Australians, too, were encouraged to change their superannuation holdings from defined benefit plans in the 1990s to a choice of investment portfolios involving a greater or lesser proportion of shares. In 2005, workers had the further choice of opting out of industry or employer-based superannuation schemes and choosing from a range of commercial superannuation schemes. Australians also flocked to mutual funds during the 1990s when the stock market was booming.

Through the 1990s the number of Australians who owned shares increased as insurance companies demutualized, public enterprises were privatized with

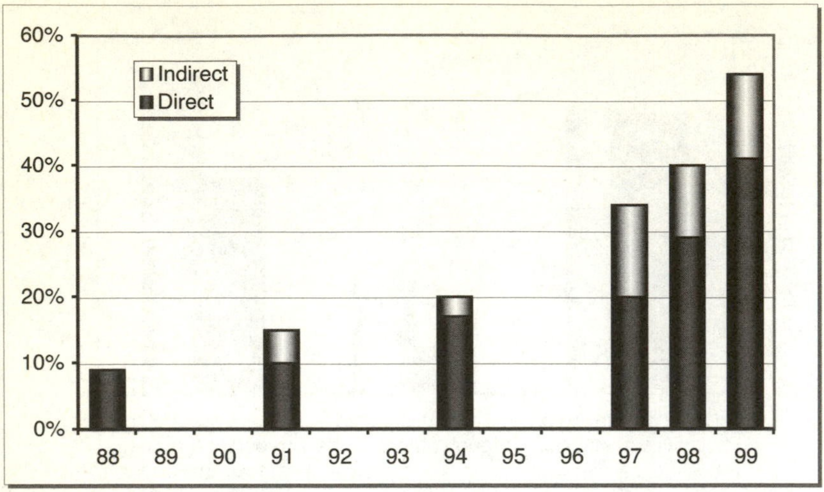

Figure 11.3 *Ownership of shares in Australia*

NB: Figures don't include compulsory superannuation system

Source: Andrew White, 'Great Aussie Stockocracy', *The Australian*, 9 February 2000.

share floats, and because of compulsory superannuation (see Figure 11.3).[61] When Australia surpassed Canada and the US in 1999 with its percentage of the adult population with shares, *The Australian* ran a feature article with the headline 'We lead the world in owning shares, Great Aussie stockocracy'.[62] The *Australian Financial Review* ran an editorial in 2000 entitled 'We are all capitalists now', extolling 'the great transformation of the Australian economy: the rise of the worker-rentier class' which had come about, largely through privatizations of government enterprises. It argued that 40 per cent of adult Australians had become 'stakeholders in capitalism', either through direct share ownership or indirectly through managed funds and private superannuation funds.[63]

Today there are groups and organizations promoting wider share ownership in various countries. The US-based Capital Ownership Group (COG) calls itself a 'virtual think tank' that 'works to broaden ownership to deal with the negative effects of globalization'. It is based at Kent State University and is funded by the Ford Foundation. It claims to be 'a non-profit network of professionals, business, labor and government leaders and staff, academics and activists on six continents'.[64] Similarly, the group Third Millennium, whose board is peopled with young Wall Street professionals but which claims to represent Generation X, has campaigned for the privatization of social security and the right of taxpayers to invest their social security funds in shares.[65]

The Shared Capitalism Institute is another US-based organization promoting wider share ownership. It argues that this will 'result in a more inclusive and

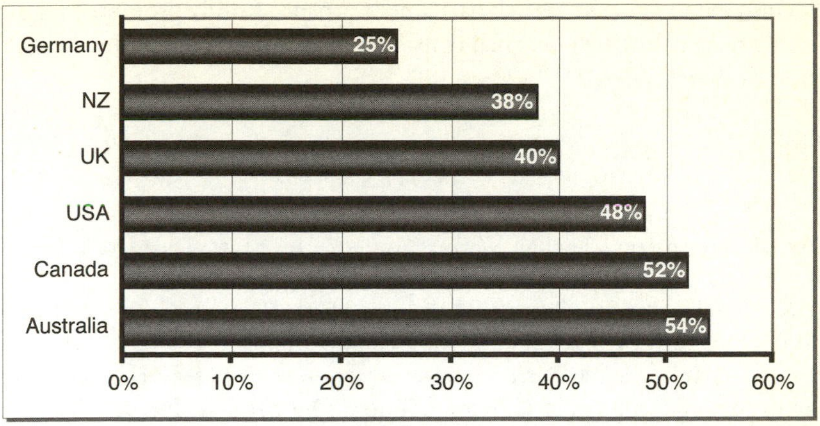

Figure 11.4 *Percentage of adult population owning shares – selected countries*

NB: Australian figures don't include compulsory superannuation system

Source: Samantha Magnusson and Andrew White, 'A Nation of Investors Takes Stock', *The Australian*, 9 February 2000, p1.

sustainable free enterprise system both in the United States and abroad'. It writes policy papers and engages in education and public relations activities to this end. Its president, Jeff Gates, calls himself a 'specialist in ownership engineering' who has advised 'in more than 30 countries' on privatization, restructuring and corporatization.[66]

In his 1998 book, *The Ownership Solution*, Gates argues that 'the central problem of capitalism is that it doesn't create enough capitalists' and that the widening gulf between the haves and have-nots creates alienation and cynicism, and thereby threatens the viability of the whole free enterprise system. His solution is widening share ownership to give everyone a personal stake in the economic system. He claims his book is 'making its way onto both liberal and conservative agendas, as well as the platforms of think tanks, philanthropic foundations, environmental groups, and international banks, among many other organizations'. Gates' second book, *Democracy at Risk: Rescuing Main Street from Wall Street – a Populist Vision for the 21st Century* (2000), makes a similar argument, and has been endorsed by people as diverse as Klaus Schwab, president of the World Economic Forum, and consumer rights' advocate Ralph Nader.[67]

The European Commission is also keen to encourage shareholder democracy, and to this end is seeking to harmonize corporate government codes in Europe to make it easier for lay people to invest. Frits Bolkestein, European commissioner for the internal market, said in 2002: 'I want to have a European market in shares, a shareholder democracy, one share one vote.' Jean-Pierre Thomas, an investment banker and member of the French parliament, unsuccessfully promoted legislation 'to establish tax-subsidized personal pension funds in hopes of turning France into a nation of shareholders'.[68]

NOTES

1 Ronald Brownstein, 'Though Workers Are Now Investors, They Don't Think Like Capitalists', *Los Angeles Times*, 15 November 1999, pA5.
2 IRC, 'Profile: Empower America', Interhemispheric Resource Center, 22 November 2003, http://rightweb.irc-online.org/org/empower.php.
3 Empower America, 'Mission', Empower America, www.empoweramerica.org/about accessed 26 December 2002; FreedomWorks, 'Our Mission', FreedomWorks, www.freedomworks.org/know/mission.php accessed 11 January 2005.
4 Richard Nadler, 'Investor Class Act', *National Review*, 22 May 2000b; Richard W. Stevenson, 'Bush's Social Security Plan Is Said to Require Vast Borrowing', *New York Times*, 28 November 2004.
5 David S. John, 'How to Fix Social Security', *Heritage Foundation Backgrounder*, no 1811, 2004.
6 Edmund L. Andrews, 'Social Security Reform, with One Big Catch', *New York Times*, 12 December 2004; Paul Krugman, 'Borrow, Speculate and Hope', *New York Times*, 10 December 2004.
7 Charles Pope, 'Bush Kicks Off Push for Social Security Proposal', *Seattle Post-Intelligencer*, 12 January 2005; Jim VanderHei, 'A Big Push on Social Security', *Washington Post*, 1 January 2005, pA01; 'National Association of Manufacturers', *PR Week*, 10 January 2005, http://prweek.com/news/news_story.cfm?ID=231878&site=3; Heidi Przybyla, 'Companies to Spend over $5 Million to Back Bush on Social Security', *Bloomberg*, 20 January 2005.
8 Przybyla, 'Companies to Spend over $5 Million to Back Bush on Social Security'.
9 VanderHei, 'A Big Push on Social Security', pA01.
10 David E. Rosenbaum, 'Bush to Return to "Ownership Society" Theme in Push for Social Security Changes', *New York Times*, 16 January 2005.
11 Jack Kemp, 'Building a Shareholder Democracy in America: Personalizing Social Security', Empower America, 10 March, 2000, www.freedomworks.org/informed/issues_template.php?issue_id=1852.
12 *Ibid.*
13 Quoted in Richard Nadler, 'Portfolio Politics', *National Review*, 4 December 2000.
14 *Ibid.*; Editorial, 'We Are All Capitalists Now', *Australian Financial Review*, 6 March 1998.
15 Quoted in Adele Horin, 'Paying a High Price for a Shareholder Democracy', *Sydney Morning Herald*, 25 March, 2000, p49.
16 Richard Nadler, 'The Rise of Worker Capitalism', *Policy Analysis*, 1 November 1999, p22.
17 Horin, 'Paying a High Price for a Shareholder Democracy', p49.
18 Dennis Fox, 'Your Politic Vs. Your Portfolio', *Alternet*, 26 April 2000, www.alternet.org/print.html?StoryID=9065.

19 Richard Nadler, 'Special (K)', *National Review*, 19 April 1999a; Nadler, 'The Rise of Worker Capitalism', p22.
20 Editorial, 'Worker Capitalists', *Wall Street Journal*, 30 November, 1999, pA26.
21 Shawn Tully, 'Europe Goes Wild over Privatisation', *Fortune*, vol 115, no 5, 1987, p68.
22 Padraic P. McGuinness, 'Every Man and His Dog Gets a Share of the Action', *Sydney Morning Herald*, 20 November 1997, p21.
23 *Ibid.*
24 Cited in Editorial, 'Worker Capitalists', pA26 and Brownstein, 'Though Workers Are Now Investors, They Don't Think Like Capitalists'.
25 Nadler, 'Portfolio Politics'.
26 Pete Du Pont, 'People's Capitalism on the March', *Human Events*, 10 December 1999, p9.
27 George Melloan, 'Europe's New Shareholder Culture Spurs Big Changes', *Wall Street Journal*, 9 May 2000, pA27.
28 *Ibid.*, pA27.
29 George Melloan, 'Assessing the Pitfalls of People's Capitalism', *Wall Street Journal*, 22 July 1996, pA15.
30 Cited in Nadler, 'The Rise of Worker Capitalism', p16.
31 Carl D. Thompson, *Confessions of the Power Trust*, New York, E. P. Dutton & Co., 1932, pp192–4; Allen Myers, 'Sharing the Wealth?' *Green Left Weekly*, 25 August 1999, p11.
32 Theodore Kinni, 'Why we work', *Training*, vol 35, no 8, 1998; Edward O. Welles, 'Motherhood, Apple Pie and Stock Options', *Inc.*, vol 20, February 1998; Arthur H. Kroll, 'Exploring Options', *HR Magazine*, vol 42, October 1997, p96.
33 ProShare, 'What Questions Do People Have in Relation to Employee Share Ownership?' ProShare, www.proshare.org/eso/faqs.asp accessed 29 December 2002; Douglas I. Kruse, 'Research Evidence on Prevalence and Effects of Employee Ownership', Ownership Associates Inc, 13 February, 2002, http://ownershipassociates.com/kruse.shtm.
34 Quoted in House of Commons' Library, 'The Employee Share Schemes Bill: Bill 13 of 2001–02', Research Paper 02/05, 16 January 2002, pp8–9.
35 Thomas Frank, *One Market under God: Extreme Capitalism Market Populism, and the End of Economic Democracy*, New York, Doubleday, 2000, pp100–1.
36 Kruse, 'Research Evidence'.
37 Quoted in House of Commons Library, 'The Employee Share Schemes Bill', pp7, 10, 19.
38 ESA, 'The Employee Share Alliance Backs Share Incentive Plan', Employee Share Alliance, www.jobownership.co.uk/esa/html/page1.htm accessed 29 December 2002.
39 ProShare, 'Welcome to ProShare!' ProShare, www.proshare.org/about/background.asp accessed 29 December 2002.
40 ProShare, 'What Questions Do People Have in Relation to Employee Share Ownership?'; ProShare, 'At Work', ProShare, www.proshare.org/about/ar01-02/work.asp accessed 29 December 2002.
41 HM Treasury, 'Boosting Productivity and Fairness: Employee Share Ownership', HM Treasury, 21 March 2000, www.hm-treasury.gov.uk/Budget/Budget_2000/Press_

Notices/bud_bud00_pressrev3.cfm; House of Commons' Library, 'The Employee Share Schemes Bill', pp11, 14; ESA, 'The Employee Share Alliance Backs Share Incentive Plan'; Legislation Watch, 'Employee Share Schemes Bill (P)', Legislation Watch, 19 June 2001, www.epolitix.com/data/Legislation/articles/.

42 ProShare, 'Our Values', ProShare, www.proshare.org/about/ar01-02/default.asp accessed 29 December 2002.

43 JOL, 'Job Ownership', Job Ownership Ltd, 2001, www.jobownership.co.uk/html/about.htm accessed 29 December 2002.

44 NCEO, 'Welcome to the NCEO', The National Center for Employee Ownership, www.nceo.org/ accessed 29 December 2002.

45 Ownership Associates, 'Trust and Ownership', *The Ownership Culture Report*, Spring/Summer, 1998, www.ownershipassociates.com/pdf/ocr1.pdf, pp1–2; Ownership Associates, 'Ownership and Motivation', *The Ownership Culture Report*, Winter, 2001, www.ownershipassociates.com/pdf/ocr4.pdf, p1.

46 Wray quoted in Nadler, 'The Rise of Worker Capitalism', p2; FED, 'About Us', Foundation for Enterprise Development/Beyster Institute, www.fed.org/aboutus/aboutus.htm accessed 29 December 2002; FED, 'All About Employee Ownership', Foundation for Enterprise Development/Beyster Institute, www.fed.org/allabout/allabout.htm accessed 29 December 2002.

47 Brendan Nelson, 'A Speech by Dr Brendan Nelson', Paper presented at the IIR/AEOA Conference and Workshop on Employee Share Ownership Plans, Sydney, 23 February 2000, pp4–5.

48 *Ibid.*, p6.

49 'Employee Share Ownership in Australian Enterprises', House of Representatives, Parliament of Australia Standing Committee on Employment, Education and Workplace relations, 13–14 July 1999, p182.

50 BCA submission to *Ibid.*, p4.

51 BCA submission to *Ibid.*, p2.

52 Alan Deans, 'Share Day's Pay', *The Bulletin*, 2000, p55.

53 BHP submission to 'Employee Share Ownership in Australian Enterprises', p4.

54 *Ibid.*, pp134–5.

55 Aaron Bernstein, 'Why ESOP Deals Have Slowed to a Crawl', *Business Week*, 18 March 1996.

56 Nadler, 'The Rise of Worker Capitalism', p4; Melloan, 'Assessing the Pitfalls of People's Capitalism', pA15; Editorial, 'Worker Capitalists', pA26; Thomas L. Friedman, *The Lexus and the Olive Tree*, New York, Farrar, Straus and Giroux, 1999, p52.

57 Nadler, 'Special (K)'; Margaret M. Blair and Douglas I. Kruse, 'Worker Capitalists?' *The Brookings Review*, Fall, 1999.

58 John M. Templeton, 'Plans Play Role in "People's Capitalism"', *Pensions & Investment Age*, vol 11, no 22, 1983.

59 Editorial, 'Worker Capitalists', pA26; Jeffrey Garten, 'A New Year; a New Agenda', *The Economist*, 4 January, 2003; John Hood, 'Investor Politics', NR Book Service, www.nrbookservice.com/popPrintasp?prod_cd=C5970 accessed 26 December 2002; John Locke Foundation, 'The Staff of the John Locke Foundation', John Locke Foundation, www.johnlocke.org/staff.html accessed 26 December 2002.

60 Nadler, 'Special (K)'.

61 Jeremy Philips and James Hooke, 'More Players – but Where Are the Benefits?' *Australian Financial Review*, 22 June 1998, p21.
62 Andrew White, 'Great Aussie Stockocracy', *The Australian*, 9 February, 2000.
63 Editorial, 'We Are All Capitalists Now', p34.
64 COG, 'The Capital Ownership Group', Capital Ownership Group, http://cog.kent.edu/index.html accessed 29 December 2002.
65 Frank, *One Market under God*, pp137–140.
66 Shared Capitalism Institute, 'Associates', Shared Capitalism Institute, 2001, www.sharedcapitalism.org/assoc.html.
67 Shared Capitalism Institute, 'Book Information', Shared Capitalism Institute, 2001, www.sharedcapitalism.org/book.html.
68 Francesco Guerrera and Simon Targett, 'The European Is Looking to Pave the Way for a Shareholder Democracy', *Financial Times*, 25 February, 2002a; Bolkestein quoted in Francesco Guerrera and Simon Targett, 'Generating Shareholder Power', *Financial Times*, 25 February 2002b; John Tagliabue, 'Europe Rethinks Its Pensions', *New York Times*, 26 December 2000.

12

Shareholder Democracy

An unprecedented demographic revolution is happening right under our noses. It is the emergence of the first mass class of worker–stockholders in history, wage-earners who derive a substantial proportion of their income from investments ... The rise of the worker–rentier is an enormous conservative opportunity. RICHARD NADLER[1]

The idea of a 'shareholder democracy' has been used to promote free enterprise and portray it as democratic, accountable and equitable. However, the term shareholder democracy is clearly a distortion of the term 'democracy'. Rather than meaning a sharing of power and decision-making, it generally refers to widespread access and participation in the stock market. *New York Times'* columnist Thomas Friedman uses the term 'democratization of finance' in his 1999 book *The Lexus and the Olive Tree*. He points to the way the public were able to buy corporate bonds from the late 1960s, invest in securitized home mortgages in the 1970s, buy junk bonds in the 1980s, and invest in third world debt in the 1990s – either directly or more often through mutual funds and pension funds: 'This gave you, me and my Aunt Bev a chance to buy a slice of these deals that had previously been off-limits to the little guy.'[2]

The new trend towards internet-based share trading which offers greater access to shares to those who do not have a stock broker has also been hailed as a democratic, levelling trend. E*Trade promoted its services as part of a revolution akin to women's liberation. It claimed to be 'leveling the playing field and democratizing individual personal financial services'. Share ownership was equated with power. E*Trade asserted in its advertisements that 'the power is in your hands'.[3]

The view that the stock market is democratic because it reflects people's choices through their investments has been propagated by free market missionaries who argue that in the stock exchange people 'vote every hour, every day through their mutual funds, their pension funds, their brokers, and, more and more, from their own basements via the internet'. Donald Schwartz noted in the *California Management Review* that 'both law and literature pay formal homage to the notion of shareholder democracy'.[4]

The notion of shareholder democracy is also promoted as a way of countering the perception that powerful corporations are not accountable to anyone.

Corporations are represented as being subject to democratic governance through the voting procedures at shareholder meetings and the exercise of investment and disinvestment. Although it is obvious that managers determine much of what corporations do, not shareholders, corporate managers like to point to the supposedly democratic processes of shareholder meetings. In theory, shareholders can exercise their displeasure with management performance or activities by selling their shares. 'This not only protects their interests but works as a sort of voting mechanism. A large-scale sale by shareholders will punish managers through its effect on the securities market and on the market for corporate control.'[5]

In this way, corporate managers are able to deflect attention from their own power. Thomas Frank points out that: 'Belief that a democratic system functions may provide a false sense of comfort to the public, to wit, that the managers – who, after all, exercise substantial power over our lives – are responsive to a governance process that we understand from another context.'[6]

By representing shares as the major source of wealth of a nation's elites and showing that this route to wealth is accessible to anyone, the inequality produced by the free market is legitimized. Shares are portrayed as a major mechanism for wealth sharing and widening social inclusiveness. Pension and superannuation schemes, managed funds and employee share schemes give working people access to this route to riches and enable business people and financial journals to extol the spread of share ownership as a sign that capitalism is indeed benefiting everyone.

However, it is a distorted picture that business interests paint, because ownership of a few shares in a mutual fund is not a route to wealth. As share prices rose in the 1990s, it was the wealthy people, who owned most of the shares already, who became wealthier. A US Federal Reserve study found that as the share market boomed between 1998 and 2001 the net worth of the top 10 per cent of families increased by 69 per cent ($833,600), while the net worth of the lowest 20 per cent only rose by 24 per cent ($7900).[7]

Similarly, despite widening share ownership in Australia, inequalities have increased. During the 1980s and 1990s as share prices rose so did the gap between rich and poor because of the concentration of shares in the hands of the wealthiest people. Between 1993 and 1998 the share of the wealth owned by the richest 10 per cent of the population rose from 43.5 per cent to 48 per cent, while that owned by the top 1 per cent went from 12 per cent to 15 per cent. During the same period, the middle-income, share-owning Australians had a declining share of the wealth.

Far from spreading wealth more equitably, share ownership has concentrated it in the hands of those who are already wealthy. Nevertheless, the myth of the great shareholder democracies spreading wealth to the underclasses is perpetuated. And although share ownership is spreading, that ownership does not confer any real accountability or power over corporations as corporate propaganda would have us believe.

Edward Wolff points out in *The American Prospect* that 'It is the very rise in corporate profitability – which comes at the expense of workers' wages – that has fueled the record boom in the stock market ... In other words, as the returns to work have atrophied, returns to capital have climbed, shifting ever more power to the rich and contributing to the rising inequality of income in this country.'[8] Yet somehow many of the new class of small shareholders have been persuaded that rises in the stock market matter more than employment levels, wage increases and social capital when it comes to government policy.

'PUBLIC' OWNERSHIP

In the US there is a long history of using propaganda techniques to make out that market transactions are equivalent to some sort of democratic expression:

> *In the 1920s, Wall Street made its first audacious bid to entice small investors, with banks setting up securities affiliates that promoted stocks with the subtlety of carnival barkers and blurred the distinction between saving and speculating.*
>
> *Tempted by easy margin requirements and the moonshine rhetoric of unending prosperity, people dabbled in mutual funds called investment trusts, which invested in other trusts, in an endless chain of speculation.*[9]

The resulting popularity of share investment and widespread participation in the late 1920s, which fuelled the boom preceding the crash, allowed the market to be portrayed as some sort of democratic process or expression.[10]

The privately owned telephone utility company AT&T pioneered the idea of 'investor democracy'. Rather than the corporation being owned by a few wealthy men, AT&T emphasized the number of its shareholders – hundreds of thousands – to portray itself as an organization owned by the people. It depicted its shareholders as ordinary people, including workers and housewives. Its advertisements were headlined 'Democracy' and 'Our Stockholders', and one, showing an older country woman shelling peas, was headlined 'She's a partner in a great American business.' The message was that AT&T was owned and controlled by the people it served, and so, far from being a private monopoly, it was virtually a public company. AT&T deliberately attracted a broader base of shareholders than most other corporations. However, most AT&T shareholders owned only a few shares, while 5 per cent of the shareholders owned 50 per cent of the shares.[11]

The ploy was so attractive that other large corporations, such as US Steel, General Electric and Du Pont, also sought to emulate AT&T in the 1920s, distributing shares widely and then promoting themselves as industrial democracies. Employee stock-owning programmes helped this goal. General Motors advertised that 'More than 68,000 investors own General Motors and divide its earnings. They live in every state in the Union, in Canada and in 16 foreign lands. Of these General Motors stockholders, 58,000 own 100 shares or less. More than 18,000 stockholders are women – mothers, sisters, wives.'[12]

The electricity companies also encouraged the public to buy shares in their utilities in the 1920s. Originally this was to raise money, but it soon became a very useful public relations tool. Wide share ownership by the community could be promoted as a substitute for public ownership of electricity systems. 'In the new language of utilities, "real public ownership" meant customer ownership, not political ownership.'[13] Power company literature frequently associated advocacy of public ownership with socialism and Bolshevism. And it repeatedly implied that private power companies were owned by the public because members of the public owned stock in the utilities, or had bank deposits and life insurance with banks and insurance companies that invested in utility securities.[14]

The electricity companies in the US recognized in the 1920s that wider share ownership would mean more people would have a self-interest in the advantage of the utilities. Customers who bought securities became 'an army of friends for utilities'.

> *Once these plain people added their voices to the hue and cry of denunciation of the utility raised by the professional agitators, socialists, and public ownership advocates. Today they say with pride, 'This is my company; I'm one of its stockholders!'*[15]

The National Electric Light Association (NELA), a coalition of private electricity companies, called broadening share ownership 'an extraordinarily clever and astute flank attack upon the forces which advocate and fight for public ownership'. Selling shares to consumers created, according to NELA's customer ownership committee, 'A stalwart army of sound-thinking owners of private property' that was 'the nation's greatest defense against socialism or communism'.[16]

NELA argued that 'customer ownership' provided real public ownership through direct investment, so public ownership through government was unnecessary. Of course these 'customer owners' could not vote at general meetings, since it was mainly bonds, securities or non-voting stock that they invested in. Nor were they otherwise able to exercise any ownership control over the companies.[17] In reality, all they were doing was lending money to the power companies.

The power companies even courted children as 'customer owners'. Not only did it encourage children to be future investors but it gave a sentimental value to the stock so that parents who bought such stock in their children's name were less likely to sell it. The chair of one of NELA's Customer Ownership Committees wrote to NELA's managing director in 1925:

> *I believe that you appreciate the great psychological value of having minors as stockholders ... I know that it has been your personal experience if you once buy something for your children, and place it in their names, it immediately takes on a sentimental aspect that the balance of your properties do not possess ... This is one field of investment that is of importance to us, for a new crop of investors is being born every day.*[18]

The share market crash that ushered in the Great Depression put many middle-class investors off share investment for many years. The New York Stock Exchange tried to win them back in the early 1950s through promoting the idea of 'people's capitalism' through share ownership. They advertised that share investment was the way to 'own your share of America'. George Keith Funston, head of the Exchange (1951–1967), was a man with 'a powerful voice and a flair for public relations' and the one who came up with the term 'people's capitalism'. During the Cold War years he argued that investing in American companies was a way of fighting communism. The numbers of shareholders tripled during his term of office.[19]

In Britain during the 1980s privatization was partly justified on the grounds of widening share ownership in the community. This was supposed to establish, in the words of one Conservative minister, 'a new breed of owners' and have 'an important effect on attitudes', thereby breaking down 'the divisions between owners and earners'.[20] The Confederation of British Industry (CBI) formed a wider share ownership taskforce and the government formed the Wider Share Ownership Council. The float of shares in privatized companies was said to have 'given a boost to popular capitalism unimaginable in the pre-Thatcher era' and the profits made by millions of small investors made it 'difficult to question the logic underpinning privatisation'.[21]

Conservatives used the rhetoric that privatization would spread wealth more widely in the community and create 'real public ownership' of government enterprises to sell privatization to the electorate and to take away public ownership. Shares for British Telecom and British Gas, for example, were sold using massive advertising campaigns to gain public support for the sale and to counteract union opposition. And as more pension funds invested in privatized corporations, workers were 'led to believe that [strike] action against these companies' would threaten their pensions.[22]

Shares were sold below market value so that new shareholders could experience an immediate financial gain when the shares were floated and the price increased. This increased the popularity of privatization amongst those who benefited or hoped to benefit from future share floats, and was seen by some as a deliberate bribe. 'The fact that huge values had been transferred from taxpayers to shareholders was not deemed troublesome.'[23]

In 1991 John Redwood, minister for corporate affairs, described the changing nature of the Stock Exchange:

> *The Stock Exchange of the 1960s was all top hats, champagne at lunch, double-barrelled names and invitations to the select few to become clients. The market of the 1990s is all filofaxes and mobile phones, long working days and draught lager on the pavements ... but does Middle England recognise the Stock Exchange as its own?*[24]

The business-serving government wanted Middle England to identify with the Stock Exchange, and Redwood called 'for new legions of private shareholders to come forward and join the long march towards the new shareholder democracy'.[25]

There was an increase in Conservative voters amongst the new shareholders of the utilities. 'Prime Minister Thatcher, as she then was, made no secret of her desire to alter the balance of political power by creating a "share-owning democracy", with more shareholders than there were trade union members.'[26] However, the new shareholders quickly realized their gains (made at the expense of taxpayers) by selling their shares. In the electricity industry, for example, the number of individual shareholders dropped from 7 million at privatization in 1990 to 2 million in 1997.[27]

In Australia, Prime Minister John Howard announced in 1998 the goal of making Australia 'the greatest share-owning democracy in the world' as a way of justifying the privatization of the remaining two-thirds of Telstra that was still owned by the government: 'I can't think of a better way of enhancing Australians' ownership than to let Australians buy something.'[28] Senator Richard Alston argued that the public would actually have more control over the way Telstra was run once it was fully privatized.[29]

In Germany, share ownership trebled between 1991 and 1995. Then in 1996 when shares in Deutsche Telekom (DT) were offered to the public they were promoted as 'people's shares'. 'This exercise in people's capitalism created more new shareholders than any other single event' causing the number of shareholders to double again by 1997. The number of shareholders increased by 500,000 in 1999 as investment clubs proliferated.[30]

By 2000 *The Economist* had reported that 'Germany was share-crazy. Gone is the image of a nation dourly stuffing its spare cash into a safe-as-houses, low-interest Sparbuch savings account. Money poured into initial public offerings ... Germans were opening share-dealing accounts – online, naturally – at a furious rate.' It noted that evidence of a 'spreading equity culture' was clear in the media: 'Since last autumn a live, four-minute bulletin on the Tops und Flops of the day, that runs just before the evening news, has become a fixture on national public television.'[31]

The French government also extolled the benefits of wider share ownership during the 1980s when it was proposing to sell off government-owned industries. It ran 'weeks of slick television advertisements, often featuring glamorous models, that extol share ownership'. Its sale of shares in glass manufacturer Saint-Gobain was promoted in a $6 million advertising campaign that included television ads that sold the shares 'the way US companies market soap or toothpaste ... A network of more than 20,000 banks and post offices pushed shares' to customers conducting their normal business.[32]

Finance Minister Edouard Balladur declared his campaign for 'popular capitalism' a success when floats of these industries were heavily oversubscribed by people wanting to buy shares in them. As in the UK, small shareholders quickly sold their shares when the price went up. Even then, the share floats could be seen as a success in that ordinary people had tasted 'the fruits of capitalism', which some said was one of the aims of the exercise – an effort to lure people away from socialism. The manager of Drexel Burnham Lambert in Paris pointed out 'The privatization campaign is making capitalism seep down through the social structure of France.'[33]

THE REALITY OF SHARE OWNERSHIP

Owning shares in a company does not give small shareholders any control in the company. They are not owners, in any real sense, but merely investors. Shareholders elect the board of directors, which in turn hires the top management of a company. They also get to vote on major changes in direction of the company but little else.[34]

The decisions at annual general meetings generally fall into four categories: election of directors, selection of accountants, approval of changes to executive pay and benefits, and shareholder resolutions. Only the last category is initiated by shareholders and such resolutions are generally opposed by management. Executive compensation resolutions are deliberately made too complex for the average shareholder to understand.[35]

Because few people are able to attend company meetings, most votes are cast by mailed proxies. Proxies enable shareholders who do not attend meetings to appoint someone else to vote for them at the meeting. The company sends them forms to enable them to do this. However, soliciting proxies from shareholders is expensive, and while management can use company funds for this, shareholders who want to solicit proxies have to pay for it themselves. Needless to say, this seldom happens.[36] Corporate management also controls the flow and content of information to shareholders, including reports that are done largely for shareholder relations' purposes.

Although theoretically shareholders elect the board of directors, what generally happens in practice is that the CEO chooses the board by nominating who should be on it and not providing alternatives for shareholders to vote for. Board members are then beholden to the CEO for their positions.[37] Increasingly, companies have adopted staggered boards, with only one-third of the seats filled each year, so that any organized opposition amongst shareholders cannot control the board after a single vote.

When it comes to election of the board of directors, any shareholder wishing to propose alternative candidates has to pay the expense of mailing proxy forms and campaign literature to many thousands of shareholders. In contrast, company management can use company funds to hire firms that specialize in contacting shareholders personally and persuading them to send in their proxies for a particular result. Ralph Nader and Joel Seligman noted in 1983: 'company insiders have so totally dominated the proxy machinery that corporate elections have come to resemble the Soviet Union's "communist ballot," on which only one slate of candidates appears'.[38]

The people nominated by CEOs for board membership tend to be senior executives of other companies (sometimes retired), many with only nominal shareholdings in the company themselves.[39] Lewis Braham writes in *Business Week*:

> *Americans like to believe we have shareholder democracy. The people who own a company have a say in how it's run. Right? Well, just try to win a seat on a corporate board without management backing. A tangle of rules and procedures stifle all but the wealthiest and most persistent voices.*[40]

In addition, institutional investors tend to vote with management, further reducing the say of individual shareholders. In the US and the UK, institutional investors dominate stock holdings (see Figure 12.1). In the US, pension funds alone owned 25 per cent of all corporate stock in 1990 and the largest 20 owned 16 per cent of shares in the 10 largest corporations. Such institutional investors have become permanent shareholders because they don't move their investments around. This is partly because their holdings are so large that such movements would affect the share price unfavourably for them.[41]

Martin Lipton, a New York lawyer, noted in the *New York Times* in 1987:

> *Corporate securities in the hands of large institutions in effect removes all public say by smaller shareholders. The old concept of shareholders' democracy related to a time when there was a diverse group of shareholders not dominated by any small group that has a single interest. Today the shareholders of corporations are dominated by a small group of institutions, all of whom have only one interest – to realise short-term gains.*[42]

Similarly, in Britain, share ownership has become more concentrated in the hands of financial institutions such as banks, pension funds, insurance companies and investment trusts. Insurance companies own a third of all shares in Britain. Although the number of people owning shares in Britain increased during the 1980s (see Figure 12.2) the actual proportion of shares in listed British companies owned by individuals, as opposed to institutions, decreased (see Figures 12.3 and 12.4).[43]

Erratum

The text on Figure 12.1 (page 199) has printed incorrectly; a corrected version of the figure is below.

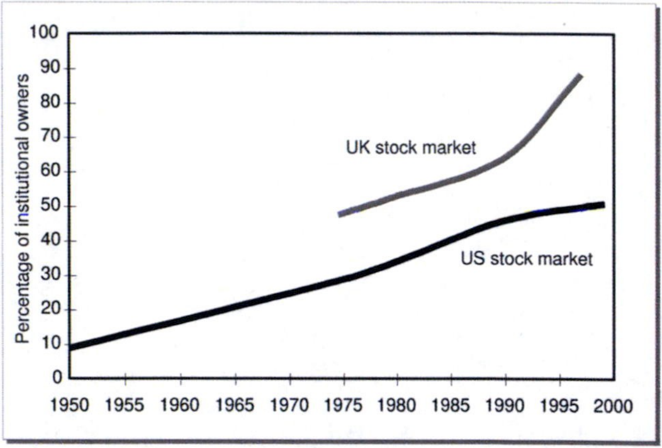

Figure 12.1 *Institutional ownership of corporate equity*

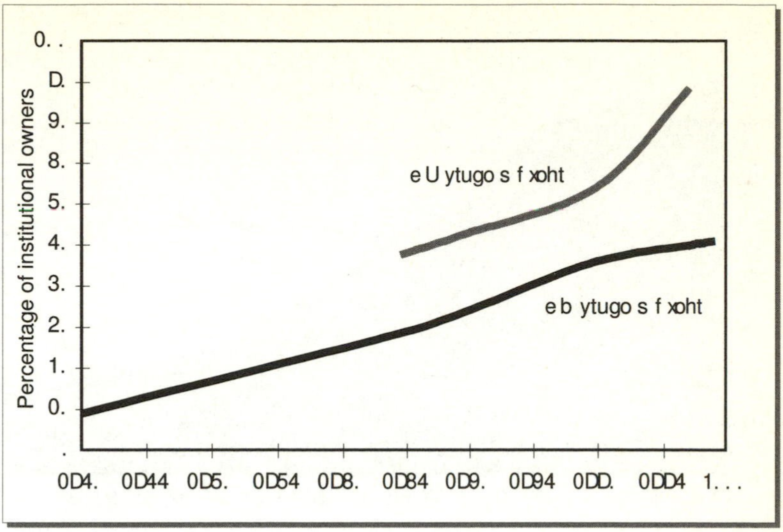

Figure 12.1 *Institutional ownership of corporate equity*[44]

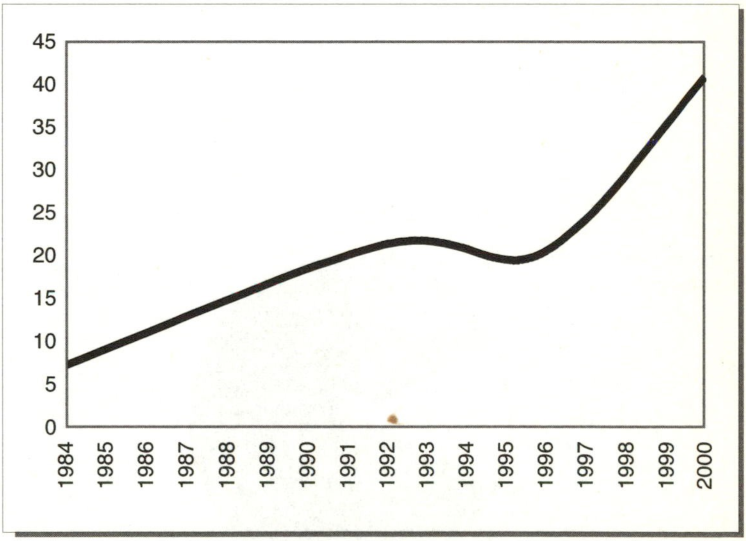

Figure 12.2 *Percentage of population owning shares in Britain*

Not only do institutional investors, including fund managers, tend to vote with corporate management but so do brokers, who are able – in the US – to vote on behalf of their clients if they don't have instructions from them.[45]

What is more, some companies have two classes of shares that allow voting power to be concentrated in the hands of loyal executives. Owners of the so-called

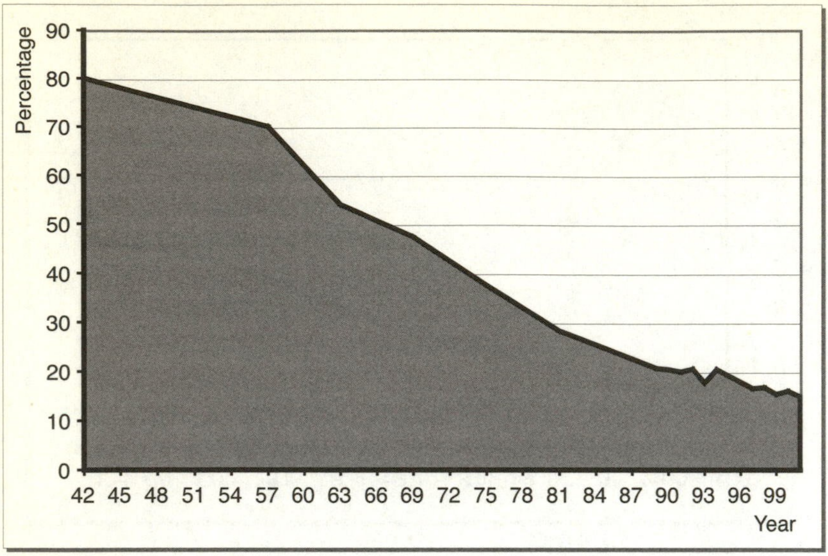

Figure 12.3 *Percentage of British shares owned by individuals*[46]

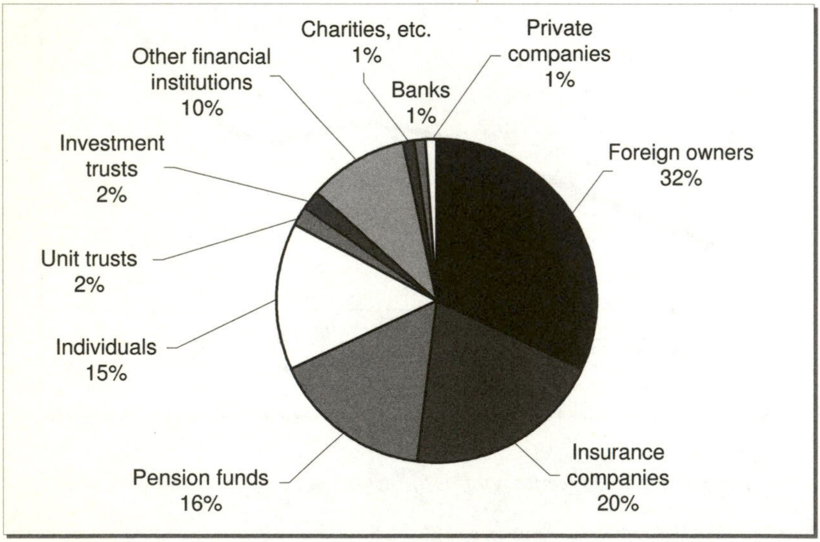

Figure 12.4 *Distribution of ownership of British shares 2001*

Source: 'Share Ownership: A Report on Ownership of Shares as at 31st December 2001', Newport, Office for National Statistics, 2002, p9.

'Supervote stock' get more votes per share or the right to elect the majority of directors. The tactic is used by companies that want to raise capital from investors but at the same time want to retain full control of the company. Family companies have traditionally used dual-class shares but the practice is spreading.[47]

The same effect can be achieved through holdings within shareholdings. 'News Corporation is controlled by Cruden Investments, Rupert Murdoch's very private company – he even bought out his sisters.' While shares in News Corporation are publicly traded, it is Cruden Investments that determines the decisions that matter.[48]

Both the level of control derived from the ownership of shares and the extent to which share ownership has been spread to lower-income brackets have been misrepresented. Although more people own shares, the majority of shares are still owned by very few people. One per cent of those who own shares owned 42 per cent of them in 1998, and the top 5 per cent owned two-thirds of all shares (see Figure 12.5).[49]

Similarly, despite widening share ownership in Australia, the richest 10 per cent own 90 per cent of the shares, and the richest 1 per cent own almost 60 per cent of the shares (see Table 12.1).[50]

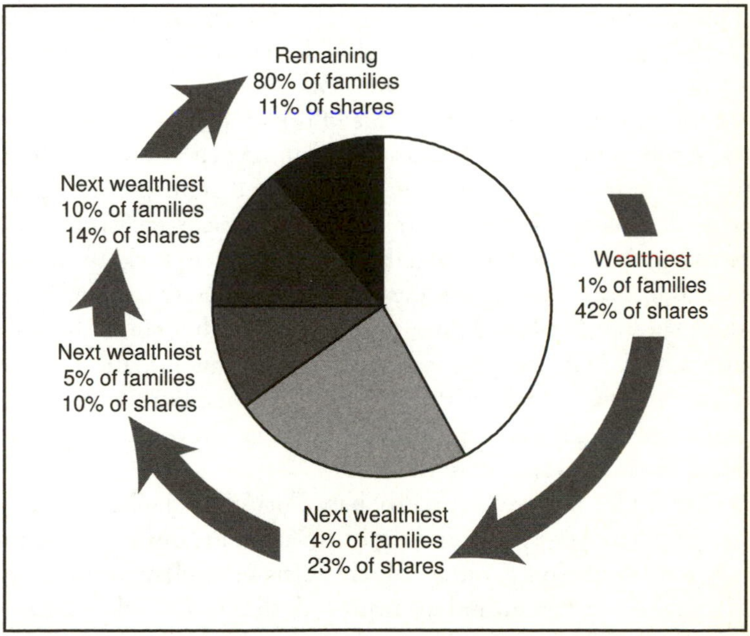

Figure 12.5 *Distribution of shares by value in the US in 1998*

Source: Edward N. Wolff, 'The Rich Get Richer: And Why the Poor Don't', *The American Prospect,* February 2001.

Table 12.1 *Distribution of wealth and shares in Australia 1993–1998*

	Wealth in 1993	*Wealth in 1998*	*Shares in 1998*
Wealthiest 10 per cent	43.5%	48%	90%
Wealthiest 1 per cent	12%	15%	60%

Source of data: Stephen Long, 'For Richer and Poorer', *Australian Financial Review*, 9 January 1999, p21.

SCHOOL EDUCATION

The propaganda power of share ownership by children has been recognised in the business community. In an opinion piece in the *Australian Financial Review* Christopher Pearson argued: 'There's a strong case for saying that any experience of share ownership is worthwhile for its educative value alone … At least they'll have begun to understand more about how market economies work than a public education is likely to have taught them.'[51]

School materials on share ownership and the stock market achieve a similar aim to that of broadening share ownership in the general community. School children practice the identity of being 'owners' and appreciate some of the goals and requirements of free enterprise. This provides a useful adjunct to the economic education discussed in chapters 4 to 6 and 13.

In the UK ProShare plays a major role in bringing ideals of share investment to schools through its Student Investor Programme, sponsored by the London School of Economics, the Department of Trade and Industry, the HSBC Bank and Foreign & Colonial – 'one of the largest investment specialists in Europe'. ProShare provides all schools in the UK with a Resource Pack on investing and runs four national school competitions, including an essay competition. It runs the Proshare Forecast Challenge three times a year for children in the 13–15-year age group. In it students compete for a cash prize by 'guestimating' which shares will perform the best and which will perform the worst during the weeks of the competition. It is designed to help teachers 'introduce the concepts of the business and financial worlds to younger students'.[52]

For older students there is the ProShare Portfolio Challenge, 'designed to increase young people's understanding of investment, business and the stock market'. It is a simulation game in which teams of students invest a notional £100,000 in the share market, and the team with the greatest value share portfolio at the end wins. In 2002, 3500 school teams entered, the winning team receiving a trip to New York as part of its prize.[53]

ProShare also provides teacher resources, case studies, worksheets and lesson plans to help teachers incorporate material about investing and the role of business into a variety of subjects including economics and mathematics. There is a dedicated website and enough material to provide for 'an entire term's work' or, alternatively, teachers can use the material for individual lessons.[54]

Share market school materials are also widely available in the US: 'Every year more than a million US primary, middle, and high school students play the stock market at school.' The experience is simulated but the numbers are taken from real stock exchanges. The games come with lesson plans, worksheets and teachers' guides as well as expert stockbroking advice and there are often prizes for those that 'win'.[55] Teams of students begin the game with an initial stake, usually $100,000, which they use to invest in shares and trade them. They research the stock market and company performance, and seek to maximize their portfolio.

These materials 'present a rosy, one-sided picture of Wall Street, in which everyone starts out rich and all that matters is short-term profits'. They suggest that winning on the stock market is a matter of intelligence and ingenuity and willingness to take risks and therefore, by extension, wealth in the wider society is deserved by those who acquire it. The fact that many people don't have enough money to invest in the stock market to start with is not covered, nor is the fact that most of the shares are owned by very few people (10 per cent of shareholders own 90 per cent of stock, while 1 per cent of shareholders own more than half).[56]

In the games 'the stock market is portrayed as a wise judge, rewarding those who make the right choices' and providing companies with much-needed capital at the same time. The fact that the stock market actually provides only a very small percentage of business capital is not examined, nor are problems caused by stock market speculation. Instead, students are taught to regard gambling in shares as company ownership, despite the lack of influence individual shareholders have. In this way the idea of shareholder democracy is perpetuated.[57]

Most importantly, students learn to interpret world events and government policy from the point of view of an investor. One stock market game producer boasts:

> *Students find that economic concepts such as supply and demand, inflation and recession, and competition come alive for them as they manage their hypothetical investments. They gain understanding of the benefits and tradeoffs of different financial instruments and strategies. They start to see the impact of world events on their investments.*[58]

Such games are often free and financed by website advertisements for a company's actual stock-broking activities. One of the best known US finance games for schools is 'The Stock Market Game'. It is distributed with curriculum activities, lesson plans and teachers' newsletters and workshops developed by the National Council on Economic Education (NCEE).[59] It is a product of the Securities Industry Foundation for Economic Education (SIFEE) which states:

> *The Stock Market Game enables participants to discover the risks and rewards involved in decision-making, the sources and uses of capital, and other related economic concepts ... The flexibility of the program allows you to use it with a variety of subjects, including social studies, mathematics, business, and language arts, as well as for economics. It can also be integrated into school clubs, lunch or rainy day programs, after school and gifted student activities.*[60]

SIFEE 'was established to foster among the public a better understanding of the American economic system' and the role of the securities industry. Since 1976 SIFEE claims to have taught 6 million children from Grade 4 upwards in 16 countries 'how financial markets work and how capital is raised to fund business growth'.[61]

The immediate impact of such games is that more children than ever before now own shares. 'A growing number of financial planners and investment companies are tailoring their products and services to suit the youth market. Some even visit schools, armed with videos and comic books aimed at an ever-younger audience.'[62]

Anne and Gerard Henderson from the Australian think tank the Sydney Institute claim that it was the shares in Telstra that their daughter bought, rather than parental guidance or her general education, that changed their daughter from someone who would have 'gone with the flow against globalization' to someone who is 'interested in what happens in Wall Street because that affects her now'.[63]

Notes

1 Richard Nadler, 'Stocks Populi', *National Review*, 9 March 1998.
2 Thomas L. Friedman, *The Lexus and the Olive Tree*, New York, Farrar, Straus and Giroux, 1999, pp47–50.
3 Quoted in Thomas Frank, *One Market under God: Extreme Capitalism Market Populism, and the End of Economic Democracy*, New York, Doubleday, 2000, p91 and Friedman, *The Lexus and the Olive Tree*, p58.
4 Free market proponents quoted in Frank, *One Market under God*, p93; Donald E. Schwartz, 'Shareholder Democracy: A Reality or Chimera?' *California Management Review*, vol XXV, no 3, 1983, p54.
5 Schwartz, 'Shareholder Democracy', p56.
6 *Ibid.*, p54.
7 Cited in 'The Rich Get Richer Faster Than the Poor Get Richer in the US', *Sydney Morning Herald*, 24 January 2003, p19.
8 Edward N. Wolff, 'The Rich Get Richer: And Why the Poor Don't', *The American Prospect*, February, 2001, www.prospect.org/print-friendly/print/V12/3/wolff-e.html.
9 Ron Chernow, 'Lambs among the Bulls and Bears', *New York Times*, 26 July 1996, pA29.

10 Frank, *One Market under God*, p105.
11 Roland Marchand, *Creating the Corporate Soul: The Rise of Public Relations and Corporate Imagery in American Big Business*, Berkeley, University of California Press, 1998, pp74–80.
12 *Ibid.*, pp80, 116, 140.
13 Alan R. Raucher, *Public Relations and Business 1900–1929*, Baltimore, The Johns Hopkins Press, 1968, pp88–89.
14 Carl D. Thompson, *Confessions of the Power Trust*, New York, E. P. Dutton & Co., 1932, pp390–1.
15 Quoted in *Ibid.*, p212.
16 Quoted in *Ibid.*, pp209–10.
17 *Ibid.*, pp213–5.
18 Quoted in *Ibid.*, p214.
19 Chernow, 'Lambs among the Bulls and Bears'; Frank, *One Market under God*, p104; Barnaby J. Feder, 'Keith Funston, Head of the Big Board through '50 Revival, Dies at 81', *New York Times*, 16 May 1992, p10.
20 John Moore, Tory Minister, quoted in Peter M. Jackson and Catherine M. Price (eds) *Privatisation and Regulation: A Review of the Issues*, London and New York, Longman, 1994, p14.
21 'View from City Road: Making Share Ownership Work', *The Independent*, 18 December 1990, p19.
22 Michael G. Pollitt, 'A Survey of Liberalisation of Public Enterprises in the UK since 1979', University of Cambridge, January 1999, p5; Dexter Whitfield, *Making It Public: Evidence and Action against Privatisation*, London, Pluto Press, 1983, pp24, 28.
23 Irwin Stelzer, 'A Review of Privatization and Regulation Experience in Britain', Institute of Economic Affairs, 7 November 2000, 2000, www.iea.org.uk/record.php?type=article&ID=54.
24 Quoted in 'Looking Forward to a True People's Market', *Investors Chronicle*, 28 June 1991, p8.
25 *Ibid.*, p8.
26 Stelzer, 'A Review of Privatization and Regulation Experience in Britain'.
27 Steve Thomas, 'The Privatization of the Electricity Supply Industry', in John Surrey (ed) *The British Electricity Experiment*, London, Earthscan Publications, 1996, pp41, 52; Jackson and Price, 'Privatisation and Regulation', p15; John Cryer, 'Utilities (Foreign Ownership)', House of Commons' Hansard Debates, 25 February 1998, www.parliament.the-stationery-office.co.uk/pa/cm199798/cmhansard/vo900225/debtext/80225-12.htm.
28 Quoted in Christopher Pyne, 'Options', SA Liberal Party, May, 2002, www.sa.liberal.org.au/pyne/default.asp?Menu=op13_1; John Howard, 'Address at Opening of Western Mining Corporation's Olympic Dam Expansion', Prime Minister's Office, 26 March 1999, www.pm.gov.au/speeches/1999/damexpansion.htm.
29 Senator Richard Alston, Parliament of Australia, broadcast on ABC Radio, 16 March 1998.
30 'A Sapling's Sound Roots; Germans Take to Shares', *The Economist*, 10 March 2001, p1; George Melloan, 'Europe's New Shareholder Culture Spurs Big Changes', *Wall Street Journal*, 9 May 2000, pA27.

31 'A Sapling's Sound Roots', p1.
32 Steven Greenhouse, 'France Embraces "Popular Capitalism"', *New York Times*, 8 June 1987; Shawn Tully, 'Europe Goes Wild over Privatisation', *Fortune*, vol 115, no 5, 1987.
33 Greenhouse, 'France Embraces "Popular Capitalism"'.
34 Hagaman T. Carter, 'The Myth of Shareholder Democracy', *Management Accounting*, vol 72, no 11, 1991.
35 *Ibid.*
36 Ralph Nader and Joel Seligman, 'The Myth of Shareholder Democracy', in Mark Green, *et al.* (eds) *The Big Business Reader: On Corporate America*, New York, Pilgrim Press, 1983, p378.
37 *Ibid.*, p377.
38 *Ibid.*, pp378–9.
39 Carter, 'The Myth of Shareholder Democracy'.
40 Lewis Braham, 'Bring Democracy to Boardroom Elections', *Business Week*, 21 October 2002, p126.
41 William Taylor, 'Can Big Owners Make a Difference', *Harvard Business Review*, September/October, 1990; James McRitchie, 'Enhancing the Return on Capital through Increased Accountability', Corporate Governance, 26 March 2000, www.corpgov.net/.
42 Nathaniel Nash, 'Shareholders' Rights: Three Views: Vying for Control of the Public Corporation', *New York Times*, 15 February 1987.
43 Kerry Capell and David Fairlamb, 'Everyone Is Selling, No One Is Buying', *Business Week*, 22 July 2002; Colin Robinson, 'Pressure Groups and Political Forces in Britain's Privatisation Programme', Paper presented at the Japan Public Choice Society International Conference, Chiba University of Commerce, 22–23 August 1997, p8; Whitfield, *Making It Public*, p30; Thomas, 'The Privatization of the Electricity Supply Industry', p41; Julia Flynn, 'Will Britain Ever Be a Nation of Stock-Keepers?' *Business Week*, 19 August 1996, p42.
44 Taylor, 'Can Big Owners Make a Difference', p70; McRitchie, 'Enhancing the Return on Capital through Increased Accountability'; Cryer, 'Utilities (Foreign Ownership)'.
45 Braham, 'Bring Democracy to Boardroom Elections'.
46 C. Robinson. 'Pressure Groups and Political Forces in Britain's Privatisation Programme', p8; S. Thomas. 'The Privatization of the Electricity Supply Industry', p41; J. Flynn. 'Will Britain Ever Be a Nation of Stock-Keepers?' *Business Week*, 19 August 1996, p42; 'Share Ownership: A Report on Ownership of Shares as at 31st December 2001', Newport, Office for National Statistics, 2002, www.statistics.gov.uk/downloads/theme_economy/ShareOwnership2001.pdf, p9.
47 Nash, 'Shareholders' Rights'; Japonica Partners, 'The Killer B's', Japonica Partners, www.japonica.com/network/killerb.html accessed 8 May 2000.
48 Allen Myers, 'Sharing the Wealth?' *Green Left Weekly*, 25 August 1999, p11.
49 Wolff, 'The Rich Get Richer'.
50 Stephen Long, 'For Richer and Poorer', *Australian Financial Review*, 9 January 1999, p21.
51 Christopher Pearson, 'Shares and Shares Alike', *Australian Financial Review*, 15 January 2001, p26.

52 ProShare, 'ProShare Student Investment Sponsors', ProShare, www.proshare.org/schools/sponsors.asp accessed 29 December 2002; ProShare, 'Welcome to ProShare!' ProShare, www.proshare.org/about/background.asp accessed 29 December 2002; ProShare, 'The ProShare Forecast Challenge', ProShare, www.proshare.org/comps/forecast.asp accessed 29 December 2002.

53 ProShare, 'The ProShare Portfolio Challenge', ProShare, www.proshare.org/comps/portfolio.asp accessed 29 December 2002.

54 ProShare, 'At School', ProShare, www.proshare.org/about/ar01-02/school.asp accessed 29 December 2002; ProShare, 'Your Money, Be Wise', ProShare, yourmoneybewise.org/ accessed 29 December 2002.

55 Mark Maier, 'Teaching About Stocks - for Fun and Propaganda', *Dollars & Sense*, March, 2001.

56 *Ibid.*

57 *Ibid.*

58 SIFEE, 'Teachers Only', Securities Industry Foundation for Economic Education, www.smgww.org/frm_teachers.html accessed 3 January 2003.

59 Maier, 'Teaching About Stocks'; SIFEE, 'Teachers Only'.

60 SIFEE, 'The Stock Market Game', Securities Industry Foundation for Economic Education, www.smgww.org/ accessed 3 January 2003; SIFEE, 'Teachers Only'.

61 SIFEE, 'The Stock Market Game'.

62 Tom Rhodes, 'Building Family Bonds', *The Australian*, 23 August 2000.

63 Quoted in Friedman, *The Lexus and the Olive Tree*, p291.

13

Fiddling with Kiddy Minds

Economics is the fourth 'R' in education. There's Reading, 'Riting and 'Rithmetic, and then there's Reality. Economics is reality . . .

NATIONAL COUNCIL ON ECONOMIC EDUCATION[1]

We are here today to begin the exploration of what we should encourage our citizenry to think about, act on and, in essence, be happy about.

MICHAEL J. CASLIN, III, CEO OF THE NATIONAL FOUNDATION FOR TEACHING ENTREPRENEURSHIP[2]

Efforts at teaching young people to love and defend the free enterprise system, which began more than a century ago, continue today. Economic education has become mainstream. It is no longer an obvious expression of a campaign to sell free enterprise. Instead the campaign is disguised as a means to give children and young adults the necessary economic knowledge to live successful lives and understand the world around them. Who could fault such a noble motive? Most people agree that basic economics should be taught in schools and the support for business education and enterprise education has widespread support.[3]

Nonetheless, the groups that are pushing for economic and business education to be mandatory in schools have an ideological agenda and the economic standards they are promoting have an ideological bias that supports the market story outlined in the introduction of this book. In the US many of these groups were established during earlier economic education campaigns. In Australia, Canada and the UK, such groups have more recent origins.

The US-based National Council on Economic Education (NCEE) is at the forefront of this endeavour and operates both in the US and internationally. It was formed in 1949 as the Joint Council on Economic Education (JCEE – see Chapter 5). Organizations such as Procter & Gamble, American Express, the Ford Motor Company Fund, the International Paper Company, the Exxon Educational Foundation, Unilever, Georgia-Pacific, Chrysler, AT&T, 3M, Olin, the Business Roundtable and the US Department of Education are long-time contributors. Its life directors include Harold Burson, founder of PR giant Burson-Marsteller.[4]

NCEE trains teachers; forms networks and partnerships with like-minded organizations; sets economics curriculum standards for schools; publishes teaching materials including internet-based programmes; and has a university-based training programme for teachers to keep up to date with changing teaching requirements. It runs EconomicsAmerica (begun in 1949) which claims to train 120,000 teachers how to teach economics to eight million students, through 'a vast network of state councils and university-based centers'. NCEE is also working on distance learning and internet technologies to reach thousands more teachers in the US. 'More than 2,600 school districts, teaching about 40 per cent of the nation's students, conduct comprehensive programmes in economic education with assistance from the network.'[5]

The NCEE also has an international programme, EconomicsInternational, supported mainly by the US Department of Education, which reaches millions of students in 21 countries. It trains teachers; translates and adapts American instructional materials; and advises on the development of standards, curricula and assessment. It is mainly aimed at the former communist countries in Europe 'helping our international partners reform their educational systems and educate their citizens for the transition to a market economy'.[6]

Free enterprise education, that is, teaching students to love business and the free enterprise system, is today conducted under the guise of teaching children the skills, beliefs and attitudes to become entrepreneurs and start their own businesses.[7] Often this involves visits to businesses or team exercises where students run a simulated business. Such curricula are embraced by educational departments in Australia, the UK and the US. Enterprise education gives the students the impression that they can become successful entrepreneurs if only they have enough knowledge, ambition and talent.

ENTERPRISE EDUCATION

Junior Achievement (JA) began its operations in the US in 1919 (see Chapter 4) and has since become an international organization. It claims to reach over 6 million students each year in over 100 countries on 6 continents, 4 million in the US alone.[8]

> *We are the passionate people behind a movement that seeks to educate and inspire young people to value free enterprise, business and economics to improve the quality of their lives ... From this, we articulate our mission: to ensure that every child in America has a fundamental understanding of the free enterprise system.*[9]

JA's funding comes from a variety of corporations including Best Buy, Deloitte, AIG, Mastercard International, 3M, PricewaterhouseCoopers and Morgan Stanley; most of which have people on the very large board of directors.[10]

JA's programmes cover all school levels, beginning with kindergarten. For high school there is JA Economics, a semester-long course – complete with textbooks and study guides – teaching economic fundamentals such as 'the nature of the free enterprise system'; 'how voluntary exchange markets allocate resources' and set prices; 'the role of entrepreneurs'; and the 'costs and benefits of international trade'. JA also has a programme for middle grades called the International Marketplace that includes a game called 'Trade Wins'. The programme teaches things such as 'why trade barriers inhibit economic growth' and 'the roles of private ownership and markets in promoting economic growth and directing the use of environmental resources'.[11]

JA has equivalents in over 100 countries. In Australia, Young Achievement Australia (YAA) was introduced by the American Chamber of Commerce in Australia and it is currently sponsored by BHP Billiton, Westpac, IBM Australia and hundreds of other corporations as well as various government departments. This amounts to some $2.5 million in sponsorship and donations each year, and together with the voluntary labour of some 1,600 business people as mentors, enables YAA to offer its programmes free of charge, including to 'youth at risk', the unemployed and Aboriginal groups. It has state and regional offices throughout the country and claims to have reached 170,000 young Australians. It offers economics programmes from primary school up and enjoys the glowing endorsement of Prime Minister John Howard.[12]

In the UK the JA member is Young Enterprise, which was founded in 1963 as a charity. It reaches 280,000 young people each year with the support of 11,500 business volunteers and more than 3000 businesses, including HSBC, Cadbury Schweppes, Hewlett Packard, Nestlé UK, Procter & Gamble and TNT Express. It has programmes for all levels of schooling, beginning with primary school. The six primary school modules teach children how to be good workers and consumers and the benefits of international trade.[13]

For more senior students aged 14–16 years, Young Enterprise's *Project Business* helps students to better understand business from a business point of view. It can be presented as a one- or two-day seminar or spread over six weeks in one-hour modules with titles such as 'Why do we need business?' Its aims are to enable young people to:

- *gain a practical, activity-based insight into economic and business life;*
- *appreciate the role of business and enterprise in our society;*
- *discover how businesses interact with investors, customers, employees and society in general;*
- *understand how businesses work and wealth is created;*
- *experience business life in their community and gain an insight into the working life of a local business person;*
- *develop team working, communication, and presentation skills;*

- *build a bridge between school and the business world;*
- *develop skills and understanding that are directly relevant to enterprise and work-related learning.*[14]

Another international enterprise education programme is the National Foundation for Teaching Entrepreneurship (NFTE) which was founded in 1987 by a business executive-turned-school teacher. It now has over '3200 Certified Entrepreneurship Teachers' in 14 countries. It offers an online curriculum – BizTech; a textbook; various school and after school programmes; and business camps. Its website explains its philosophy:

> *When young people participate in our programs they begin to unlock their unique entrepreneurial creativity, have a greater understanding of the free enterprise system, improve the quality of their lives, and dare to dream for bright futures.*[15]

In the US, where it focuses on young people from low-income communities, it is supported by the Goldman Sachs foundation (over $2 million), Microsoft Corporation (over $1million), Merrill Lynch, Scaife Family Foundation, Morgan Stanley Foundation, and many others. It claims to have 'reached over 100,000 young people'. NFTE's UK branch, NFTE-UK opened in 2000. Its advisers come from Goldman Sachs International, HSBC and the International Business Leaders Forum as well as from the education sector. Its sponsors include Vodafone, JP Morgan, Merrill Lynch, McKinsey & Company and Marks and Spencer.[16]

Michael J. Caslin, III, CEO of the NFTE, testified to a US congressional hearing that 63 per cent of students who had taken NFTE courses viewed the market economy more favourably, while 33 per cent didn't change their view:

> *An entrepreneurial culture promotes a personally productive and responsible lifestyle. The Culture of Entrepreneurship brings with it traditions, beliefs, values, attitudes, morals, interests, lifestyle, an innovative and opportunity-obsessed, problem-solving skill set, value exchange, private property rights and voluntary trade.*[17]

In Australia, Australian Business Week (ABW) involves teams of students managing a simulated company and competing with other teams of students in school, state and national championships. There is now also a primary school programme that is supposed to help children 'become flexible, good communicators, entrepreneurial and more able to take calculated risks'. They run a simulated sandwich shop.[18]

ABW was conceived at a chamber of commerce meeting in 1992 as a way to 'help young people get a better appreciation of business'. It has been sponsored throughout its life by Coca-Cola. Other corporate sponsors have included IBM,

Unilever, Boeing, Ernst & Young, PricewaterhouseCoopers, American Express, Konica Minolta, Hallmark Cards, Rio Tinto, Shell and Woolworths. ABW is now expanding overseas and in 2002 began operations in Scotland. It has also expanded to include corporate programmes for the employees of corporations such as IBM, Holiday Inn, Telecom NZ and Crane Metals.[19]

ABW founder and chair Norman Owens, who travelled to the US early in the life of ABW to see how such programmes were run there, has been awarded an Order of Australia Medal. ABW's web page includes a letter of support from Prime Minister John Howard, who congratulates ABW 'on giving more than 75,000 participants over the past decade an insight into the enterprise skills required to be successful in business'. It is also supported by state departments of education and several universities that host its programmes and even offer them to their own students.[20]

The Australian Commonwealth Government actively promotes enterprise education. It initiated an Enterprise in Schools programme in 1995 aimed at 'the inculcation of enterprising cultures, mindsets and qualities in young people' and allocated $3.2 million for the 1997–99 triennium. In 1998 it launched an Enterprise Education Programme Awareness Package developed by the Curriculum Corporation that was sent to every school. It was entitled 'Making it Happen: An Introduction to Enterprise Education'. The package included a video, CD-ROM and booklet that showcased enterprise education efforts at schools around the country.[21]

A School–Industry Link Demonstration Programme was also set up by the government agency AusIndustry. The programme 'is designed to give students a better understanding of the value to the community of local business and industry'. The state education departments also embraced enterprise education during the 1990s. In Victoria, the Curriculum and Standards Framework incorporated enterprise education at various stages and subjects from kindergarten to year ten. A dedicated subject, Industry and Enterprise Studies, was introduced for senior students. Enterprise education has also been integrated throughout the curriculum in South Australia and a programme called 'Ready Set Go' implemented.[22]

In the UK, according to the Qualifications and Curriculum Authority, 'Enterprise education is a key element' of the work-related learning framework, which became a statutory requirement in 2004. 'Enterprise education consists of enterprise capability, supported by financial capability and economic and business understanding.' The government has allocated £60 million per year from September 2005 'to support a new focus on enterprise education in English secondary schools'.[23]

Enterprise education in the UK, as elsewhere, has been driven by business. In a paper on 'Creating an Enterprise Culture', Enterprise Insight and the Small Business Service argue that the challenge for the UK is 'to be the best environment for business with ever more positive attitudes towards enterprise':[24]

> *... corporate opinion believes that attitudes in the UK are less positive than elsewhere. In an international survey of CEOs, 68% of UK senior executives said that entrepreneurial behaviour and entrepreneurs are not highly regarded here, well above the global average of 41% and 23% for the US.*
>
> *In addition, a significant proportion of the UK population believes that those successful in business have low morals or ethics.*[25]

Enterprise Insight was founded by the British Chambers of Commerce (BCC), the Confederation of British Industry (CBI), the Institute of Directors and the Federation of Small Businesses, which also fund and run it. It organizes a national Enterprise Week each year with over 1000 events around the country. It also seeks to 'engage young people in the main spaces they occupy in their lives – work, education, leisure and media' through the use of personal stories, role models, and workshops. It has full government support.[26]

Enterprise Insight has partnered with various other pro-enterprise education organizations including the Academy of Enterprise – which aims to 'to assist schools and higher education institutions develop an enterprise culture'; businessdynamics – 'a business education and enterprise charity that aims to bring business to life for young people'; the National Federation of Enterprise Agencies; Business in the Community – which aims to 'support business in continually improving its positive impact on society'; the National Education Business Partnership Network; Shell LiveWire; and Young Enterprise.[27]

ECONOMIC LITERACY

Those who advocate economic education seek not only to ensure that people think in an economic way but also that government policies be judged according to free market principles. Wolfgang Kasper, a senior fellow at the Australian think tank, the Centre for Independent Studies (CIS – see Chapter 9), argued that economic literacy includes understanding 'that ballot democracy must therefore not be allowed to subvert the dollar democracy of the market place'.[28] David S. Dahl, public affairs economist with the Federal Reserve Bank of Minneapolis, argues that, with the collapse of communist states, 'the debate is now about the degree and effectiveness of government action within a market-oriented economy rather than a stark choice of state vs. market'. He therefore sees a major aim of economic literacy as being 'to teach people how to ascertain when a government policy will improve market outcomes'.[29]

An economic literacy symposium, organized by the Economic Literacy Project concluded that the better-informed people were, the fewer mistakes there would be in public policy and that 'economic literacy is not just about teaching people how to react to certain policies or ideas, but how to put them into context and evaluate them'.[30] Similarly, William Walstad, past president of NCEE and director of the National Center for Research in Economic Education, argues:

> *Economic knowledge, whether measured by an overall score or by knowledge of a specific question, may be the most critical factor determining public opinion on economic issues, perhaps more important and more consistently influential than other personal characteristics such as age, sex, race, education, income or political party.*[31]

Walstad argued that if people 'understood' economics (by which he presumably meant if they share his free market views) they would be more likely to accept market outcomes. For example, when young people are asked what they think of a bicycle manufacturer raising prices of bikes because demand is increasing, even though the cost of producing the bikes remains the same, two-thirds said he shouldn't be allowed to. However, most of those who 'understood' how markets work said he should be allowed to raise his prices. They were more accepting of market outcomes.[32]

In 1999 the US-based NCEE embarked on a five-year campaign for economic literacy, which it said was equivalent to the national campaign that was underway to improve reading literacy. The idea was to ensure students would possess 'economic ways of thinking' when they left school. The advisory committee for the campaign included the CEOs of American Express, Merrill Lynch, International Paper Co. and Bank of America as well as the president of the American Federation of Teachers.[33]

The goal of the campaign was to 'ensure that economic literacy becomes a priority on the national education agenda' and that 'quality, standards-based economic education is effectively taught in every state, in every school, and at every grade level'. To achieve this NCEE implemented a 'communications program, to create public awareness of the need and intensify the public demand for economic education'. It mobilized relevant constituencies 'to help magnify the significance of economic education'. It also sought to develop materials; make use of volunteers, new technologies and partner organizations; and measure progress towards its goals.[34]

Regular statements from a variety of sources about how students lack understanding of the economic system, and how this threatens American prosperity, have been successful in having economics courses introduced into schools. The NCEE states that 'The shocking reality is that American high school and college students know precious little about how the American economic system actually works' and gives the example that 'Sixty percent do not understand the purpose of profits'.[35]

JCEE conducted a survey in 1989 when 28 states required secondary students to receive some instruction on economics and found what *US News & World Report* referred to as 'a burgeoning nation of economic dunces'. The given answers to the test, however, were attacked by economists of different persuasions as misleading or incorrect. NCEE's 1999 survey of economic literacy amongst students and the general public was funded by Merrill Lynch and conducted by Louis Harris & Associates. It found that half of the adults surveyed and two-thirds of the high school students failed when tested.[36]

Of course, when NCEE and others are testing economic knowledge they are in fact testing adherence to free-market gospel. The survey found that 61 per cent of adults but only 48 per cent of students 'understand that in the United States it is a combination of consumers, producers and government that determines what goods and services should be produced'. Similarly, a majority of adults but a minority of students 'correctly' 'understand that investing in more research and development, and not taxing inventions or increasing government regulation, would most likely accelerate innovation'.[37] Clearly, the survey was testing the degree to which the population subscribed to the 'market story' rather than their real knowledge. Here are some sample questions which people did badly on, with the 'correct' answer shown:

If your city government sets a maximum amount landlords can charge in rent, what is the most likely result?
( ) *There will be more apartments available than people want to rent*
(✓) *There will be fewer apartments available than people want to rent*
( ) *The number of apartments available will be equal to the number of people that want to rent*
( ) *Don't know*

The stock market is an example of an institution within our economy that exists to help people achieve their economic goals. The existence of this institution:
( ) *Results in an increase in the price of stocks*
(✓) *Brings people together who want to buy stocks together with those who want to sell stocks*
( ) *Helps predict stock earnings*
( ) *Don't know*

NCEE's Test of Economic Literacy (TEL) has become a standard for many schools wishing to evaluate student knowledge of economics. Developed in 1987, 64,000 copies were distributed over the following four years, and it has been given official status in some states. For example, students who can pass the TEL in New York do not have to take the compulsory economics class at high school.[38] However, as is obvious from the above sample, this test is not so much a test of economic knowledge so much as a test of a particular economic view or ideology.

Economists Nelson and Sheffrin examined the test in 1991 and found it to have a 'pronounced ideological slant'. For example:

> *In a market economy, the social purpose of profits is to*
> *(a) get businesses to follow government regulations*
> *(b) get businesses to provide what consumers demand*
> *(c) provide funds to pay workers better wages*
> *(d) transfer income from the poor to the rich*

According to free market ideology and the test authors, (b) is the correct answer but the answer (d) might indicate a different ideological standpoint rather than economic illiteracy. Similarly:

> *Which of the following is the most essential for a market economy?*
> *(a) Effective labour unions*
> *(b) Good government regulation*
> *(c) Active competition in the marketplace*
> *(d) Responsible action by business leaders*

Nelson and Sheffrin argue that 'while the test writers (and perhaps most economists) prefer (c), it is certainly arguable that a minimal level of social responsibility and cooperation and a regulatory infrastructure are necessary to create the 'playing field' on which competition take place, and are hence even more basic than competition'.[39] Others might reasonably argue that for a high standard of living and a cohesive society (a) is actually the most essential of all.

The assumption that the public interest is served by individuals pursuing their own interest is not open to question in the test and some of the questions have the propaganda embedded in them so that it would be impossible to give any answer at all without accepting the free market premises. For example:

> *In a market economy, the public interest is likely to be served even when individuals pursue their own private economic goals because of*
> (✓) *the operation of competitive markets*
> ( ) *the social responsibility of business leaders*
> ( ) *careful planning and coordination of market activity*
> ( ) *individuals who understand what is in the public interest*

The Business Roundtable commissioned the NCEE to survey employees of seven companies. NCEE found that 28 per cent of them 'failed to see the connection between their companies' interests and their own. They would have failed if the survey had been a test. Those are adults who are likely to make poor personal financial decisions.'[40]

Some of NCEE's earlier surveys also included a section 'measuring' 'Economic Attitude Sophistication'. For example, according to the NCEE, the economically sophisticated student should disagree with the following statements:[41]

> *Free medical care should be provided for all Americans.*
> *When a business gets big, it should be controlled by government.*
> *When a strike occurs, the government should step in and settle the dispute.*

Other organizations have used similarly ideologically slanted questions to survey economic literacy. For example, the Federal Reserve Bank of Minneapolis' national telephone survey of economic literacy awarded an average score of 45 per cent to respondents. Sample questions which those surveyed failed included:[42]

> *What would happen to employment if the government mandated a minimum wage above what employers currently pay?*
> ( ) *Employment would go up*
> (✓) *Employment would go down*
> ( ) *Employment would stay the same*
>
> *Which of the following approaches to pollution control makes the best use of a country's economic resources:*
> ( ) *Abolishing the use of toxic chemicals*
> ( ) *Using resources to reduce all pollution damage*
> (✓) *Controlling pollution as long as the extra benefits are greater than the extra costs*
> ( ) *Prohibiting economic activities that cause pollution or harm the environment*

The 'Great Nebraskan National Economics Test' can be found on the internet. It asks multiple choice questions such as 'The prices of meat products in a competitive market are determined by . . .?' The 'correct' answer being 'Supply and Demand'. Or 'Which of the following is most likely to improve the wages of American workers?' The 'correct' answer being 'An increase in productivity'.[43]

Such surveys are also done in other countries. At the end of 1997 the Canadian Bankers Association and the Canadian Foundation for Economic Education (CFEE) conducted a survey of the level of economic literacy amongst Canadians and found them lacking.[44] In Australia economics is an elective high school subject in all states. A survey of the economic literacy in Queensland high school students (years 11 and 12) was conducted in 1998. It was adapted from JCEE's 1987 Test of Economic Literacy (TEL) discussed above.[45] A more recent version of the TEL was used to test the economic literacy of Japanese senior high school students in 2001 and of Korean students in 2002.[46] The TEL has also been used on New Zealand first-year university students.[47]

ECONOMIC EDUCATION STANDARDS

In 1997 a coalition of NCEE, the National Association of Economic Educators, the Foundation for Teaching Economics, which has close associations with a number of conservative think tanks and is funded by corporate and right wing foundations, and the American Economic Association's Committee on Economic Education established National Voluntary Content Standards for Pre-College Economics Education in the US. This consisted of 20 standards specifying knowledge to be obtained and benchmarks for what students should understand and be able to do at various stages of their schooling.[48]

For example, Content Standard 13 states: 'Income for most people is determined by the market value of the productive resources they sell. What workers earn depends, primarily, on the market value of what they produce and how productive they are.' Benchmarks for this standard include that by Grade 4 students will know things like 'Labor is a human resource used to produce goods and services.' By Grade 8 they will know things like 'People's incomes, in part, reflect choices they have made about education, training, skill development, and careers. People with few skills are more likely to be poor.' And by Grade 12 they will know things like 'Changes in demand for specific goods and services often affect the incomes of the workers who make those goods and services.'[49]

This is a version of the market gospel, which promotes the view that the market sets wages automatically and anonymously according to supply and demand (as opposed to wage setting being the result of a power struggle between employers and workers), and that everybody gets what they deserve on the basis of their talents, education and effort (as opposed to poverty being the result of injustice, discrimination, lack of opportunities, bad luck, or a lack of adequately paid jobs being available). The idea that workers' wages depend on the market value of what they produce and their productivity ignores the reality of sweatshop labour, for example, where goods are sold at many times the cost of production and wages bear no relation to market value or productivity.

Content Standard 2 teaches that 'Effective decision-making requires comparing the additional costs of alternatives with the additional benefits' and the youngest students are taught 'A cost is what you give up when you decide to do something', while 'A benefit is something that satisfies your wants.' By the end of school students will know that when marginal benefits exceed marginal costs of an activity, then people will be better off doing it, and that public policy programmes should be based on this principle.[50]

Just because the benefits of an action outweigh the costs, it does not mean that the decision is morally correct. Exploiting the vulnerability of a weaker person to gain a benefit for oneself, for example, may not be the right thing to do. The role of morality and equity and other non-economic factors in decision-making is ignored in such analyses and the world is reduced to a balancing of economic costs and benefits.[51] These are very dubious standards for guiding the education of school children.

Content Standard 4 states 'People respond predictably to positive and negative incentives' and by Grade 8 students know this is because 'people usually pursue their self-interest'.[52] This is based on the fallacious assumption that there is no such thing as the common good outside of individual wants and preferences. However, people often consider wider interests than their own self-interest. They are concerned with the 'good of society'. This is why people support ideas such as public education, when they do not have children, and environmental protection that has significance beyond their own lifetimes.[53]

The economic education standards also expect students to learn that 'most prices in market economies are established by interaction between buyers and sellers' and that price controls 'reduce the quantity of goods and services consumed, thus depriving consumers of some goods and services ...'. They will learn that 'Property rights help ensure that people bear the costs and reap the benefits of their decisions' and that while increased government spending may increase employment and output in the short run, in the long run it will lead to increased interest rates that will reduce private sector investment, offsetting 'partially, if not entirely' those gains in employment and output.[54]

NCEE produces lessons on teaching economics in civics and government, history and geography courses and correlates the economics standards with these lessons. For example, the NCEE's 73 lessons on US history are each designed to convey one or more of the economics standards.[55]

Bonnie Meszaros, associate director of the Center for Economic Education and Entrepreneurship at the University of Delaware, was on the Writing Committee for the standards. She claims that the standards stress 'the importance of learning how to reason about economic issues' using economic knowledge and skills such as comparing costs and benefits. They teach students to be willing to compromise and trade off. In the case of environmental pollution, for example, this means optimizing pollution levels for economic benefit rather than environmental protection. Armed with this sort of thinking students will supposedly be better able to evaluate environmental regulations.[56]

In an article on the standards in the *Journal of Economic Education*, two of the authors of the standards admitted that the standards reflected a neoclassical model of economic behaviour but defended this by stating that in order to produce 'a single, coherent set of standards to guide the teaching of economics' it was necessary to use a majority paradigm:

> *Including strongly held minority views of economic processes risk undermining the entire venture. With too many qualifications and alternatives, teachers and their students may abandon economics entirely out of frustration born of confusion and uncertainty.*[57]

They agreed that in the area of macroeconomics they were struggling to find a 'consensus paradigm' and that some economists would criticize their standards in this area. Similarly they omitted many of the assumptions on which the economic principles were based:

> *Almost all economics principles are conditioned on assumptions. To report all of those assumptions each time would detract from the effectiveness of the standards ... So, in numerous cases, assumptions are omitted, leaving standards and benchmarks implying as 'always true' principles that are usually but not always true as they are stated.*[58]

In 2002 the number of US states with economics standards increased to 48. Three-quarters of these states required the standards to be implemented. Seventeen states required economics subjects to be offered in high school and 14 states required students to do such a subject. These 14 states included the largest 4 states and accounted for a third of all school children in public schools. Twenty-seven states required students to be tested for economic knowledge.[59]

Like NCEE, CFEE runs a programme, supported by the Royal Bank of Canada and the Canadian government, entitled EconomicsCanada, which has produced a proposed consensus Canadian 'guideline for economic literacy' that outlines target economic concepts that students need 'to understand in order to understand economic events and realities' such as comparative advantage, economic efficiency and economic freedom. It has also produced a curriculum framework/database and draft economics life skills courses/themes.[60]

OTHER ECONOMIC LITERACY PROGRAMMES

These efforts are augmented by many other programmes. The Foundation for Economic Education (FEE – see Chapter 4) is still going strong. It is 'dedicated to the preservation of individual freedom and the private property order' and follows the teachings of Austrian libertarian economist Ludwig von Mises, an early mentor of Friedrich von Hayek (see Chapter 7). It also promotes limited government and free trade and produces 'a multitude of educational resources in the form of classic and contemporary books and essays, articles, op-ed columns' as well as student seminars, discussion clubs, lesson plans for teachers and weekend classes for undergraduate students.[61]

On its website, The Association of Private Enterprise Education (APEE) takes partial credit for the increasing conservatism of young people: 'For over two decades, the Association of Private Enterprise Education has been teaching that markets work and that maximum society benefits come from individuals' efforts to achieve their own goals with minimal governmental interference. APEE's teachings are bearing fruit.'[62] APEE claims to reach millions of people each year with its message.

The APEE provides information, enables interaction and offers support for this network through newsletters, conferences, publications, membership directories and other means. It is also involved in employee education. Its particular interest though, has been in creating Chairs and Centers of Private Enterprise at universities. It was a group of people with such chairs, along with committed business people and other educators, who founded the APEE in the 1970s.[63]

Students in Free Enterprise (SIFE) is another advocacy group aimed at university students. Founded in 1975 in the US, it is today global in reach and claims to be 'literally changing the world through highly dedicated student teams on more than 1600 university campuses in 40 countries'. SIFE members learn, practice and teach others the principles of free enterprise, 'thereby improving the standard of living for millions in the process'. Its board of directors is made up of business people, including the vice-chairmen of transnational corporations KPMG, 3M, AT&T, Gillette, GE, Nestlé, Pfizer, Philip Morris, Procter and Gamble, Shell and Wal-Mart.[62]

The Foundation for Teaching Economics (FTE) is yet another organization that pushes the free enterprise story in schools and subscribes to NCEE voluntary standards. It was formed in the US in 1975 'in response to a concern that too many young people lack an understanding of the basic concepts of market economics'. It runs workshops for 'leaders' and teachers covering topics such as market solutions to environmental problems. Its purpose is to introduce selected high school students 'to an economic way of thinking about national and international issues'.[65]

FTE lessons on economic forces in American history teach that the push for regulation of big business in the late 19th century came from small businesses and their success 'in securing protection against competition from big business imposed significant costs on consumers'.[66] Similarly, its lesson on the Great Depression diverges quite markedly from the normal scholarly interpretation of history, in order to make its ideological points:

> *The Depression itself resulted from disruptions to international trade and faulty government economic policies before and after the downturn came. Curiously, even though government policies had much to do with bringing on the Depression and making it more severe, the economic crisis of the early 1930s became ground for greatly expanding the role of government in American life ... Unfortunately, New Deal programs did not fulfil expectations and, indeed, may have delayed recovery as they further disabled market operations.*[67]

In its lesson on 'The use and abuse of natural resources in historical perspective' FTE teaches that if natural resources are not privately owned then 'the value of the resource dissipates, unless access can be limited. While government would seem the natural and appropriate vehicle for limiting access, it has met with varying degrees of success in protecting our natural resources from exploitation.' Corruption and the absence of specified property rights are blamed for this. FTE holds four-day residential programmes for teachers to learn similar ways of looking at environmental problems and to 'learn how to use economic principles to analyze environmental issues'.[66]

FTE teaches public choice theory (see Chapter 7). This theory seeps into other lessons including the history lessons FTE offers: 'The nature of the system of incentives within the electoral process is such that, as government grows, it becomes increasingly responsive to the demands of special interest groups, often at the expense of the general public.'[69] Of course, general business interests are not special interests because what's good for business is good for the public.

FTE works in partnership with the various state Councils on Economic Education as well as federal banks in several states. It is also partnered with a variety of neoconservative think tanks such as the Cato Institute, the Center for Strategic and International Studies, Citizens for a Sound Economy, the Competitive Enterprise Institute and the Heritage Foundation.[70] So it is little surprise to find FTE lessons are very much in tune with the views and ideologies advocated by these think tanks.

The John Templeton Foundation is one of FTE's major sponsors. It 'supports free enterprise education and development internationally . . . and other programmes that encourage free-market principles'. In 2003 the John Templeton Foundation gave FTE $550,000 to produce a set of classroom materials entitled 'Is Capitalism Good for the Poor?', based on the NCEE standards. The materials are to help teachers explain the 'innate fairness of capitalism' to students.[71]

A number of other foundations also support FTE including the Citigroup Foundation, the GE Fund and the Sarah Scaife Foundation.[72] In this way FTE can offer its programmes free to teachers and cover their accommodation costs for out-of-town workshops and conferences as well.

The Gillette Company is another of FTE's major sponsors. Together with FTE it has put together an instructional programme called 'Is Anything Ever Really Free? Explaining the Basics of Economics to Children', which explains seven key economic principles, including private property rights, incentives, voluntary exchange and competition. Each concept is explained in a different way for different age groups. For example, competition is explained to 5 to 8 year-olds in terms of buying a cat. If there is only one pet store in town then the store can charge whatever it wants because there is no competition. In a neighbouring town there are five pet stores and the prices for cats are much lower there because of competition.[73] This reduction of the value of pet cats to interchangeable commodities to be bought on the basis of lowest price is typical of the economic way of thinking being promoted in schools.

The US 2002 No Child Left Behind Act provides some encouragement for economic education including funding of awards for Excellence in Economic

Education and a programme of teacher training, research and assessment to promote economic and financial literacy in schools at all levels from kindergarten up.[74]

In Canada the CFEE produces educational resources including teaching kits and student materials – print, video and CD-ROM – on the economy, economics and entrepreneurship. It also holds seminars, workshops, leadership forums for teachers and conferences; provides strategic planning and advisory services; and develops curricula. CFEE claims that its resource materials reach some 300,000 Canadian students each year and that 'it works in collaboration with provincial Ministries and Departments of Education' as well as private organizations such as Finance Canada, the Canadian Banker Association, and Investors Group. It is also supported by a number of corporations including Imperial Oil, Shell Canada and Suncor.[75]

In Australia the Centre for Economic Education, a 'Melbourne-based, national education centre ... dedicated to promoting economic literacy within the community and, in particular, supporting economics education in Australian schools', operated until 2004. It provided teaching and learning resources to teachers, travel awards to the annual US Economics America Conference and student essay competitions. Its board included academics, teachers and business people as well as the General Manger of the Uranium Information Centre, a front organization for the uranium mining industry.[76]

Its publications included materials on work and wealth in Australia, as well as the benefits from international trade and the benefits of foreign investment: 'As countries compete with each other to become the best at what they do, they drive down the costs of production. This makes the price of their goods and services lower. This improves our standard of living.' It argued that 'lower tariffs can lead to increased total sales' with sales for both foreign and local companies increasing, because the increased competition encourages companies to produce the best possible quality goods for the lowest cost, thus reducing prices. As a result 'customers are more satisfied, and employment levels rise'.[77]

The propagation of the market story to children is insidious because, while it promotes the virtues of the pursuit of self-interest and profit, and therefore raises the status and benefits of business enterprises in the minds of the children, it subverts their ability to look after their own interests in the world of work. Most children and young people will become employees and their interests will often conflict with those of employers and corporate executives. Their self-interest may well involve joining unions and fighting management to protect their pay and work conditions, particularly as labour markets around the world are deregulated.

However, corporate-sponsored economic education, business studies and enterprise education seek to get young people to view the world through the eyes of those employers and assume that what is good for employers is good for them. The aim of business propaganda in the schools is to persuade young people that it is in their interests to eschew their own power as workers and citizens, and forgo their democratic power to restrain and regulate business activity. This deprives them of the ability to protect and fight for their self-interest.

NOTES

1 National Council on Economic Education, 'Economic Literacy', *Business Week Special Advertising Section*, 1999, www.businessweek.com/adsections/education/econlit/econhome.htm.
2 Michael J. Caslin, 'Where Will Our Next Generation of Entrepreneurs, Our Next Generation of National Wealth Creators and Manufacturers Come From? A Call to Action for the Development of an Entrepreneurial Culture for All Americans', New York, National Foundation for Teaching Entrepreneurship (NFTE), 2 June 2004, p13.
3 National Council on Economic Education, 'About NCEE: Campaign for Economic Literacy', National Council on Economic Education, www.ncee.net/cel/ accessed 25 July 2004.
4 *Ibid.*; National Council on Economic Education, 'National Council on Economic Education', www.nationalcouncil.org/ accessed 1 June 1998; National Council on Economic Education, 'About NCEE'.
5 National Council on Economic Education, 'About NCEE'; National Council on Economic Education, 'Affiliated Councils & Centers', National Council on Economic Education, www.ncee.net/network/network.php accessed 25 July 2004; Economics America, 'Economics America', www.economicsamerica.org/schools.html accessed 1 June 1998.
6 National Council on Economic Education, 'Economics International', National Council on Economic Education, www.ncee.net/ei/ accessed 25 July 2004; National Council on Economic Education, 'National Council on Economic Education'.
7 NFTE UK, 'Network for Teaching Entrepreneurship', NFTE UK, www.nfte.co.uk/ accessed 25 September 2005.
8 Junior Achievement, 'Junior Achievement International', Junior Achievement, www.jaintl.org/home.asp accessed 25 July 2004.
9 Junior Achievement, 'Who We Are: Our Mission', Junior Achievement, www.ja.org/about/about_who.shtml accessed 25 July 2004.
10 Junior Achievement, 'Contributors: Who Contributes?' Junior Achievement, www.ja.org/involved/involved_contrib_who.shtml accessed 25 July 2004.
11 Junior Achievement, 'JA Programs', Junior Achievement, www.ja.org/programs/programs.shtml accessed 25 July 2004.
12 Young Achievement Australia, 'YAA: Young Achievement Australia', Young Achievement Australia, www.yaa.org.au accessed 25 July 2004.
13 Young Enterprise, 'Young Enterprise, United Kingdom', Young Enterprise, www.young-enterprise.org.uk/ accessed 26 September 2005; Young Enterprise, 'Primary Programme', Young Enterprise, United Kingdom, www.young-enterprise.org.uk/programmes/primary.asp accessed 26 September 2005.

14 Young Enterprise, 'Project Business', Young Enterprise, United Kingdom, www.young-enterprise.org.uk/programmes/pb.asp accessed 26 September 2005.

15 NFTE, 'NFTE – Teaching Entrepreneurship to Youth', National Foundation for Teaching Entrepreneurship, www.nfte.com/ accessed 25 September 2005.

16 *Ibid.*; NFTE UK, 'Network for Teaching Entrepreneurship'.

17 Caslin, 'Where Will Our Next Generation of Entrepreneurs, Our Next Generation of National Wealth Creators and Manufacturers Come From? A Call to Action for the Development of an Entrepreneurial Culture for All Americans', p22.

18 ABW, *ABW News*, Spring, 2002, www.abw.org.au/pdf/newsletter/2002_Spring.pdf; ABW, 'ABW Enterprise Education', Australian Business Week, www.abw.org.au accessed 24 September 2005.

19 ABW, 'ABW Enterprise Education'.

20 *Ibid.*

21 Jim Cumming, 'National Education Agenda 1997–8', Australian Principals Association's Professional Development Council, August, 1997, ww3.beecoswebengine.org/servlet/Web?s=157573&p=RE_nateduag97; Curriculum Corporation, *Enterprise Education*, March, 1998, www.curriculum.edu.au/enterprise/eenwsltr/eenws7.htm.

22 Curriculum Corporation; Cumming, 'National Education Agenda 1997–8'.

23 QCA, 'Enterprise Education', Qualifications and Curriculum Authority, www.qca.org.uk/14-19/11-16-schools/110_2032.htm accessed 26 September 2005; Teachernet, 'National Guidance on Enterprise Education', Teachernet, www.teachernet.gov.uk/teachingandlearning/14to19/ks4/enterpriseeducation/guidance/ accessed 26 September 2005.

24 'Creating an Enterprise Culture: Discussion Paper', Enterprise Insight, Small Business Service, HM Treasury, 26 January 2004, p3.

25 *Ibid.*, p3.

26 Enterprise Insight, 'Make Your Mark: Start Talking Ideas', Enterprise Insight, www.starttalkingideas.org/ accessed 26 September 2005; 'Creating an Enterprise Culture: Discussion Paper', p6.

27 Enterprise Insight, 'Make Your Mark'.

28 Wolfgang Kasper, 'Economic Literacy in One Mighty Lesson', *Policy*, vol 17, no 2, 2001, p45.

29 David S. Dahl, 'Why Johnny Can't Choose', *The Region*, December, 1998, http://minneapolisfed.org/pubs/region/98-12/dahl.cfm.

30 David Fettig, 'A Report on the Economic Literacy Symposium', *The Region*, June, 1999, http://minneapolisfed.org/pubs/region/99-06/blueprint.cfm.

31 Quoted in Dahl, 'Why Johnny Can't Choose'.

32 William Walstad, 'Why It's Important to Understand Economics', *The Region*, December, 1998, http://minneapolisfed.org/pubs/region/98-12/walstad.cfm.

33 National Council on Economic Education, 'About NCEE'; National Council on Economic Education, 'Economic Literacy'.

34 National Council on Economic Education, 'About NCEE'.

35 Robert Rothman, 'High-School Students "Fail" Test of Basic Economics', *Education Week*, vol 8, no 16, 1989, p8; National Council on Economic Education, 'National Council on Economic Education'.

36 'Adam Smith? Never Heard of the Guy', in *US News & World Report*, 1989, p14; Robert W. Reinke, *et al.*, 'Essential Tools for High School Economics', *School*

Education, February, 1990, p93; National Council on Economic Education, 'About NCEE'.

37 National Council on Economic Education, 'About NCEE'.

38 Julie A. Nelson and Steven M. Sheffrin, 'Economic Literacy or Economic Ideology', *Journal of Economic Perspectives*, vol 5, no 3, 1991, pp157–8.

39 *Ibid.*, p159.

40 National Council on Economic Education, 'Economic Literacy'.

41 Quoted in Nelson and Sheffrin, 'Economic Literacy or Economic Ideology', pp163–4.

42 Dahl, 'Why Johnny Can't Choose'; 'Economic Literacy Survey', *The Region*, December, 1998, http://minneapolisfed.org/pubs/region/98-12/survey.cfm.

43 Fettig, 'A Report on the Economic Literacy Symposium'.

44 Bruce McDougall, 'What Canadians Want to Know', *Canadian Banker*, Jan/February, 1998.

45 Petra Lietz, *et al.*, 'Levels of Economic Literacy: From Items to Global Indicators', Paper presented at the Australian Association for Research in Education (AARE) annual meeting, Adelaide, 29 November–3 December 1998.

46 Tadayoshi Asano, *et al.*, 'Economic Literacy of High School and University Students: An International Comparison Based on TEL3', Paper presented at the What We Teach and How We Teach It: Perspectives on Economics from Around the Globe, University of South Australia, 2004, p24.

47 Stephen Lim and Choon Tan, 'Tests of Economic Literacy: Their Use in Revising a University Economics Syllabus', Paper presented at the Economic Education Conference, University of South Australia, 2004.

48 Foundation for Teaching Economics, *et al.*, 'National Voluntary Content Standards for Pre-College Economics Education', Foundation for Teaching Economics, 12 June, 1998, www.fte.org/standards.html.

49 *Ibid.*

50 *Ibid.*

51 Sharon Beder, *Environmental Principles and Policies: An Interdisciplinary Approach*, UNSW Press, Sydney and Earthscan, London, 2006, Chapter 8.

52 Foundation for Teaching Economics, *et al.*, 'National Voluntary Content Standards for Pre-College Economics Education'.

53 Beder, *Environmental Principles and Policies*, p140.

54 Foundation for Teaching Economics, *et al.*, 'National Voluntary Content Standards for Pre-College Economics Education'.

55 Bonnie Meszaros, 'Economic Standards', *Social Education*, vol 61, no 6, 1997.

56 *Ibid.*

57 John J. Siegfried and Bonnie T. Meszaros, 'Voluntary Economics Content and Standards for America's Schools: Rationale and Development', *Journal of Economic Education*, vol 29, no 2, 1998.

58 *Ibid.*

59 National Council on Economic Education, 'Survey of the States: Economic and Personal Finance Education in Our Nation's Schools in 2002', National Council on Economic Education, April 2003, p4.

60 CFEE, 'EconomicsCanada: Introduction and Overview', Canadian Foundation for Economic Education, www.cfee.org/economicscanada/intro2.html accessed 25 July 2004.
61 FEE, 'Foundation for Economic Education', Foundation for Economic Education, www.fee.org accessed 12 August 2004.
62 APEE, 'The Association of Private Enterprise Education', Association of Private Enterprise Education, www.apee.org/about/main.html accessed 6 December 2001.
63 *Ibid.*
64 SIFE, 'SIFE: Changing the World', Students in Free Enterprise, www.sife.org/ accessed 12 August 2004.
65 Foundation for Teaching Economics, 'The Foundation for Teaching Economics', Foundation for Teaching Economics, www.fte.org/ accessed 12 June 1998; Foundation for Teaching Economics, 'Annual Review', Foundation for Teaching Economics 2002.
66 Foundation for Teaching Economics, 'Big Business and Regulation', Foundation for Teaching Economics, http://fte.org/teachers/programs/history/lessons/lesson04.htm.
67 Foundation for Teaching Economics, 'The Great Depression and the New Deal', Foundation for Teaching Economics, http://fte.org/teachers/programs/history/lessons/lesson09.htm.
68 Foundation for Teaching Economics, 'The Use and Abuse of Natural Resources in Historical Perspective', Foundation for Teaching Economics, http://fte.org/teachers/programs/history/lessons/lesson11.htm; Foundation for Teaching Economics, 'Environment and the Economy', Foundation for Teaching Economics, http://fte.org/teachers/programs/environment.
69 Foundation for Teaching Economics, 'Rise of Big Government in the 20th Century', Foundation for Teaching Economics, http://fte.org/teachers/programs/history/lessons/lesson10.htm.
70 Foundation for Teaching Economics, 'Annual Review'.
71 John Templeton Foundation, 'John Templeton Foundation', John Templeton Foundation, www.templeton.org/ accessed 10 August 2004; Foundation for Teaching Economics, 'Annual Review'.
72 FEE, 'Foundation for Economic Education'.
73 The Gillette Company, 'Is Anything Ever Really Free? Explaining the Basics of Economics to Children', Gillette, www.gillette.com/community/ecochildren/ accessed 25 July 2004.
74 Ed.gov, 'Subpart 13 – Excellence in Economic Education', Ed.gov, www.ed.gov/print/policy/elsec/leg/esea02/pg78.html accessed 24 July 2004, 'Economic and Financial Literacy Moves from the Schoolhouse to the Statehouse', *The Region*, September, 2002, http://minneapolisfed.org/pubs/region02-09/literacy.cfm.
75 CFEE, 'About CFEE', Canadian Foundation for Economic Education, www.cfee.org/en/about.shtml accessed 25 July 2004.
76 CEE, 'Centre for Economic Education', Centre for Economic Education, www.cee.org.au accessed 22 January 2001.
77 CEE, 'International Trade', Centre for Economic Education, www.cee.org.au/globalisation/trade.htm accessed 25 October 2004.

14

Conclusion

Faith in idealized market structures has spawned a political jihad intent upon stripping away the community and governmental safeguards against market abuses and imperfections ... RICHARD C. LEONE[1]

When we blindly adopt a religion, a political system, a literary dogma, we become automatons. We cease to grow. ANAÏS NIN[2]

The revolutionary shift that we are witnessing at the beginning of the 21st century from democracy to corporate rule is as significant as the shift from monarchy to democracy, which ushered in the modern age of nation states. It represents a wholesale change in cultural values and aspirations. Despite the rhetoric of corporate accountability and shareholder or consumer democracy, corporations are not democratic organizations. There is no free flow of ideas or open debate about decisions within their hierarchies. The purpose of corporations is to make profits and thereby increase shareholder value, not to serve the public or national interest.

This eclipse of democratic values by corporate values is not a natural evolution but the consequence of a deliberate strategy employed by corporate executives who have combined their financial and political resources to spread free market ideology. Corporations, individually and in concert, have utilized all the major communication institutions of a modern society – including the media and education – to shape community beliefs, values and behaviour. This has enabled corporations 'to enthral and becloud the understanding' of large numbers of citizens[3] so that it is commonly believed that large corporations are benevolent institutions that should be minimally regulated because what is good for them is good for society as a whole.

Corporate values emphasize mass conformity, subordination to authority, obedience and loyalty. Ironically, these values, which undermine individuality and freedom of expression, have been encouraged in the name of individuality and freedom. The market values of competition, salesmanship and deception have replaced the democratic ideals of truth and justice. Economic relationships have replaced social relationships. The power of the State has become subordinate to corporate interests. The realm of politics has increasingly narrowed as all major political parties are enrolled in the service of corporate interests.

The conflict between democratic values and corporate values is even more evident at a personal level. In the new global culture – where people are rewarded for their greed, their ruthlessness and their ambition to climb career ladders, their ability to deceive and manipulate others, their willingness to suck up and network with the right people and keep their personal opinions to themselves – increasingly there is little room for the expression of higher human values and qualities such as generosity, compassion, selflessness, willingness to seek out and expose the truth, and courage to fight for justice.

Robert Nelson, in his book *Economics as Religion* notes that the 'new emphasis on uninhibited self-expression for individual gain' has 'meant that traditional ethical commitments to honesty, personal sacrifice, duty to country, civic participation, political involvement, and so forth' have 'a declining role in society.' Nelson argues, as others have done, that economics is the new religion. He claims that economics teaches and reinforces the norms of behaviour and values necessary to sustain a market system, including adherence to contracts, defence of property rights, and condemnation of corruption and collusion and price fixing. The Market itself is seen by economists, he says, as the instrument of economic progress, and is the pathway to a 'secular salvation' where there is material abundance and where market failure is seen as the root of most social problems including crime, drug addiction, war and conflict.[4]

However, in reality, the Market is simply a framework for corporate acquisition of wealth and power. Markets may serve as a means of distributing goods and services. But they also redistribute wealth and power, concentrating them most when there is an absence of regulation to protect weaker members of the community.

According to economist Robert Heilbroner in *The Nature and Logic of Capitalism*, it is not that economics legitimates activities that business people know to be wrong. Rather, it offers 'definitions of right and wrong that exonerate the activities and results of market activity'. It does this partly by judging material gain as being of more benefit to society than any moral deterioration that might arise from concentrating on material goals, or from equating 'goodness' with '*private* happiness, absolving all licit activity from any need to justify itself on other grounds'. This gives the ruling class 'a moral self assurance without which it could not carry on its historic mission with such dedicated conviction'.[5]

Australian economist and commentator Ken Davidson argues that economists became the new priesthood bestowing morality on the pursuit of self-interest and providing a rationale for why it was in everyone's interest for them to do so:

> *Economists extol the virtues of the market, and just as priests sought out and expunged heresies which might question the beliefs on which the authority of their masters rested, the main task of economists is to find and root out 'market failure'.*[6]

Traditionally, religion, which has been a force for social cohesion as well as a source of conflict, has taught that the pursuit of self-interest was sinful, or at least morally inferior. Even Protestantism, within which modern capitalism took root, did not condone acquisitiveness and the accumulation of goods for individual satisfaction.[7] Therefore, modern economics developed as a 'secular religious' way of giving the Market social legitimacy and a way for self-interest to be not only accepted but applauded. Within such a view the costs of economic progress, including unemployment and the psychological pain of changes and losses incurred by individuals and communities in the face of profit-seeking economic activity, should not be allowed to impede economic progress because such progress is in the interests of the greater good of society.[8]

Nevertheless, many people still stubbornly adhere to a past code of morals and values and find it hard to equate the relentless pursuit of self-interest with high moral standards. In the UK, for instance, according to a survey by the Small Business Service, more than a third of the people surveyed in the UK agreed that 'People who are highly successful in business often have low morals or ethics.'[9] Apparently, there is much work still to be done by free market missionaries if the new global order is to be made permanently safe for corporations.

NOTES

1 Richard C. Leone, 'Preface' in Robert Kuttner, *Everything for Sale: The Virtues and Limits of Markets*, New York, Alfred A. Knopf, 1998, pxi.
2 Anaïs Nin, *The Diary of Anaïs Nin, Volume IV (1944–47)*, edited by Gunther Stuhlmann, New York, Harcourt Brace Jovanovich, 1971, p10.
3 Robert L. Heilbroner, *The Nature and Logic of Capitalism*, New York, W.W. Norton & Co., 1985, p106.
4 Robert H. Nelson, *Economics as Religion: From Samuelson to Chicago and Beyond*, Pennsylvania, Pennsylvania State University Press, 2001, pp9, 12, 232.
5 Heilbroner, *The Nature and Logic of Capitalism*, p117.
6 Kenneth Davidson, 'Defrocking the Priests', in Donald Horne (ed) *The Trouble with Economic Rationalism*, Newham, Victoria, Scribe, 1992, p60.
7 Sharon Beder, *Selling the Work Ethic: From Puritan Pulpit to Corporate PR*, London, Zed Books, 2000.
8 Nelson, *Economics as Religion*, pp70, 88, 279–80.
9 NOP Social & Political, 'SBS Household Survey of Entrepreneurship 2003', London, Small Business Service, DTI 2004, p 81.

Bibliography

Abelson, D. E. (1995) 'From Policy Research to Political Advocacy: The Changing Role of Think Tanks in American Politics', *Canadian Review of American Studies*, vol 25, no 1, pp93–126

Advertising Council (1976) *The American Economic System. And Your Part in It*, Advertising Council and the US. Department of Commerce, New York

Aitkin, D. (1980) 'A Sea-Change on Tax Cuts', *National Times*, 10–16 February

Aitkin, D. (1980) 'Why Labor Should Cut Union Ties', *National Times*, 17–23 February

Alterman, E. (1994) 'Fighting Smart', *Mother Jones*, vol 19, no 4, pp59–61

American Economic Foundation (undated) 'Ten Pillars of Economic Wisdom: A Blueprint for Understanding', American Economic Foundation, New York

American Federation of Labor (1913) 'National Association of Manufacturers Exposed: Revelations of Senate Lobby Investigation', American Federation of Labor, Washington, DC

Andrews, E. L. (2004) 'Social Security Reform, with One Big Catch', *New York Times*, 12 December, p6

Ashford, N. (1997) 'Politically Impossible? How Ideas, Not Interests and Circumstances, Determine Public Policies', *Policy*, Autumn, pp21–25

Australian Financial Review (1998) 'We Are All Capitalists Now', editorial, *Australian Financial Review*, 6 March, p34

Bates, D. (2002) '"Mini-Me" History: Public Relations from the Dawn of Civilization', Institute for Public Relations, www.instituteforpr.com/pdf/HistoryofPublic%20Relation--Institute.pdf

Battin, T. (1991) 'What Is This Thing Called Economic Rationalism?' *Australian Journal of Social Issues*, vol 26, no 4, pp294–307

Baum, D. (2001) *Citizen Coors: A Grand Family Saga of Politics, Business, and Beer*, Perennial, New York

Beder, S. (1996) *The Nature of Sustainable Development*, 2nd edn, Scribe Publications, Melbourne

Beder, S. (2000) *Selling the Work Ethic: From Puritan Pulpit to Corporate PR*, Zed Books, London

Beder, S. (2002) *Global Spin: The Corporate Assault on Environmentalism*, 2nd edn, Green Books, Dartington, Devon

Beder, S. (2003) *Power Play: The Fight to Control the World's Electricity*, Scribe Publications, Melbourne and The New Press, New York

Beder, S. (2006) *Suiting Themselves: How Corporations Drive the Global Agenda*, Earthscan, London

Beder, S. (2006) *Environmental Principles and Policies: An Interdisciplinary Approach*, UNSW Press, Sydney and Earthscan, London

Bello, W. and Cunningham, S. (1994) 'The World Bank & the IMF', *Z Magazine*, July, www.zmag.org/zmag/articles/july94bello.htm

Berger, M. T. (2004) *The Battle for Asia: From Decolonization to Globalization*, RoutledgeCurzon, New York

Berlet, C. and Lyons, M. N. (2000) *Right-Wing Populism in America: Too Close for Comfort*, The Guilford Press, New York

Bernays, E. L. (1928) *Propaganda*, Horace Liveright, New York

Bernstein, A. (1996) 'Why ESOP Deals Have Slowed to a Crawl', *Business Week*, 18 March, p101

Bittlingmayer, G. (1996) 'Antitrust and Business Activity: The First Quarter Century', *Business History Review*, Autumn, pp363–401

Blair, M. M. and Kruse, D. I. (1999) 'Worker Capitalists?' *The Brookings Review*, Fall, pp23–26

Blazey, P. (1985) 'Now It's Stirrer Stone, Company Director', *The Bulletin*, 27 August, p44–45

Blumenthal, S. (1986) *The Rise of the Counter-Establishment: From Conservative Ideology to Political Power*, Time Books, New York

Blundell, J. (1990) 'Waging the War of Ideas: Why There Are No Shortcuts', Atlas Economic Research Foundation, January, www.atlasusa.org/toolkit/waging_war.php

Blustein, P. (2002) 'IMF's "Consensus" Policies Fraying', *Washington Post*, 26 September, pE01

Blyskal, J. and Blyskal, M. (1985) *PR: How the Public Relations Industry Writes the News*, William Morrow and Co., New York

Bollard, A. (1994) 'New Zealand', in J. Williamson (ed) *The Political Economy of Policy Reform*, Institute for International Economics, Washington, DC, pp73–110

Boston, J., and Uhr, J. (1996) 'Reshaping the Mechanics of Government', in F. G. Castles, R. Gerritsen and J. Vowles (eds) *The Great Experiment: Labour Parties and Public Policy Transformation in Australia and New Zealand*, Allen & Unwin, Sydney, pp48–67

Braham, L. (2002) 'Bring Democracy to Boardroom Elections', *Business Week*, 21 October, pp126

Broadway, F. (1978) 'Defending Free Enterprise: An Approach to the Schools', in M. Ivens (ed) *International Papers on the Revival of Freedom and Enterprise*, Aims for Freedom and Enterprise (AIMS), London, pp63–64

Brownstein, R. (1999) 'Though Workers Are Now Investors, They Don't Think Like Capitalists', *Los Angeles Times*, 15 November, pA5

Burks, D. B. (1977) 'Disenchantment with Business: A Mandate for Christian Ethics', *The Entrepreneur*, August, pp1–4

Burton, B. (1995) 'Right Wing Think Tanks Go Environmental', *Chain Reaction*, no 73–74,

Burton, T. (1988) 'How We Packaged Nick', *Sydney Morning Herald*, 26 March, p65

Butler, D. (1995) 'Radicals without Reins', *Accountancy*, vol 116, no 1224, pp36–38

Cahill, D. (2004) 'In the Vanguard', *Workers Online*, August, workers.labor.net.au/features/200408/b_tradeunion_neocons.html

Cahill, D. (2005) 'The Right Values in Education: Neo-Liberal Think Tanks and the Assault Upon Public Schooling', *Overland*, June, pp21–26

Capell, K. and Fairlamb, D. (2002) 'Everyone Is Selling, No One Is Buying', *Business Week*, 22 July, pp54

Carey, A. (1987) 'Conspiracy or Groundswell?' in K. Coghill (ed) *The New Right's Australian Fantasy*, McPhee Gribble and Penguin Books, Fitzroy, Victoria, pp3–19

Carey, A. (1987) 'The Ideological Management Industry', in K. D. Buckley and E. L. Wheelwright (eds) *Communications and the Media in Australia*, Allen and Unwin, Sydney, pp156–179

Carey, A. (1995) *Taking the Risk out of Democracy*, A. Lohrey (ed) UNSW Press, Sydney

Carey, M. and Powis, T. (1985) 'The New Right Thinktanks', *National Times*, 13–19 September, pp14–15

Carlisle, J. (1993) 'Public Relationships: Hill and Knowlton, Robert Gray, and the CIA', *CovertAction*, no 44, pp19–25

Carr, C. C. (1949) 'Translating the American Economic System', *PR Journal*, vol 5, no 6, pp1–4

Carrier, J. G. (1997) 'Introduction', in J. G. Carrier (ed) *Meanings of the Market: The Free Market in Western Culture*, Oxford University Press, New York, pp1–67

Carroll, J. (1992) 'Economic Rationalism and Its Consequences', in J. Carroll and R. Manne (eds) *Shutdown: The Failure of Economic Rationalism and How to Rescue Australia*, The Text Publishing Company, Melbourne, pp7–26

Carter, H. T. (1991) 'The Myth of Shareholder Democracy', *Management Accounting*, vol 72, no 11, p20

Caslin, M. J. (2004) 'Where Will Our Next Generation of Entrepreneurs, Our Next Generation of National Wealth Creators and Manufacturers Come From? A Call to Action for the Development of an Entrepreneurial Culture for All Americans', National Foundation for Teaching Entrepreneurship (NFTE), New York, 2 June, www.nfte.com/downloads/publicpolicy_06022004.pdf

Castles, F. G., Gerritsen, R. and Vowles, J. (eds) (1996) *The Great Experiment: Labour Parties and Public Policy Transformation in Australia and New Zealand*, Allen & Unwin, Sydney

Catley, B. (1996) *Globalising Australian Capitalism*, Cambridge University Press, Cambridge

Cellier, F. S. (1953) 'The Story of Sears in America: An Economic Education Program', *American Management Association Personnel Series*, no 152, pp29–40

Chandler, A. D. and Tedlow, R. S. (1985) *The Coming of Managerial Capitalism: A Casebook History of American Economic Institutions*, Richard D. Irwin, Homewood, Illinois

Chemical Week (1978) 'Teaching the Teachers', *Chemical Week*, 18 October, p27

Chernow, R. (1996) 'Lambs among the Bulls and Bears', *New York Times*, 26 July, pA29

Clark, A. (2001) 'In Their Own Image', *Australian Financial Review Magazine*, 23 February, pp30–37

Clark, D. (1986) 'Direct the Public Subsidies to Left and Right – Then Let the Arrows Fly', *Australian Financial Review*, 15 December, p16

Cochran, T. and Miller, W. (1942) *The Age of Enterprise*, Macmillan, New York

Cockett, R. (1994) *Thinking the Unthinkable: Think-Tanks and the Economic Counter-Revolution 1931–1983*, Harper Collins, London

COG (2002) 'The Capital Ownership Group', The Capital Ownership Group, http://cog.kent.edu/index.html accessed 29 December

Committee on Education and Labour (1939) 'Violations of Free Speech and Rights of Labor', report by Committee on Education and Labour, US Senate, Washington, DC
Commonwealth of Australia (1999) *Employee Share Ownership in Australian Enterprises*, Standing Committee on Employment, Education and Workplace Relations, Official Committee Hansard, House of Representatives, Commonwealth of Australia, Canberra, 26 August, www.aph.gov.au/hansard/reps/commttee/r2493.pdf
Compton Advertising (1974) 'National Survey on the American Economic System', Advertising Council, New York
Compton Advertising (1976) 'Study on Advertising Awareness and Understanding of the American System: Benchmark, Phase I', Compton Advertising, New York, June
Compton Advertising (1977) 'Study on Advertising Awareness and Understanding of the American System: Post Study, Phase II', Compton Advertising, New York, June
Cooke, B. L. (1954) 'Economic Education in Industry', PhD thesis, University of Minneapolis
Coultran, M. (1992) 'Greiner Steps Back from the Precipice', *Sydney Morning Herald*, 28 March, p26
Cran, W. and Yergin, D. (2002) 'The Commanding Heights: The Battle for the World Economy', Public Broadcasting Service, www.pbs.org/wgbh/commandingheights/
Crichton-Brown, R. (1977) 'Looking to the Future – the Institute's Role in the Corporate Sphere', *Australian Director*, October/December, pp11–15
Crittenden, A. (1978) 'The Economic Wind's Blowing toward the Right – for Now', *New York Times*, 16 July, pp3.1, 3.9
Cryer, J. (1998) 'Utilities (Foreign Ownership)', House of Commons Hansard Debates, London, 25 February, www.parliament.the-stationery-office.co.uk/pa/cm199798/cmhansard/vo900225/debtext/80225-12.htm
Cumming, J. (1997) 'National Education Agenda 1997–8', Australian Principals Association's Professional Development Council, [August, ww3.beecoswebengine.org/servlet/Web?s=157573&p=RE_nateduag97
Cummings, B. A. (1979) 'The Advertising Council's Campaign on Economic Education', Advertising Council, New York, April
Curriculum Corporation (1998) *Enterprise Education*, March, www.curriculum.edu.au/enterprise/eenwsltr/eenws7.htm
Da Silva, W. (1996) 'The New Social Focus', *Australian Financial Review Magazine*, May, pp18–28
Dahl, D. S. (1998) 'Why Johnny Can't Choose', *The Region*, December, http://minneapolisfed.org/pubs/region/98-12/dahl.cfm
Davidson, K. (1992) 'Defrocking the Priests', in D. Horne (ed) *The Trouble with Economic Rationalism*, Scribe, Newham, Victoria, pp58–62
Deans, A. (2000) 'Share Day's Pay', *The Bulletin*, pp54–56
Desai, R. (1994) 'Second-Hand Dealers in Ideas: Think-Tanks and Thatcherite Hegemony', *New Left Review*, vol 203, Jan–Feb, pp27–64
Dodd, T. (1992) 'Greiner's Top Man Quits to Become Policy Consultant', *Sydney Morning Herald*, 25 September, p5
Domhoff, G. W. (2002) *Who Rules America? Power and Politics*, 4th edn, McGraw Hill, New York
Duncan, T. (1985) 'Western Mining's Messiahs of the New Right', *The Bulletin*, 2 July, pp67–70

Duncan, T. (1986) 'Mark of Cain in Attack on New Right Academics', *The Bulletin*, 14 October, pp26–28

Duncan, T. and McAdam, A. (1985) 'New Right: Where It Stands and What It Means', *The Bulletin*, 10 December, pp38–45

Dusevic, T. (1990) 'The Idea Factories', *Australian Financial Review*, 25 May, pp1, 3

Easton, B. (1988) 'From Reaganomics to Rogernomics', in A. Bollard (ed) *The Influence of United States Economics on New Zealand*, NZ–US Educational Foundation and the New Zealand Institute of Economic Research, Wellington, pp69–95

Easton, B. (1993) 'From Rogernomics to Ruthanasia: New Right Economics in New Zealand', in S. Rees, G. Rodley and F. Stilwell (eds) *Beyond the Market: Alternatives to Economic Rationalism*, Pluto Press, Leichhardt, NSW, pp149–162

Easton, B. and Gerritsen, R. (1996) 'Economic Reform: Parallels and Divergences', in F. G. Castles, R. Gerritsen and J. Vowles (eds) *The Great Experiment: Labour Parties and Public Policy Transformation in Australia and New Zealand*, Allen & Unwin, Sydney, pp22–47

The Economist (1989) 'Of Policy and Pedigree', *The Economist*, 6 May, pp52–54

The Economist (1991) 'Think-Tanks: The Carousels of Power', *The Economist*, May 25, pp23–26

The Economist (1992) 'The Good Think-Tank Guide', *The Economist*, vol 321, no 7738, pp49–53

The Economist (2001) 'A Sapling's Sound Roots; Germans Take to Shares', *The Economist*, 10 March, p1

Edwards, L. (2002) *How to Argue with an Economist: Reopening Political Debate in Australia*, Cambridge University Press, Cambridge

Edwards, L., Simon, W. E. and Buckley, W. F. (1998) *The Power of Ideas: The Heritage Foundation at 25 Years*, Jameson Books, Ottawa, IL

Eichbaum, C. (1992) 'Market Liberalisation in New Zealand: Fightback! In Practice?' in P. Vintila, J. Phillimore and P. Newman (eds) *Markets, Morals & Manifestos: Fightback! & the Politics of Economic Rationalism in the 1990s*, Institute for Science and Technology Policy, Murdoch University, Murdoch, WA, pp221–236

Eldean, F. (1943) 'The Next Job for Institutional Advertising', Paper presented at the Pennsylvania Newspaper Publisher's Association, Harrisburg, Pennsylvania, 4 October

Enterprise Australia (1982) 'Action 1982', Enterprise Australia, Sydney

Enterprise Australia (1982) 'The Facts of the Enterprise Australia Schools and Colleges Programme', Enterprise Australia, Sydney, September

Enterprise Australia (1983) 'The Capitalist Crisis: Meeting the Challenge', Enterprise Australia, Sydney

Enterprise Insight (2004) 'Creating an Enterprise Culture: Discussion Paper', Enterprise Insight, Small Business Service, HM Treasury, London 26 January, www.hm-treasury.gov.uk/media/053A0/ent_paper_0104.pdf#page=8

Enterprise Insight (2005) 'Make Your Mark: Start Talking Ideas', Enterprise Insight, www.starttalkingideas.org/ accessed 26 September

ESA (2002) 'The Employee Share Alliance Backs Share Incentive Plan', Employee Share Alliance, www.jobownership.co.uk/esa/html/page1.htm accessed 29 December

Ewen, S. (1996) *PR! A Social History of Spin*, Basic Books, New York

Feder, B. J. (1992) 'Keith Funston, Head of the Big Board through '50 Revival, Dies at 81', *New York Times*, 16 May, p10

Ferguson, T. W. (1989) 'New Zealand's Unfinished Economic Experiment', *Wall Street Journal*, 1 December

Fettig, D. (1999) 'A Report on the Economic Literacy Symposium', *The Region*, June, http://minneapolisfed.org/pubs/region/99-06/blueprint.cfm

Feulner, E. J. (1985) 'Ideas, Think-Tanks and Governments: Away from the Power Elite, Back to the People', *Quadrant*, November, pp22–26

Flynn, J. (1996) 'Will Britain Ever Be a Nation of Stock-Keepers?' *Business Week*, 19 August, p42

Fones-Wolf, E. A. (1990) 'Beneath Consensus: Business, Labor, and the Post-War Order', PhD thesis, University of Massachusetts

Fones-Wolf, E. A. (1994) *Selling Free Enterprise: The Business Assault on Labor and Liberalism, 1945–60*, University of Illinois Press, Urbana and Chicago

Ford, L. G. (1967) 'A Survey of Organizations Active in Economic Education', PhD thesis, Western Reserve University

Forero, J. (2002) 'Still Poor, Latin Americans Protest Push for Open Markets', *New York Times*, 19 July, pA–1

Forsyth, M. (1978) 'Defending Freedom in Higher Education', in M. Ivens (ed) *International Papers on the Revival of Freedom and Enterprise*, Aims for Freedom and Enterprise (AIMS), London, p65

Fortune (1949) 'Business Is Still in Trouble', editorial, *Fortune*, May, pp67–71, 196–200

Fortune (1977) 'The Last Great Free-Enterprise Campaign', *Fortune*, June, pp188

Foundation for Teaching Economics (1999) 'Big Business and Regulation', Foundation for Teaching Economics, http://fte.org/teachers/programs/history/lessons/lesson04.htm

Foundation for Teaching Economics (1999) 'Environment and the Economy', Foundation for Teaching Economics, http://fte.org/teachers/programs/environment

Foundation for Teaching Economics (1999) 'The Great Depression and the New Deal', Foundation for Teaching Economics, http://fte.org/teachers/programs/history/lessons/lesson09.htm

Foundation for Teaching Economics (1999) 'Rise of Big Government in the 20th Century', Foundation for Teaching Economics, http://fte.org/teachers/programs/history/lessons/lesson10.htm

Foundation for Teaching Economics (1999) 'The Use and Abuse of Natural Resources in Historical Perspective', Foundation for Teaching Economics, http://fte.org/teachers/programs/history/lessons/lesson11.htm

Foundation for Teaching Economics (2002) 'Annual Review', Foundation for Teaching Economics, www.fee.org

Foundation for Teaching Economics, the National Council of Economic Education, the National Association of Economic Educators, and the American Economic Association's Committee on Economic Education (1998) 'National Voluntary Content Standards for Pre-College Economics Education', Foundation for Teaching Economics, 12 June, www.fte.org/standard.html

Fox, D. (2000) 'Your Politics Vs. Your Portfolio', *Alternet*, 26 April, www.alternet.org/print.html?StoryID=9065

Frank, T. (2000) *One Market under God: Extreme Capitalism, Market Populism, and the End of Economic Democracy*, Doubleday, New York

Friedman, T. L. (1999) *The Lexus and the Olive Tree*, Farrar, Straus and Giroux, New York

Galambos, L. (1975) *The Public Image of Big Business in America, 1880–1940*, The Johns Hopkins University Press, Baltimore

Galbraith, J. K. (1956) *American Capitalism: The Concept of Countervailing Power*, Sentry edn, Houghton Mifflin, Boston

Galbraith, J. K. (1984) *The Anatomy of Power*, Hamish Hamilton, London

Galbraith, J. K. (1992) *The Culture of Contentment*, Penguin, London

Garnaut, R. (1994) 'Australia', in J. Williamson (ed) *The Political Economy of Policy Reform*, Institute for International Economics, Washington, DC, pp51–72

Garrett, P. W. (1938) 'Public Relations – Industry's No. 1 Job', Paper presented at the Twenty-First Annual Convention of the American Association of Advertising Agencies, White Sulphur Springs, West Virginia

Garten, J. (2003) 'A New Year; a New Agenda', *The Economist*, 4 January, p56

Gellner, W. (1995) 'The Politics of Policy "Political Think Tanks" and Their Markets in the US Institutional Environment', *Presidential Studies Quarterly*, vol 25, no 3, pp497–510

George, S. (1997) 'How to Win the War of Ideas', *Dissent*, vol 44, no 3, pp47–73

George, S. (1999) 'A Short History of Neoliberalism', Paper presented at the Conference on Economic Sovereignty in a Globalising World, Bangkok, 24–26 March

Georges, C. (1995) 'Conservative Heritage Foundation Finds Recipe for Influence: Ideas Plus Marketing Equal Clout', *Wall Street Journal*, August 10, p10

Gerritsen, R. (1994) 'Microeconomic Reform', in S. Bell and B. Head (eds) *State, Economy and Public Policy*, Oxford University Press, Melbourne, pp269–290

Giddens, K. R. (1978) 'International Radio and Free Enterprise', in M. Ivens (ed) *International Papers on the Revival of Freedom and Enterprise*, Aims for Freedom and Enterprise (AIMS), London, pp36–37

Golden, L. L. L. (1968) *Only by Public Consent*, Hawthorn Books, New York

Gray, J. (2002) *False Dawn: The Delusions of Global Capitalism*, Granta Books, London

Greenhouse, S. (1987) 'France Embraces "Popular Capitalism"', *New York Times*, 8 June, pD10

Greer, D. F. (1988) 'Contestability in Competition Policy: Replacement, Supplement, or Impediment?' in A. Bollard (ed) *The Influence of United States Economics on New Zealand*, NZ–US Educational Foundation and the New Zealand Institute of Economic Research, Wellington, pp39–68

Greider, W. (1992) *Who Will Tell the People: The Betrayal of American Democracy*, Simon & Schuster, New York

Griffith, R. (1983) 'The Selling of America: The Advertising Council and American Politics, 1942–1960', *Business History Review*, Autumn, pp388–412

Guerrera, F. and Targett, S. (2002) 'Brussels Set to Shake Up Corporate Governance', *Financial Times*, 25 February, p1

Guerrera, F. and Targett, S. (2002) 'Generating Shareholder Power', *Financial Times*, 25 February, p4

Haass, R. N. (2002) 'Think Tanks and US Foreign Policy: A Policy-Maker's Perspective', *US Foreign Policy Agenda*, vol 7, no 3, http://usinfo.state.gov/journals/itps/1102/ijpe/pj73haass.htm

Haley, M. A. (2001) *Freedom and Finance: Democratization and Institutional Investors in Developing Countries*, Palgrave, New York

Halligan, J. and Power, J. (1992) *Political Management in the 1990s*, Oxford University Press, Oxford

Harman, E. (1993) 'The Impact of Public Sector Reforms on Australian Government', in P. Weller, J. Forster and G. Davis (eds) *Reforming the Public Service: Lessons from Recent Experience*, Macmillan Education Australia, South Melbourne, pp16–36

Hazlitt, H. (1983) 'Leonard E. Read, RIP', *National Review*, 10 June, p668

Hazlitt, H. (1984) 'The Early History of FEE', *The Freeman*, March, www.libertyhaven.com/theoreticalorphilosophicalissues/history/earlyhistory.html

Heilbroner, R. L. (1985) *The Nature and Logic of Capitalism*, W.W. Norton & Co., New York

Himmelstein, J. L. (1990) *To the Right: The Transformation of American Conservatism*, University of California Press, Berkeley, California

Hirsch, G. K. (1975) 'Only You Can Prevent Ideological Hegemony: The Advertising Council and Its Place in the American Power Structure', *Insurgent Sociologist*, vol V, no III, pp64–82

HM Treasury (2000) 'Boosting Productivity and Fairness: Employee Share Ownership', HM Treasury, 21 March, www.hm-treasury.gov.uk/Budget/Budget_2000/Press_Notices/bud_bud00_pressrev3.cfm

Holmes, J. W. and Wileman, T. A. (2001) 'Reform in the Australian Public Service 1983–1996', Office of the Auditor General of Canada, www.oag-bvg.gc.ca/domino/other.nsf/html/aus.html accessed 29 June

Hood, J. (2002) 'Investor Politics', NR Book Service, www.nrbookservice.com/popPrintasp?prod_cd=C5970 accessed 26 December

Horin, A. (2000) 'Paying a High Price for a Shareholder Democracy', *Sydney Morning Herald*, 25 March, p49

Howard, J. (1999) 'Address at Opening of Western Mining Corporation's Olympic Dam Expansion', Prime Minister's Office, 26 March, www.pm.gov.au/speeches/1999/damexpansion.htm

The Independent (1990) 'View from City Road: Making Share Ownership Work', editorial, *The Independent*, 18 December, p19

Institute for International Economics (2001) 'About the Institute for International Economics', Institute for International Economics, www.iie.com/ADMINIST/aboutiie.htm accessed 6 January

Investors Chronicle (1991) 'Looking Forward to a True People's Market', *Investors Chronicle*, 28 June, p8

Ivens, M. (ed) (1978) *International Papers on the Revival of Freedom and Enterprise*, Aims for Freedom and Enterprise (AIMS) London

Jackson, H. (2003) 'Joseph Coors: The Man Who Bought the White House for Ronald Reagan', *The Guardian*, 19 March, p27

Jackson, P. M. and Price, C. M. (1994) 'Privatisation and Regulation: A Review of the Issues', in P. M. Jackson and C. M. Price (eds) *Privatisation and Regulation: A Review of the Issues*, Longman, London and New York, pp1–34

James, S. (1993) 'The Idea Brokers: The Impact of Think Tanks on British Government', *Public Administration*, vol 71, Winter, pp491–506

Japonica Partners (2000) 'The Killer B's', Japonica Partners, www.japonica.com/network/killerb.html accessed 8 May

Jay, C. (1986) 'New Right Policy Moves out of the Politician's Hand', *Australian Financial Review*, 11 February, pp16–17

John, D. S. (2004) 'How to Fix Social Security', *Heritage Foundation Backgrounder*, no 1811

Jones, B. M. (1948) 'Community Drives in 150 New Plants', *New York Times*, 5 June, p3-1, 3-7

Jones, B. M. (1948) 'Nation-Wide Advertising Campaign Aimed at Combating Communism', *New York Times*, 17 October, p3F

Kangas, S. (2001) 'Milton Friedman and Monetarism', *Liberalism Resurgent*, www.huppi.com/kangaroo/L-chimonetarism.htm accessed 11 June

Kangas, S. (2004) 'Chile: The Laboratory Test', *Liberalism Resurgent*, www.huppi.com/kangaroo/L-chichile.htm accessed 15 August

Kangas, S. (2004) 'Milton Friedman and the Natural Rate of Unemployment', *Liberalism Resurgent*, www.huppi.com/kangaroo/L-chinairu.htm accessed 15 August

Kasper, W. (2001) 'Economic Literacy in One Mighty Lesson', *Policy*, vol 17, no 2, pp45–49

Katz, J. L. (1992) 'The Conservative Idea Machine', *Governing*, February, pp51–55

Keating, M. (1993) 'Mega-Departments: The Theory, Objectives and Outcomes of the 1987 Reforms', in P. Weller, J. Forster and G. Davis (eds) *Reforming the Public Service: Lessons from Recent Experience*, Macmillan Education Australia, South Melbourne, pp1–15

Keating, R. J. (1995) 'A Walk on the Supply Side', *The Freeman*, vol 45, no 5, www.liberty.com/theoreticalorphilosophicalissues/supplysideeconomics/walksupply.html

Keavney, J. (1978) 'Enterprise Australia: A Case Study in Mobilisation', in M. Ivens (ed) *International Papers on the Revival of Freedom and Enterprise*, Aims for Freedom and Enterprise (AIMS), London, pp66–69

Kellow, A. (1990) 'Changing Conceptions of Responsibility in Government', in J. Porter (ed) *Public Administration in Australia: A Watershed*, Hale & Iremonger, Sydney

Kelly, P. (1992) *The End of Uncertainty: The Story of the 1980s*, Allen & Unwin, St Leonards, NSW

Kelsey, J. (1995) *Economic Fundamentalism*, Pluto Press, London

Kelsey, J. (1999) *Reclaiming the Future: New Zealand and the Global Economy*, Bridget Williams Books, Wellington

Kemp, D. (1988) 'Liberalism and Conservatism in Australia since 1944', in B. Head and J. Walter (eds) *Intellectual Movements and Australian Society*, Oxford University Press, Melbourne, pp322–362

Kemp, J. (2000) 'Building a Shareholder Democracy in America: Personalizing Social Security', Empower America, 10 March, www.empoweramerica.org/stories/storyreader$344?print-friendly=true

Kemp, M. (2000) 'Out of Service', *The Advertiser*, 29 July, p65

Kerr, R. (1993) 'Taking Part in the Public Policy Debate in the 1990s', *Independent Business Weekly*, 26 November, p11

Kilpatrick, J. J. (1975) 'Why Students Are Hostile to Free Enterprise', *Nation's Business*, July, pp11–12

Knight, N. (1978) 'Using Commercial Radio on Behalf of Freedom and Enterprise', in M. Ivens (ed) *International Papers on the Revival of Freedom and Enterprise*, Aims for Freedom and Enterprise (AIMS), London, pp38–39

Knoerle, J. (2002) 'Local Family Endows Chair at Hoover Institution', *The Almanac*, 26 June, www.almanacnews.com/morgue/2002/2002_06_26.hoover.html

Kohler, A. (1997) 'The Radical Right Wing Speeds the Kennett Revolution', *The Age*, 14 February, p15

Kolko, G. (1998) 'Ravaging the Poor: IMF Indicted by Its Own Data', *Multinational Monitor*, June, pp20–23

Krugman, P. (1994) *Peddling Prosperity: Economic Sense and Nonsense in the Age of Diminished Expectations*, W. W. Norton, New York

Krugman, P. (1996) 'The Dismal Science', *Slate Magazine*, 15 August, http://slate.msn.com/code/story/actions

Krugman, P. (2004) 'Borrow, Speculate and Hope', *New York Times*, 10 December, pA41

Kruse, D. I. (2002) 'Research Evidence on Prevalence and Effects of Employee Ownership', Ownership Associates Inc., 13 February, http://ownershipassociates.com/kruse.shtm

Kuttner, R. (1998) *Everything for Sale: The Virtues and Limits of Markets*, Alfred A. Knopf, New York

Landay, J. M. (2002) 'The Powell Manifesto', Mediatransparency.org, 20 August, www.mediatransparency.org/stories/powell.htm

Landay, J. M. (2004) 'Simon Said', Mediatransparency.org, 23 June, www.mediatransparency.org/stories/neocons.html

Langmore, J. (1991) 'The Labor Government in a De-Regulatory Era', in B. Galligan and G. Singleton (eds) *Business and Government under Labor*, Longman Cheshire, Melbourne, pp75–90

Lapper, R. (2002) 'Piling on the Pressure', *Financial Times*, 5 October, p1

Lever, C. W. (1978) 'Fighting for Free Enterprise in America: The USIC Approach', in M. Ivens (ed) *International Papers on the Revival of Freedom and Enterprise*, Aims for Freedom and Enterprise (AIMS), London, pp71–72

Lietz, P., Kotte, D. and Helbers, D. (1998) 'Levels of Economic Literacy: From Items to Global Indicators', Paper presented at the Australian Association for Research in Education (AARE) annual meeting, Adelaide, 29 November–3 December

Lim, S. and Tan, C. (2004) 'Tests of Economic Literacy: Their Use in Revising a University Economics Syllabus', Paper presented at the Economic Education Conference, University of South Australia, 12–16 July

Lindsay, G. (1996) 'The CIS at Twenty: Greg Lindsay Talks to Andrew Norton', *Policy*, Winter, pp16–21, www.cis.org.au/glint.htm

Lindsay, G. (1997) 'Threats to Freedom Then and Now', *Policy*, Autumn, pp18–20, www.cis.org.au/Policy/mps.html

Lippman, W. (1955) *Essays in the Public Philosophy*, Little Brown, Boston

Logan, B. (2000) 'Power Behind the Premier's Throne', *Sydney Morning Herald*, 3 April, p6

Long, S. (1999) 'For Richer and Poorer', *Australian Financial Review*, 9 January, p21

Lyons, J. (1991) 'Think-Tank Commanders', *Sydney Morning Herald*, 9 March, p43

Maier, M. (2001) 'Teaching About Stocks – for Fun and Propaganda', *Dollars & Sense*, March, p28

Mandell, M. A. (undated) 'A History of the Advertising Council', Doctor of Commercial Science, School of Business, Indiana University

Marchand, R. (1998) *Creating the Corporate Soul: The Rise of Public Relations and Corporate Imagery in American Big Business*, University of California Press, Berkeley

Massey, P. (1995) *New Zealand: Market Liberalization in a Developed Economy*, St Martin's Press, New York

Matthews, T. (1994) 'Employers' Associations, Corporatism and the Accord: The Politics of Industrial Relations', in S. Bell and B. Head (eds) *State, Economy and Public Policy*, Oxford University Press, Melbourne, pp194–224

McDougall, B. (1998) 'What Canadians Want to Know', *Canadian Banker*, January/February, pp15–19

McEachern, D. (1991) *Business Mates: The Power and Politics of the Hawke Era*, Prentice Hall, Sydney

McGuinness, P. P. (1997) 'Every Man and His Dog Gets a Share of the Action', *Sydney Morning Herald*, 20 November, p21

McKnight, D. (1986) 'The New Right: A Consumer's Guide', *Sydney Morning Herald*, 9 June, p41

McRitchie, J. (2000) 'Enhancing the Return on Capital through Increased Accountability', Corporate Governance, 26 March, www.corpgov.net/

Melloan, G. (1996) 'Assessing the Pitfalls of People's Capitalism', *Wall Street Journal*, 22 July, pA15

Melloan, G. (2000) 'Europe's New Shareholder Culture Spurs Big Changes', *Wall Street Journal*, 9 May, pA27

Meszaros, B. (1997) 'Economic Standards', *Social Education*, vol 61, no 6, p324

Metcalf, L. and Reinemer, V. (1967) *Overcharge: How Electric Utilities Exploit and Mislead the Public*, David McKay Company, New York

Miliband, R. (1969) *The State in Capitalist Society*, Quartet Books, London

Miliband, R. (1982) *Capitalist Democracy in Britain*, Oxford University Press, Oxford

Moore, B. and Carpenter, G. (1987) 'Main Players', in K. Coghill (ed) *The New Right's Australian Fantasy*, McPhee Gribble and Penguin Books, Fitzroy, Victoria, pp145–160

Moore, D. and Porter, M. (eds) (1991) *Victoria: An Agenda for Change*, Tasman Institute and the Institute of Public Affairs for Project Victoria, Melbourne

Moore, M. (1990) 'Greiner's Muscle Man Toughs It Out', *Sydney Morning Herald*, 18 August, p69

Moore, M. (1991) 'Greiner Adviser Blamed', *Sydney Morning Herald*, 29 June, p4

Murray, G. and Pacheco, D. (2001) 'Think Tanks in the 1990s', Australian National University, www.anu.edu.au/polsci/marx/interventions/thinktanks.htm accessed 23 January

Myers, A. (1999) 'Sharing the Wealth?' *Green Left Weekly*, 25 August, p11

Nader, R. and Seligman, J. (1983) 'The Myth of Shareholder Democracy', in M. Green, R. K. Massie, Jr and M. Waldman (ed) *The Big Business Reader: On Corporate America*, Pilgrim Press, New York, pp377–384

Nadler, R. (1998) 'Stocks Populi', *National Review*, 9 March, pp36–39

Nadler, R (1999) 'The Rise of Worker Capitalism', *Policy Analysis*, 1 November, pp1–27

Nadler, R (1999) 'Special (K)', *National Review*, 19 April, pp52–54

Nadler, R (2000) 'Investor Class Act', *National Review*, 22 May, pp24–26

Nadler, R (2000) 'Portfolio Politics', *National Review*, 4 December, pp38–40

Nash, N. (1987) 'Shareholders' Rights: Three Views: Vying for Control of the Public Corporation', *New York Times*, 15 February, pp4–5

National Council on Economic Education (1999) 'Economic Literacy', *Business Week Special Advertising Section*, www.businessweek.com/adsections/education/econlit/econhome.htm

National Council on Economic Education (2003) 'Survey of the States: Economic and Personal Finance Education in Our Nation's Schools in 2002', National Council on Economic Education, April, www.ncee.net/about/survey2002/NCEESurvey2002webB.pdf

National Education Program (undated) 'Activity Suggestions for Citizenship Leaders', National Education Program, Searcy, Arkansas

NCEO (2002) 'Welcome to the NCEO', National Center for Employee Ownership, www.nceo.org/ accessed 29 December

Nelson, B. (2000) 'A Speech by Dr Brendan Nelson', Paper presented at the IIR/AEOA Conference and Workshop on Employee Share Ownership Plans, Sydney, 23 February

Nelson, J. A. and Sheffrin, S. M. (1991) 'Economic Literacy or Economic Ideology', *Journal of Economic Perspectives*, vol 5, no 3, pp157–165

Nelson, R. H. (2001) *Economics as Religion: From Samuelson to Chicago and Beyond*, Pennsylvania State University Press, University Park, PA

Nin, A. (1971) *The Diary of Anaïs Nin, Volume IV (1944–47)*, Gunther Stuhlmann (ed), Harcourt Brace Jovanovich, New York, p10

Noah, H. J. and Eckstein, M. A. (1988) 'Business and Industry Involvement with Education in Britain, France and Germany', in J. Lauglo and K. Lillis (eds) *Vocationalizing Education: An International Perspective*, Pergamon Press, Oxford, pp45–68

NOP Social & Political (2004) 'SBS Household Survey of Entrepreneurship 2003', Small Business Service, DTI, London, www.sbs.gov.uk/SBS_Gov_files/household-survey-entrepreneur-2003-full.pdf&e=10342

Norris, F. (1954) 'Basic Economics Courses for Industry', adapted from Master's Thesis in Economics, Los Angeles, CA

Noyes, H. (1995) 'Economic Rationalism', Bachelor of Economics (Social Science) Honours, University of Sydney.

Oakley, R. (1989) 'Privatized Policy-Making for the Tory Right', *The Times*, 17 February

O'Brien, D. P. (1975) *The Classical Economists*, Clarendon Press, Oxford

Oliver, S. (1993) 'Where Do Governments Get Their Advice – Lobby Groups, Think Tanks, the Universities and the Media', *Canberra Bulletin of Public Administration*, December, pp134–137

Opinion Research Corporation (1947) 'The Company's Role in Selling Free Enterprise', Opinion Research Corporation, Princeton, January

Opinion Research Corporation (1947) 'Industry and the Social Science Teacher', Opinion Research Corporation, Princeton, April

Opinion Research Corporation (1950) 'School Children Learn About Industry', Opinion Research Corporation, Princeton, March

Opinion Research Corporation (1951) 'The High School Market for Economic Education', Opinion Research Corporation, Princeton, June

Opinion Research Corporation (1952) 'Experiment in Employee Education. Courses in American Freedoms', Opinion Research Corporation, Princeton, May

Opinion Research Corporation (1960) 'Why Too Many College Students Are Economic Illiterates', Opinion Research Corporation, Princeton, April

Opinion Research Corporation (1960) 'Word Impact for Management's Communications', Opinion Research Corporation, Princeton, January

Ownership Associates (1998) 'Trust and Ownership', *The Ownership Culture Report*, Spring/Summer, www.ownershipassociates.com/pdf/ocr1.pdf

Ownership Associates (2001) 'Ownership and Motivation', *The Ownership Culture Report*, Winter, www.ownershipassociates.com/pdf/ocr4.pdf

Palast, G. (2002) *The Best Democracy Money Can Buy*, Pluto Press, London

Parenti, M. (1986) *Inventing Reality: The Politics of the Mass Media*, St Martin's Press, New York

Parker, R. S. and Nethercote, J. R. (1996) 'The Administrative Vocation in the 1990s', in S. S. Richardson (ed) *Public Administration under Scrutiny: Essays in Honour of Roger Wettenhall*, Centre for Research in Public Sector Management, University of Canberra and Institute of Public Administration Australia, Canberra

Pearson, C. (2001) 'Shares and Shares Alike', *Australian Financial Review*, 15 January, p26

Philips, J. and Hooke, J. (1998) 'More Players – But Where Are the Benefits?' *Australian Financial Review*, 22 June, p21

Pimlott, J. (1948) 'Public Service Advertising', *POQ*, Summer, pp209–219

Piñera, J. (1994) 'Chile', in J. Williamson (ed) *The Political Economy of Policy Reform*, Institute for International Economics, Washington, DC, pp225–231

Pollitt, M. G. (1999) 'A Survey of Liberalisation of Public Enterprises in the UK since 1979', University of Cambridge, Cambridge, January

Pont, P. D. (1999) 'People's Capitalism on the March', *Human Events*, 10 December, p9

Pope, C. (2005) 'Bush Kicks Off Push for Social Security Proposal', *Seattle Post-Intelligencer*, 12 January, pA1

Powell, L. F. (1971) 'Confidential Memorandum: Attack on American Free Enterprise System', 23 August, www.mediatransparency.org/stories/powellmanifesto.htm

Probert, B. (1994) 'Globalisation, Economic Restructuring and the State', in S. Bell and B. Head (eds) *State, Economy and Public Policy*, Oxford University Press, Melbourne, pp98–118

Przybyla, H. (2005) 'Companies to Spend over $5 Million to Back Bush on Social Security', *Bloomberg*, 20 January, www.bloomberg.com/apps/news?pid=10000103&sid=aW9uFsLXQwa0&refer=us

Pusey, M. (1991) *Economic Rationalism in Canberra*, Cambridge University Press, Cambridge

Pusey, M. (1992) 'Canberra Changes Its Mind: The New Mandarins', in J. Carroll and R. Manne (eds) *Shutdown: The Failure of Economic Rationalism and How to Rescue Australia*, The Text Publishing Company, Melbourne, pp38–48

Pusey, M. (1992) 'What's Wrong with Economic Rationalism', in D. Horne (ed) *The Trouble with Economic Rationalism*, Scribe, Newham, Victoria, pp63–69

Rabbior, G. (1998) 'Knowledge: The Key to Economic Success', *Canadian Banker*, January/February, pp20–3

Raspberry, W. (1987) 'Do Blacks Have an Aversion to Capitalism?' *Houston Chronical*, 6 November, p26

Raucher, A. R. (1968) *Public Relations and Business 1900 –1929*, The Johns Hopkins Press, Baltimore

Reinke, R. W., Gilliard, J. and Morton, J. (1990) 'Essential Tools for High School Economics', *School Education*, February, pp93–95

Rhodes, T. (2000) 'Building Family Bonds', *The Australian*, 23 August, p38

Ricci, D. (1993) *The Transformation of American Politics: The New Washington and the Rise of Think Tanks*, Yale University Press, New Haven

Rippa, S. A. (1984) *Education in a Free Society: An American History*, Longman, New York

Robinson, C. (1997) 'Pressure Groups and Political Forces in Britain's Privatisation Programme', Paper presented at the Japan Public Choice Society International Conference, Chiba University of Commerce, 22–23 August

Rose, T. (1974) *Free Enterprise Economics*, Institute for Free Enterprise Education and Texas Bureau for Economic Understanding, Dallas

Rose, T. (1974) *Free Enterprise Economics: A Resource Unit for Instruction in America's Free Enterprise System*, Institute for Free Enterprise Education and Texas Bureau for Economic Understanding, Dallas

Rosenbaum, D. E. (2005) 'Bush to Return to "Ownership Society" Theme in Push for Social Security Changes', *New York Times*, 16 January, p20

Rothman, R. (1989) 'High-School Students "Fail" Test of Basic Economics', *Education Week*, vol 8, no 16, p8

Roubini, N. (1997) 'Supply Side Economics: Do Tax Rate Cuts Increase Growth and Revenues Reduce Budget Deficits?', http://equity.stern.nyu.edu/~nroubini/SUPPLY.HTM

Rowell, A. (1996) *Green Backlash: Global Subversion of the Environment Movement*, Routledge, London and New York

Rusbridger, A. (1987) 'A Thought for Tomorrow', *The Guardian*, 22 December, http://politics.guardian.co.uk/thinktanks/comment/0,,527214,00.html

Sale, K. (1993) *The Green Revolution: The American Environmental Movement, 1962–1992*, Hill and Wang, New York

Saloma, J. S. (1984) *Ominous Politics: The New Conservative Labyrinth*, Hill and Wang, New York

Sampson, A. (1996) *Company Man: The Rise and Fall of Corporate Life*, HarperCollins-Business, London

Sawer, M. (ed) (1982) *Australia and the New Right*, George Allen & Unwin, North Sydney

Schmookler, A. B. (1993) *The Illusion of Choice: How the Market Economy Shapes Our Destiny*, State University of New York Press, Albany

Schriftgiesser, K. (1951) *The Lobbyists: The Art and Business of Influencing Lawmakers*, Little, Brown & Co, Boston

Schwartz, D. E. (1983) 'Shareholder Democracy: A Reality or Chimera?' *California Management Review*, vol XXV, no 3, pp53–67

Seely, A. (2002) 'The Employee Share Schemes Bill: Bill 13 of 2001–02', Research Paper 02/05, House of Commons' Library, 16 January, www.parliament.uk/commons/lib/research/rp2002/rp02-005.pdf

Self, P. (1993) *Government by the Market? The Politics of Public Choice*, Macmillan, Hampshire and London,

Self, P. (2000) *Rolling Back the Market: Economic Dogma and Political Choice*, Macmillan Press, London

Selvage, J. (1942) 'Selling the Private Enterprise System', *Vital Speeches of the Day*, November

Sennholz, M. (1996) 'Leonard Read, the Founder and Builder', *The Freeman*, May, www.libertyhaven.com/thinkers/leonarderead/readfounder.html

Sheehan, P. (1985) 'The Right Strikes Back', *Sydney Morning Herald*, 2 March, pp37, 39

Sheil, C. (2000) *Water's Fall: Running the Risks with Economic Rationalism*, Pluto Press, Annandale, NSW

Sheils, M. (1979) 'Capitalism 101', *Newsweek*, 30 April, p62

Siegfried, J. J. and Meszaros, B. T. (1998) 'Voluntary Economics Content and Standards for America's Schools: Rationale and Development', *Journal of Economic Education*, vol 29, no 2, pp139–149

Simms, M. (1982) *A Liberal Nation: The Liberal Party & Australian Politics*, Hale & Iremonger, Sydney

Singleton, J. and Howard, B. (1977) *Rip Van Australia*, Cassell, Sydney

Smith, J. A. (1991) *The Idea Brokers: Think Tanks and the Rise of the New Policy Elite*, Free Press, New York

Smythe, D. W. (1981) *Dependency Road: Communications, Capitalism, Consciousness, and Canada*, Ablex Publishing, Norwood, NJ

Spicer, B., Emanuel, D. and Powell, M. (1996) *Transforming Government Enterprises: Managing Radical Organisational Change in Deregulated Environments*, Centre for Independent Studies, St Leonards, NSW

Spindler, C. (1995) 'Carr Government Takes Conservative Lead', *Green Left Weekly*, p6, http://jinx.sistm.unsw.edu.au/~greenlft/1995/206/206p6.htm

Stauber, J. and Rampton, S. (1995) *Toxic Sludge Is Good for You! Lies, Damn Lies and the Public Relations Industry*, Common Courage Press, Monroe, Maine

Stein, H. (1976) 'Expert Reviews "AES" Booklet', *Economic Communicator*, September/October, pp1–2

Stelzer, I. (2000) 'A Review of Privatization and Regulation Experience in Britain', Institute of Economic Affairs, 7 November 2000, www.iea.org.uk/record.php?type=article&ID=54

Stevenson, R. W. (2004) 'Bush's Social Security Plan Is Said to Require Vast Borrowing', *New York Times*, 28 November, p1.1

Stiglitz, J. E. (2002) *Globalization and Its Discontents*, W. W. Norton & Co., New York

Stilwell, F. (1993) 'Economic Rationalism: Sound Foundations for Policy?' in S. Rees, G. Rodley and F. Stilwell (eds) *Beyond the Market: Alternatives to Economic Rationalism*, Pluto Press, Leichhardt, NSW, pp27–37

Stoesz, D. (1987) 'Policy Gambit: Conservative Think Tanks Take on the Welfare State', *Journal of Sociology and Social Welfare*, vol 14, no 4, pp3–20

Stone, D. (1991) 'Old Guard Versus New Partisans: Think Tanks in Transition', *Australian Journal of Political Science*, vol 26, no 2, pp197–215

Stone, J. (1986) 'Repairing Australia', H. R. Nicholls Society, www.hrnicholls.com.au/nicholls/nichvol1/vol1repa.htm

Sturgess, G. L. (1993) 'Microeconomic Reform: An Overview', in B. Galligan, B. Lim and K. Lovegrove (eds) *Managing Microeconomic Reform*, Federalism Research Centre, ANU, Canberra, pp6–14

Sydney Morning Herald (1992) 'Exit Architect of Greinerism', editorial, *Sydney Morning Herald*, 26 September, p24

Sydney Morning Herald (2003) 'The Rich Get Richer Faster Than the Poor Get Richer in the US', *Sydney Morning Herald*, 24 January, p19

Taft, B. (1987) 'The New Right in Practice', in K. Coghill (ed) *The New Right's Australian Fantasy*, McPhee Gribble and Penguin Books, Fitzroy, Victoria, pp27–37

Tagliabue, J. (2000) 'Europe Rethinks Its Pensions', *New York Times*, 26 December, pC1

Talbott, S. (2002) 'The Brookings Institution: How a Think Tank Works', *US Foreign Policy Agenda*, vol 7, no 3, http://usinfo.state.gov/journals/itps/1102/ijpe/pj73talbott.htm

Taylor, W. (1990) 'Can Big Owners Make a Difference', *Harvard Business Review*, September/October, p70

Tedlow, R. S. (1979) *Keeping the Corporate Image: Public Relations and Business, 1900–1950*, JAI Press, Greenwich, Connecticut

Templeton, J. M. (1983) 'Plans Play Role in "People's Capitalism"', *Pensions & Investment Age*, vol 11, no 22, pp32–33

Thomas, S. (1996) 'The Privatization of the Electricity Supply Industry', in J. Surrey (ed) *The British Electricity Experiment*, Earthscan Publications, London, pp40–63

Thompson, C. D. (1932) *Confessions of the Power Trust*, E. P. Dutton & Co., New York

Thompson, E. (1992) 'Where Is the Economy?' in Horne, D. (ed) *The Trouble with Economic Rationalism*, Scribe, Newham, Victoria, pp14–17

Tobin, J. (1986) 'Economic Literacy Isn't a Marginal Investment', *Wall Street Journal*, 9 July 1986, p1

Tully, S. (1987) 'Europe Goes Wild over Privatisation', *Fortune*, vol 115, no 5, pp68–70

US News & World Report (1977)'Why Business Finds It Tough to Polish Its Own Image', *US News & World Report*, 19 September, p64

VanderHei, J. (2005) 'A Big Push on Social Security', *Washington Post*, 1 January, pA01

Vintila, P. (1992) 'Markets, Morals and Manifestos', in P. Vintila, J. Phillimore and P. Newman (eds) *Markets, Morals & Manifestos: Fightback! & the Politics of Economic Rationalism in the 1990s*, Institute for Science and Technology Policy, Murdoch University, Murdoch, WA, pp3–12

Viteles, M. S. (1953) *Motivation and Morale in Industry*, W. W. Norton & Co., New York

Vogel, D. (1989) *Fluctuating Fortunes: The Political Power of Business in America*, Basic Books, New York

Wade, M. and Freed, J. (2005) 'BHP Hits Jackpot of a Lifetime', *Sydney Morning Herald*, 25 August, p1

Walker, S. H. and Sklar, P. (1938) *Business Finds Its Voice: Management's Effort to Sell the Business Idea to the Public*, Harper & Brothers, New York and London

Wall Street Journal (1999) 'Worker Capitalists', editorial, *Wall Street Journal*, 30 November, pA26

Walstad, W. (1998) 'Why It's Important to Understand Economics', *The Region*, December, http://minneapolisfed.org/pubs/region/98-12/walstad.cfm

Weaver, R. K. (1989) 'The Changing World of Think Tanks', *PS: Political Science and Politics*, vol 22, no Sept., pp563–578

Weeks, J. (1994) 'Credit Where Discredit Is Due', *Third World Resurgence*, April, pp32–34

Weller, P., Forster, J. and Davis, G. (eds) (1993) *Reforming the Public Service: Lessons from Recent Experience*, Macmillan Education Australia, South Melbourne

Wells, K. (1948) 'Remain Silent and Die', *PR Journal*, vol 4, no 10, pp9–12

West, P. (1945) 'Needed Vitally: More Favorable Public Opinion of Corporations', *Printers Ink*, 14 September, pp106–116

Weyman-Jones, T. (1994) 'Deregulation', in P. M. Jackson and C. M. Price (eds) *Privatisation and Regulation: A Review of the Issues*, Longman, London and New York, pp99–119

White, A. (2000) 'Great Aussie Stockocracy', *The Australian*, 9 February, p23

White, F. C. (1978) 'How to Go on the Political Offensive', in M. Ivens (ed) *International Papers on the Revival of Freedom and Enterprise*, Aims for Freedom and Enterprise (AIMS), London, pp1–2

Whitfield, D. (1983) *Making It Public: Evidence and Action against Privatisation*, Pluto Press, London

Whitwell, G. (1993) 'Economic Ideas and Economic Policy: The Rise of Economic Rationalism in Australia', *Australian Economic History Review*, vol 33, no 2, pp8–28

Whitwell, G. (1994) 'The Power of Economic Ideas? Keynsian Economic Policies in Post-War Australia', in S. Bell and B. Head (eds) *State, Economy and Public Policy*, Oxford University Press, Melbourne, pp119–141

Whyte, W. H. (1952) *Is Anybody Listening? How and Why US Business Fumbles When It Talks with Human Beings*, Simon & Schuster, New York

Whyte, W. H. (1960) *The Organization Man*, 2nd edn, Penguin, Harmondsworth, Middlesex

Williams, D. and Peterfreund, S. (1954) *The Education of Employees: A Status Report*, Management Education for Itself and Its Employees, American Management Association, New York

Williams, K. D. (1974) 'The Image of Business in Australia Today', Australian Chamber of Commerce, Canberra

Williamson, J. (ed) (1994) *The Political Economy of Policy Reform*, Institute for International Economics, Washington, DC

Wolff, E. N. (2001) 'The Rich Get Richer: And Why the Poor Don't', *American Prospect*, February, www.prospect.org/print-frendly/print/V12/3/wolff-e.html

Wringe, C. (1988) 'Education, Schooling and the World of Work', in D. Corson (ed) *Education for Work: Background to Policy and Curriculum*, Dunmore Press, Palmerston North, pp33–46

Yarrow, A. (2003) 'The Big Postwar Story: "New Era" of "People's Capitalism" Dawns Where "Everybody's Rich in the U.S.," or So They Said', George Mason University, Fairfax, VA, http://mason.gmu.edu/~ayarrow/economic%20journalismform.PDF accessed 2 January

Yergin, D. and Stanislaw, J. (1998) *The Commanding Heights: The Battle between Government and the Marketplace That Is Remaking the World*, Simon & Schuster, New York

Index